KU-104-114

MATHEMATICS EXPLAINED
FOR PRIMARY TEACHERS

DEREK HAYLOCK is Senior Lecturer in Education at the University of East Anglia Norwich, where he is Chair of Primary Initial Teacher Education and responsible for the Mathematics components of the primary programmes. He has worked for 25 years in teacher education, both initial and in-service, but also has considerable practical experience of teaching in primary classrooms. His work in mathematics education has taken him to Germany, Lesotho, Kenya, Brunei and India. He was co-author (with Anne Cockburn) of *Understanding Early Years Mathematics* (Paul Chapman Publishing 1989) and author of *Teaching Mathematics to Low Attainers 8–12* (Paul Chapman Publishing 1991). His other publications include four books of Christian drama for young people and a Christmas musical (published by Church House/National Society), as well as frequent contributions to education journals. He is editor of *Mathematics Education Review*.

MATHEMATICS EXPLAINED FOR PRIMARY TEACHERS

Derek Haylock

P·C·P

Paul Chapman
Publishing Ltd

Copyright © 1995, Derek Haylock

All rights reserved

Paul Chapman Publishing Ltd
144 Liverpool Road
London
N1 1LA

Apart from any fair dealing for the purposes of research or private study, or criticism or review, as permitted under the Copyright, Designs and Patents Act, 1988, this publication may be reproduced, stored or transmitted, in any form or by any means, only with the prior permission in writing of the publishers, or in the case of reprographic reproduction in accordance with the terms of licences issued by the Copyright Licensing Agency. Inquiries concerning reproduction outside those terms should be sent to the publishers at the abovementioned address.

British Library Cataloguing in Publication Data

Haylock, Derek W.
Mathematics Explained for Primary Teachers
I. Title
372.7044

ISBN 1-85396-261-9

Typeset by Dorwyn Ltd, Rowlands Castle, Hants
Printed and bound by Athenaeum Press Ltd, Gateshead, Tyne & Wear

G H 9 8

Contents

Acknowledgements

My thanks and genuine appreciation are due to the many student-teachers and primary-school teachers with whom I have been privileged to work over the years on initial training and in-service courses in teaching mathematics: for their willingness to get to grips with understanding mathematics, for their patience with me as I have tried to find the best ways of explaining mathematical ideas to them, for their honesty in sharing their own insecurities and uncertainties about the subject, and for thereby providing me with the material on which this book is based.

Introduction

Mathematics Explained for Primary Teachers is the book which many student-teachers and primary-school teachers have asked to be written. Time and time again when I have been explaining some mathematical ideas to such audiences I have been asked, 'Is there a book which explains all this?' Many people may be surprised that there is a need for such a book as this. But all my experience of working with primary teachers and student-teachers convinces me that there is. Even well qualified graduates feel insecure and uncertain about much of the mathematics they have to teach, as is demonstrated in Chapter 1 of the book, and appreciate a systematic explanation of even the most elementary mathematical concepts and procedures of the primary curriculum. This insecurity leads to a neglect of the important teaching skill of 'explanation' in much of primary-school mathematics. So the book is written to explain mathematics to primary-school teachers, so that they in turn will have the confidence to provide appropriate, systematic and careful explanation of mathematical ideas and procedures to their pupils, with an emphasis on the development of understanding, rather than mere learning by rote.

After the introductory chapter, each of the subsequent chapters follows the same format. They each start with a reference to the programmes of study for mathematics in the National Curriculum (DfE: *Mathematics in the National Curriculum*, London, HMSO, 1995), taken mainly from Key Stage 2 and occasionally from Key Stage 1. There follows a summary of the ideas explained in the chapter. Each section of the material in the chapter is then headed by a question of the kind that I am frequently asked by primary teachers and student-teachers, and sets out to answer the question posed. Then there is a set of self-assessment questions, which will enable the reader to reinforce his or her learning from the chapter. I would strongly encourage the reader to engage with these. Answers are provided at the end of the book. Each chapter then concludes with a summary of some teaching implications for dealing with the mathematics in question in the primary classroom.

Derek Haylock
University of East Anglia, Norwich
School of Education and Professional Development

1

Primary Teachers' Insecurity about Mathematics

One of the best ways for children to learn much of the mathematics in the primary-school curriculum is for a teacher who understands it to explain it to them. Much of the criticism of primary-school teaching of mathematics in recent reports (Ofsted, 1993a; 1993b) suggests that there is too great a reliance on approaches to the organisation of pupils' activities which allow insufficient opportunities for teachers to provide this explanation. I have personally been particularly critical of the way in which some teachers rely almost exclusively on a commercial scheme to do the teaching of mathematics (Haylock, 1991). For many children, their only experience of mathematics in primary school is to work individually page by page through the scheme, hardly ever getting any substantial explanation or teaching, other than at a procedural level when they get stuck on a particular question. I may be old-fashioned, but I do actually believe that teachers are paid to teach. Of course, there is more to learning mathematics than just having a teacher explain something and then following this up with exercises. Using and applying mathematics must always be at the heart of learning the subject. But children need 'explanation' and teachers must organise their lessons and the pupils' activities in ways which give opportunities for them to provide careful, systematic and appropriate explanation of mathematical concepts, procedures and principles to groups of children. That many primary teachers neglect this aspect of teaching may possibly be associated with a prevailing primary ethos, which emphasises active learning and the needs of the individual pupil. But it is more likely to be a consequence of the insecurity about mathematics which is characteristic of many primary-school teachers and which seems to have been increased by the frequent revisions to the National Curriculum that have been experienced in England and Wales in recent years. This insecurity has made it more likely that teachers will lean heavily on the commercial scheme to do their teaching for them. This book is written, therefore, to encourage teachers to redress the balance in their teaching, and to provide more opportunities to explain mathematical ideas to their pupils. I have set out to provide explanations of all the key mathematical ideas in the National Curriculum for England and Wales for Key Stages 1 and 2 (DfE, 1995), with the aim of improving primary teachers' own understanding and increasing their personal confidence in talking to their pupils about these ideas.

The background for this book is partly my experience of working with graduates enrolled on a primary one-year initial teacher-training programme. The student-teachers I work with are highly motivated, good-honours graduates, with the subjects of their degree studies ranging across the curriculum. The ages of these student-teachers range from 23 to 40 years, with the mean age about 27. Over a number of years of working with such student-teachers, it has become clear that many of them start their course with a high degree of anxiety about having to teach mathematics. So an invitation was given for any student-teachers who felt particularly worried about mathematics to join a group who would meet for an hour a week throughout their course, to discuss their anxieties and to identify which aspects of the National Curriculum for mathematics appropriate to the age-range they would be teaching gave them most concern. A surprisingly large number of student-teachers turned up for these sessions. Discussions with these student-teachers revealed both those aspects of mathematics anxiety which they still carry around with them, derived clearly from their own experiences of learning mathematics at school, and the specific areas of mathematics which they will have to teach for which they have doubts about their own understanding.

The students' comments on their feelings about mathematics can be conveniently categorised under five headings: 1) feelings of anxiety and fear; 2) expectations; 3) teaching and learning styles; 4) the image of mathematics and; 5) language. These categories reflect closely the findings of other studies of the responses towards mathematics of adults in general and primary teachers in particular.

Mathematics anxiety in adults

Anxiety about mathematics and feelings of inadequacy in this subject are widespread amongst the adult population in Britain (Buxton, 1981). These phenomena are clearly demonstrated by surveys of adults' attitudes to mathematics (Sewell, 1981; Cockcroft, 1982). Findings indicate that many adults, in relation to mathematical tasks, admit to feelings of anxiety, helplessness, fear, dislike and even guilt. The feeling of guilt is found to be particularly marked amongst those with high academic qualifications, who feel they ought to be more confident in their understanding of this subject. There is a common feeling that there are proper ways of doing mathematics and that the subject is characterised by questions to which your answers are either right or wrong. Feelings of failure, frustration and anxiety are identified by many adults as having their roots in unsympathetic attitudes of teachers and the expectations of parents. Furthermore, there are widespread confusions about many of the basic mathematical processes of everyday life (ACACE, 1981).

Mathematics anxiety in primary teachers

Research into primary-school teachers' attitudes to mathematics reveals that many of them continue to carry around with them these same kinds of 'baggage' (Briggs and Crook, 1991). There is evidence that many primary teachers still experience feelings of panic and anxiety when faced with unfamiliar mathematical tasks (Briggs, 1993), that they are muddled in their thinking about many of the basic mathematical concepts which underpin the material they teach to children, and that they are all too aware of their personal inadequacies in mathematics (Haylock and Cockburn, 1989).

Student-teachers' anxieties

Below I have recounted many of the statements made by the primary student-teachers in my group about their attitudes towards and experiences of learning mathematics. In reading these comments it is important to remember that these are students who have come through the system with relative success in mathematics: all must have GCSE grade C, or the equivalent, and can therefore be judged to be in the top 30% for mathematics attainment. Yet this is clearly not how they feel about themselves in relation to this subject.

Feelings of anxiety and fear

When these student-teachers talk freely about their memories of mathematics at school, their comments are sprinkled liberally with such words as *frightened, terror, horrific*, and several recalled having nightmares. These memories were very vivid and still lingered in their attitudes to the subject today as academically successful adults:

I was very good at geometry, but really frightened of all the rest.

Maths struck terror in my heart: a real fear that has stayed with me from over twenty years ago.

I had nightmares about maths. They only went away when I passed my A-level!

I had nightmares about maths as well: I really did, I'm not joking. Numbers and figures would go flashing through my head. Times tables, for example. I especially had nightmares about maths tests.

It worried me a great deal. Maths lessons were horrific.

Others recalled feelings of stupidity or frustration at being faced with mathematical tasks:

I remember that I would always feel stupid. I felt sure that everyone else understood.

Things used to get hazy and frustrating when I was stuck on a question.

Those of us who teach mathematics must pause and wonder what it is that we do to pupils which produces successful, intelligent students who continue to feel like this about the subject.

Expectations

It seems as though the sources of anxiety for some student-teachers were the expectations of others:

It was made worse because Dad's best subject was maths.

> My teacher gave me the impression that she thought I was bad at maths. So that's how I was labelled in my mind. When I got my GCE result she said, 'I never thought you'd get an A!' So I thought it must just be a fluke. I still thought I was no good at maths.

But the most common experience cited by these student-teachers was the teacher's expectation that they *should* be able to deal successfully with all the mathematical tasks they were given. They recalled clearly the negative effect on them of the teacher's response to their failure to understand:

> There were few maths teachers who could grasp the idea of people not being mathematical.

> The teacher just didn't understand why I had problems.

> Teachers expect you to be good at maths if you're good at other things. They look at your other subjects and just can't understand why you can't do maths. They say to you, 'You should be able to do this . . .'

> I remember when I was 7 I had to do 100 long divisions. The headmaster came in to check on our progress. He picked me up and banged me up and down on my chair, saying, 'Why can't you do it?' After that I wouldn't ask if I couldn't understand something.

Teaching and learning styles

The student-teachers spoke with considerable vigour about their memories of the way mathematics was taught to them, recognising now, from their adult perspective, that part of the problem was a significant limitation in the teaching style to which they were subjected:

> Surely not everyone can be bad at maths. Is it just that it's really badly taught?

> I remember one teacher who was good because she actually tried to explain things to me.

It was clear that most of the student-teachers in this group felt that they had been encouraged to learn by rote, to learn rules and recipes without understanding. This rote-learning style was then reinforced by apparent success:

> I was quite good at maths at school but I'm frightened of going back to teach it because I think I've probably forgotten most of what we learnt. I have a feeling that all I learnt was just memorised by rote and now it's all gone.

> I could rote learn things, but not understand them.

> I got through the exams by simply learning the rules. I would just look for clues in the question and find the appropriate process.

> I don't think I understood any of it. I got my O-level, but that just tested rote learning.

The limitations of this rote-learning syndrome were sometimes apparent to the students:

> I found you could do simple problems using the recipes, but then they'd throw in a question which was more complex. Then when the recipe I'd learnt didn't work I became angry.

> We would be given a real-life situation but I would find it difficult to separate the maths concepts out of it.

But it seems that some teachers positively discouraged a more appropriate learning style:

> I was made to feel like I was a nuisance for trying to understand.

> Lots of questions were going round in my head but I was too scared to ask them.

> I always tried to avoid asking questions in maths lessons because you were made to feel so stupid if you got it wrong. There must be ways of convincing a child it doesn't matter if they get a question wrong.

The following remark by one student-teacher in this context highlights how the role as a student-teacher serves to focus the feeling of anxiety and inadequacy arising from the rote-learning strategy adopted in the past: 'I have a real fear of teaching young children how to do things in maths as I just learnt rules and recipes. I have this dread of having to explain why we do something.'

Image of mathematics
For some students, mathematics had an image of being a difficult subject, so much so that it was socially acceptable not to be any good at it:

> Maths has an image of being hard. You pick this idea up from friends, parents and even teachers.

> My Mum would tell me not to worry, saying, 'It's alright, we're all hopeless at maths!' It was as if it was socially acceptable to be bad at maths.

> Among my friends and family it was OK to be bad at maths, but it's not acceptable in society or employment.

For some, the problem seemed to lie with the feeling that mathematics was different from other subjects in school because the tasks given in mathematics are seen as essentially convergent and uncreative:

> Maths is not to do with the creativity of the individual, so you feel more restricted. All the time you think you've just got to get the right answer. And there is only one right answer.

> There's more scope for failure with maths. It's very obvious when you've failed, because things are either right or wrong, so you feel a fool, or look a fool in front of the others.

Language
A major problem for all the student-teachers was that mathematical language seemed to be too technical, too specific to the subject and not reinforced through their language use in everyday life:

> I find the language of maths difficult, but the handling of numbers is fine.

> Most of the words you use in maths you never use in everyday conversation.

> Some words seem to have different meanings in maths, so you get confused.

> I was always worried about saying the wrong things in maths lessons, because maths language seems to be so precise. I worry now that I'll say things wrong to children in school and get them confused. You know, like, 'Which is the bigger half?'

When we discussed the actual content of the National Curriculum order for mathematics, it became clear that the majority of the students' anxieties were related to language. Often they would not recognise mathematical ideas which they actually understood quite well, because they appeared in the National Curriculum programmes of study in formal mathematical language, which they had either never known or forgotten through neglect. This seemed to be partly because most of this technical mathematical language is not used in normal everyday adult conversation, even amongst intelligent graduates:

> I can't remember what prime numbers are . . . Why are they called prime numbers anyway?

> Is a product when you multiply two numbers together?

> What's the difference between mass and weight?

> What is congruence? A mapping? Discrete data? A measure of spread? A quadrant? An inverse? Reflective symmetry? A translation? A transformation?

Even as a 'mathematician', I must confess that it is very rare for any of this kind of technical language to come into my everyday conversation, apart from when I am actually 'doing mathematics'. When this technical language was explained to the students, typical reactions would be:

> Oh, is that what they mean? Why don't they say so, then?

> Why do they have to dress it up in such complicated language?

Mathematics explained

Recognising that amongst primary student-teachers and, indeed, amongst many primary-school teachers in general, there is this background of anxiety and confusion, a major task for initial and in-service training is the promotion of positive attitudes towards teaching mathematics in this age-range. The evidence from my conversations with student-teachers suggests that to achieve this we need to shift perceptions of teaching mathematics away from the notion of teaching recipes and more towards the development of understanding. And we need to give time to explaining mathematical ideas, to the ironing out of confusions over the content and, particularly, the language of the mathematics National Curriculum.

Some students' comments later in the year highlighted the significance to them of having mathematics explained. The emphasis on explaining and understanding paid off in shifts of attitudes towards the subject:

> It's the first time anyone has actually explained things in maths to me. I feel a lot happier about going into the classroom now.

> The course seems to have reawakened an interest in mathematics for me and exploded the myth that maths was something I had to learn by rote for exams, rather than understand.

> I was really fearful about having to teach maths. That fear has now declined. I feel more confident and more informed about teaching maths now.

These kinds of reactions have prompted me to write this book. It is my hope that the book, focusing specifically on explaining the language and content of the mathematics that we teach in the primary age-range, will, in the same way, help other student-teachers and primary-school teachers in general to develop this kind of confidence in approaching their teaching of this core subject of the curriculum to children who are at such an important stage in their educational development.

References

ACACE (Advisory Council for Adult and Continuing Education) (1981) *Adults' Mathematical Ability and Performance*, Leicester, ACACE.

Briggs, M. (1993) Bags and baggage revisited, *Mathematics Education Review*, Vol. 2, pp. 16–20.

Briggs, M. and Crook, J. (1991) Bags and baggage, in E. Love and D. Pimm (eds) *Teaching and Learning Mathematics*, London, Hodder & Stoughton.

Buxton, L. (1981) *Do You Panic About Maths?* London, Heinemann.

Cockcroft, W.H. (1982) *Mathematics Counts. Report of the Committee of Inquiry into the Teaching of Mathematics under the Chairmanship of Dr W.H. Cockcroft*, London, HMSO.

DfE (Department for Education) (1995) *Mathematics in the National Curriculum*, London, HMSO.

Haylock, D. (1991) *Teaching Mathematics to Low Attainers, 8–12*, London, Paul Chapman Publishing.

Haylock, D. and Cockburn, A. (1989) *Understanding Early Years Mathematics*, London, Paul Chapman Publishing.

Ofsted (Office for Standards in Education) (1993a) *The Teaching and Learning of Number in Primary Schools*, London, HMSO.

Ofsted (Office for Standards in Education) (1993b) *Curriculum Organisation and Classroom Practice in Primary Schools: A Follow-up Report*, London, HMSO.

Sewell, B. (1981) *Use of Mathematics by Adults in Daily Life*, Leicester, Advisory Council for Adult and Continuing Education.

2

Place Value

Pupils should be taught to: read, write and order whole numbers, understanding that the position of a digit signifies its value; extend their understanding of the number system to . . . decimals . . . in the context of measurement and money.

In this chapter there are explanations of

- the way in which our Hindu-Arabic system of numeration uses the principle of place value;
- some contrasts with numeration systems from other cultures;
- powers of ten;
- two ways of demonstrating place value with materials;
- the role of zero as a place-holder;
- the extension of the place-value principle to tenths, hundredths, etc.; and
- the decimal point used as a separator in the contexts of money and measurement.

What is meant by 'place value'?

The system of numeration we use today is derived from an ancient Hindu system which was picked up and developed by Arab traders in the ninth and tenth centuries and which spread through Europe. Of course, there have been many other systems developed by various cultures through the centuries, each with their particular features. Comparing some of these with the way we write numbers today enables us to appreciate the power and elegance of the Hindu-Arabic legacy. There is not space here to go into much detail, but the history of different numeration systems is a fascinating topic, with considerable potential for cross-curriculum work in schools, which will repay further study by the reader.

The Egyptian hieroglyphic system, used as long ago as 3000 BC, for example, had separate symbols for ten, a hundred, a thousand, ten thousand, a hundred thousand and a million. The Romans, some three thousand years later, in spite of all their other achievements, were using a numeration system which was still based on the same principle as the Egyptians, but simply had symbols for a few extra numbers, including 5, 50 and 500. Figure 2.1 illustrates how various

Egyptian hieroglyphics	Roman numerals	Hindu-Arabic
|	I	1
|| |||	V	5
∩	X	10
∩∩∩∩∩	L	50
𐎖	C	100
𐎖𐎖 𐎖𐎖 𐎖	D	500
𐎖𐎖𐎖 ∩∩∩∩∩∩ ||||||	CCCLXVI	366

Figure 2.1   Some numbers written in different numeration systems

numerals are written in these systems and, in particular, how the numeral 366 would be constructed. Clearly, the Hindu-Arabic system we use today is far more economic in its use of symbols. The reason for this is that it is based on the highly sophisticated concept of *place value*.

In the Roman system, for example, to represent three hundreds, three Cs are needed, and each of these symbols represents the same quantity, namely, a hundred. Likewise, in the Egyptian system, three 'scrolls' are needed, each representing a hundred. In the Hindu-Arabic system we do not use a symbol representing a hundred to construct three hundreds: we use a symbol representing three! Just this one symbol is needed to represent three hundreds, and we know that it represents three hundreds, rather than three tens or three ones, because of the place in which it is written. The two sixes in 366, for example, do not stand for the same number: reading from left to right, the first stands for six tens and the second for six ones, because of the places in which they are written.

So, in our Hindu-Arabic place-value system, all numbers can be represented using a finite set of *digits*, i.e. 0, 1, 2, 3, 4, 5, 6, 7, 8, 9. Like most numeration systems, no doubt because of the availability of our ten fingers for counting purposes, the system uses ten as a *base*. Larger whole numbers than 9 are constructed using *powers* of the base: ten, a hundred, a thousand, and so on. Of course, these powers of ten are not limited and can continue indefinitely with higher powers. This is how some of these powers are named, written as numerals, constructed from tens, and expressed as powers of ten in symbols and in words:

A million	$1\,000\,000 = 10 \times 10 \times 10 \times 10 \times 10 \times 10 =$	10^6 (ten to the power six)
A hundred thousand	$100\,000 = 10 \times 10 \times 10 \times 10 \times 10$	$= 10^5$ (ten to the power five)
Ten thousand	$10\,000 = 10 \times 10 \times 10 \times 10$	$= 10^4$ (ten to the power four)
A thousand	$1000 = 10 \times 10 \times 10$	$= 10^3$ (ten to the power three)
A hundred	$100 = 10 \times 10$	$= 10^2$ (ten to the power two)
Ten	$10 = 10$	$= 10^1$ (ten to the power one)

The place in which a digit is written then represents that number of one of these powers of ten. So, for example, working from right to left, in the numeral '2345' the 5 represents 5 ones, the 4 represents 4 tens, the 3 represents

3 hundreds and the 2 represents 2 thousands. Perversely, we work from right to left in determining the place values, with increasing powers of ten as we move in this direction. But, since we read from left to right, the numeral is read with the largest place value first, i.e. 'two thousands, three hundreds, four tens, and five'. Certain conventions of language then transform this into the customary form, 'two thousand, three hundred and forty-five'. So, the numeral '2345' is essentially a clever piece of shorthand, condensing a complicated mathematical expression into four symbols, as follows:

$$(2 \times 10^3) + (3 \times 10^2) + (4 \times 10^1) + 5 = 2345$$

Notice that each of the powers of ten is equal to ten times the one below: a hundred equals ten tens, a thousand equals ten hundreds, and so on. This means that whenever you have accumulated ten in one place this can be exchanged for one in the next place to the left. This principle of being able to 'exchange one of these for ten of those' as you move right to left along the powers of ten, or to 'exchange ten of these for one of those' as you move left to right, is a very significant feature of the place-value system. It is essential for understanding the way in which we count. For example, the next number after '56, 57, 58, 59 . . .' is '60', because we fill up the units position with ten ones and these are exchanged for an extra ten in the next column. This principle of exchanging is also fundamental to the ways we do calculations with numbers. It is the principle of 'carrying one' in addition (see Chapter 5). It also means that when necessary we can exchange one in any place for ten in the next lower place, for example, when doing subtraction by decomposition (see Chapter 7).

What are the best ways of explaining place value in concrete terms?

There are two sets of materials which provide particularly effective concrete embodiments of the place-value principle and therefore help us to explain the

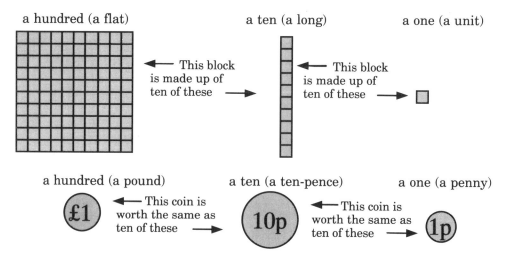

Figure 2.2   Materials for explaining place value

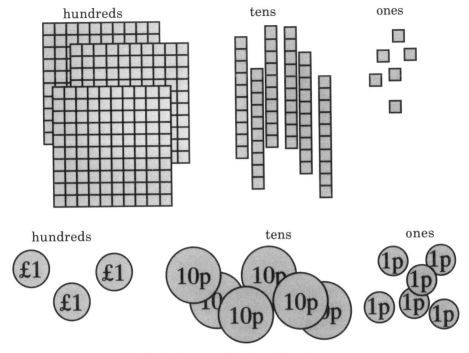

Figure 2.3   The number 366 in base-ten blocks and in coins

way our number system works. They are 1) base-ten blocks and 2) 1p, 10p and
£1 coins. Figure 2.2 shows how the basic place-value principle of exchanging
one for ten is built into these materials, for ones, tens and hundreds. Note that
the ones in the base-ten blocks are sometimes referred to as units, the tens as
longs and the hundreds as flats. With the blocks, of course, ten of one kind of
block do actually make one of the next kind. With the coins it is simply that ten
ones are *worth* the same as one ten, and so on.

Figure 2.3 shows the number 366 represented with these materials. Notice
that with both the blocks and the coins we have three hundreds, six tens and
six ones; that the blocks are equivalent to 366 units; and that the coins amount
to 366 pence. Representing numbers with these materials enables us to build
up images which help us to make sense of the way we do calculations such as
addition and subtraction, as will be seen in Chapters 5 and 7.

What is meant by saying that zero is a place-holder?

The Hindu-Arabic system was not the only one to use a place-value concept.
Remarkably, about the same time as the Egyptians, the Babylonians had developed a system which incorporated this principle, although it used sixty as a
base as well as ten. But a problem with their system was that you could not
easily distinguish between, say, three and three sixties. They did not have a
symbol for zero. It is generally thought that the Mayan civilisation of South
America was the first to develop a numeration system which included both the

concept of place value and the consistent use of a symbol for zero. Clearly, there is some rich potential here for the inclusion of a mathematical dimension for pupils studying, for example, the ancient Egyptian and Mayan civilisations.

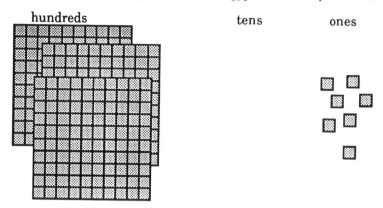

Figure 2.4   Three hundred and seven in base-ten blocks

Figure 2.4 shows 'three hundred and seven' represented in base-ten blocks. Translated into symbols, without the use of a zero, this would easily be confused with thirty-seven: '3 7'. The zero is used therefore to 'hold the place'; that is, to indicate the position of the tens' place, even though there are no tens there: '307'. It is worth noting, therefore, that when we see a numeral such as '300', we should not think to ourselves that the '00' means 'hundred'. It is the *position* of the 3 which indicates that it stands for 'three hundred'; the function of the zeros is to make this position clear whilst indicating that there are no tens and no ones. This may seem a little pedantic, but it is the basis of the confusion which leads some children to write, for example, '30045' for 'three hundred and forty-five'.

What's the difference between a 'numeral' and a 'number'?

A numeral is the symbol, or collection of symbols, which we use to represent a number. The number is the concept represented by the numeral. We have seen in Figure 2.1 that the same number (for example, the one we call 'three hundred and sixty-six') can be represented by different numerals, such as '366' and 'CCCLXVI'. Because the Hindu-Arabic system of numeration is now more or less universal, the distinction between the numeral and the number is easily lost.

How does the place-value system work for quantities less than one?

In exactly the same way. Once the principle of being able to 'exchange one of these for ten of those' is established, we can continue with it to the right of the units position, with tenths, hundredths, thousandths, and so on. These positions are usually referred to as *decimal places* and are separated from the units by the *decimal point*. Since a tenth and a hundredth are what you get if you divide a unit into ten and a hundred equal parts respectively, it follows that one unit can be exchanged for ten tenths, and one tenth can be exchanged for ten hundredths.

In this way the principle of 'one of these being exchanged for ten of those' continues indefinitely to the right of the decimal point, with the values represented by the places getting progressively smaller by a factor of ten each time.

A useful way to picture decimals is to explore what happens if we decide that the 'flat' piece in the base-ten blocks represents 'one whole unit'. In this case the 'longs' represent tenths of this unit and the small cubes represent hundredths. Then the collection of blocks shown in Figure 2.3 is made up of 3 units, 6 tenths and 6 hundredths. This quantity is represented by the decimal number 3.66. Similarly the blocks in Figure 2.4 represent the decimal number 3.07, i.e. 3 units, no tenths and 7 hundredths.

Do you have to explain tenths, hundredths and decimal places when you introduce decimal notation in the contexts of money and measurement?

If we decide to call a pound coin the 'unit', then the collection of coins in Figure 2.3 also represents the number 3.66, since the ten-penny coins are tenths of a pound and the penny coins are hundredths of a pound. This makes sense, since this amount of money written in pounds, rather than in pence, is recorded conventionally as £3.66.

Now in terms of decimal numbers in general, the function of the decimal point is to indicate the transition from units to tenths. Because of this a decimal number such as 3.66 is read as 'three point six six', with the first figure after the point indicating the number of tenths and the next the number of hundredths. It would be confusing to read it as 'three point sixty-six', since this might be taken to mean three units and sixty-six tenths. There is a different convention, however, when using the decimal point in recording money: the amount £3.66 is read as 'three pounds sixty-six'. In this case there is no confusion about what the 'sixty-six' refers to: the context makes clear that it is 'sixty-six pence'. In practice, it is in money notation like this that children first encounter the decimal point. In this form we use the decimal point quite simply as something which separates the pounds from the pennies – so that £3.66 represents simply 3 whole pounds and 66 pence – without any awareness necessarily that the first 6 represents 6 tenths of a pound and the next 6 represents 6 hundredths. It is because the decimal point here is effectively no more than a separator of the pounds from the pennies that we have the convention of always writing two figures after the point when recording amounts of money in pounds. So, for example, we would write £3.20 rather than £3.2, and read it as 'three pounds twenty (i.e. twenty pence)'. By contrast, if we were working with pure decimal numbers then we would simply write '3.2', meaning '3 units and 2 tenths'.

Since there are a hundred centimetres (cm) in a metre (m), just like a hundred pence in a pound, the measurement of length in centimetres and metres offers a close parallel to recording money. So, for example, a length of 366 cm can also be written in metres, as 3.66 m. Once again the decimal point is seen simply as something which separates the 3 whole metres from the 66 centimetres. In this context it is helpful to press the parallel quite strongly, following the same convention of writing two figures after the point when expressing lengths in metres, for example, writing 3.20 m rather than 3.2 m. We can then interpret this simply as three metres and twenty centimetres. I shall explain in Chapter 17 how this convention is very useful when dealing with additions and subtractions involving decimals.

This principle then extends to the measurement of mass (or, colloquially, weight) where, because there are a thousand grams (g) in a kilogram (kg), it is best, at least to begin with, to write a mass measured in kilograms with three figures after the point. For example, 3450 g written in kg is 3.450 kg. The decimal point can then simply be seen as something which separates the 3 whole kilograms from the 450 grams. Similarly, in recording liquid volume and capacity, where there are a thousand millilitres (ml) in a litre, a volume of 2500 ml is also written as 2.500 litres, with the decimal point separating the 2 whole litres from the 500 millilitres.

So, when working with primary-school children, it is not necessary initially to explain about tenths and hundredths when using the decimal point in the context of money, length and other measurement contexts. To begin with we can use it simply as a separator and build up the pupil's confidence in handling the decimal notation in these familiar and meaningful contexts. Later, of course, money and measurement in general will provide fertile contexts for explaining the ideas of tenths, hundredths and thousandths. For example, a decimal number such as 1.35 can be explained in the context of length by laying out in a line 1 metre stick, 3 decimetre rods (i.e. tenths of a metre) and 5 centimetre cubes (i.e. hundredths of a metre), as shown in Figure 2.5.

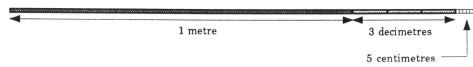

1 metre   3 decimetres

5 centimetres

Figure 2.5   The decimal number 1.35 shown as a length

Self-assessment questions

2.1: Arrange these numbers in order from the smallest to the largest, without converting them to Hindu-Arabic numbers: DCXIII, CCLXVII, CLXXXVIII, DCC, CCC. Now convert them to Hindu-Arabic, repeat the exercise and note any significant differences in the process.

2.2: Add one to four thousand and ninety-nine.

2.3: Write these numbers in Hindu-Arabic numerals, and then write them out in full using powers of ten: a) five hundred and sixteen; b) three thousand and sixty; and c) two million, three hundred and five thousand and four.

2.4: I have 34 one-penny coins, 29 ten-penny coins and 3 pound coins. Apply the principle of 'exchanging ten of these for one of those' to reduce this collection of coins to the smallest number of 1p, 10p and £1 coins.

2.5: Interpret these decimal numbers as collections of base-ten blocks (using a 'flat' to represent a unit) and then arrange them in order from the smallest to the largest: 3.2, 3.05, 3.15, 3.10.

2.6: There are a thousand millimetres (mm) in a metre. How would you write lengths of 3405 mm and 2500 mm in metres?

2.7: How should you write a) 25p in pounds; b) 25 cm in metres; c) 7p in pounds; d) 45 g in kilograms; e) 50 ml in litres; and f) 5 mm in metres?

Summary of teaching points

1. Incorporate some study of numeration systems into history-focused topics such as Egyptian and Mayan civilisations, highlighting the advantages and significance of the place-value system we use today.
2. Give appropriate credit to the non-European cultures which have contributed so much to the development of numeration.
3. Use coins (1p, 10p and £1) and base-ten blocks to develop pupils' understanding of the place-value system.
4. Use the materials to reinforce especially the principle of 'exchanging one of these for ten of those' as you move right to left along the powers of ten, and 'exchanging ten of these for one of those' as you move left to right.
5. Give particular attention to the function and meaning of zero when writing and explaining numbers to pupils.
6. Articulate the words 'tenths' and 'hundredths' very carefully when explaining decimal numbers; pupils may think you are saying 'tens' and 'hundreds'.
7. Explain decimal numbers by using the flat pieces in the base-ten materials to represent units, the longs to represent tenths and the small cubes to represent hundredths.
8. Children will first encounter the decimal point as a separator in the context of money (pounds and pence) and then length (metres and centimetres), with two figures after the point. They can use the notation in these contexts initially without having any real awareness of figures representing tenths and hundredths.
9. This can then extend to further experience of decimal notation in the contexts of mass (kilograms and grams) and liquid volume and capacity (litres and millilitres), with three figures after the point.
10. Later these contexts can be used to reinforce the explanation of the idea that the figures after the point represent tenths, hundredths and thousandths.

3

Mathematical Modelling

Pupils should be taught to: select and use the appropriate mathematics; recognise situations to which the operations (of addition, subtraction, multiplication and division) apply; understand and use the features of a basic calculator, interpreting the display in the context of the problem; develop their use of the four operations to solve problems, including those involving money and measures, using a calculator where appropriate.

In this chapter there are explanations of

- three approaches to calculations: algorithms, adhocorithms and calculators;
- the fundamental process of mathematical modelling;
- the contribution of electronic calculators to this process;
- three different kinds of answers which might be obtained from a calculation done on a calculator; and
- truncation.

What is an algorithm?

There are essentially three ways in which we can do a calculation, such as an addition, a subtraction, a multiplication or a division. For example, consider the problem of finding the cost of 16 items at 25p each. To solve this we may decide to work out '16 × 25'.

One approach to this would be to use an *algorithm*. The word 'algorithm' (derived from the name of the ninth-century Arabian mathematician, Al-Khowarizmi) refers to a step-by-step process for obtaining the solution to a mathematical problem or, in this case, the result of a calculation. In number work we use the word to refer to the formal, paper-and-pencil methods which we might use for doing calculations which, if the procedures are followed correctly, will always lead to the required result. These would include, for example, subtraction by decomposition and long division. So, solving the problem above using an algorithm might involve, for example, performing the calculation for '16 × 25' as shown in Figure 3.1, using the method known as long multiplication.

16

$$
\begin{array}{r}
1\,6 \\
\times\ \underline{2\,5} \\
3\,2\,0 \\
\underline{\ \ 8\,0} \\
\underline{\mathbf{4\,0\,0}}
\end{array}
$$

Figure 3.1   Using an algorithm for '16 × 25'

Secondly, there is a vast array of informal methods for doing calculations, most of which are not written down in textbooks or explained by teachers to pupils, but which are actually the methods which most numerate adults employ for the calculations they encounter in everyday life. For example, to solve the problem above, we might make use of the fact that four 25 pences make £1, so 16 of them must be £4. Or we might work out ten 25s (250), four 25s (100) and two 25s (50) and add these up, to get 400. Or we could reason, 'two 25s is 50, so four 25s is 100, so eight 25s is 200, so sixteen 25s is 400'. This kind of approach, in which we make *ad hoc* use of the particular numbers and relationships in the problem in question, I like to call an *adhocorithm*. These informal, *ad hoc* approaches to calculations are equally as valid as the formal, algorithmic approaches, and have the advantage that they are based on our own personal level of confidence with numbers and number operations. In Chapters 5, 7, 9 and 11, I discuss various algorithms and adhocorithms for each of the four operations.

Then, thirdly, we could just use a *calculator*.

Calculators

I'm not convinced that there's any mathematics involved in using a calculator – all you have to do is press the buttons and the machine does all the thinking for you. Isn't that cheating?

This is a common misconception about calculators. In fact, using a calculator to solve a practical problem involves us in a fundamental mathematical process called *mathematical modelling*. This is nothing to do with making shapes out of card, but everything to do with using and applying mathematics in the real world.

For example, how would you work out how many boxes you need to hold 150 calculators if each box holds just 18 calculators? Personally I would use one of the calculators to work out 150 divided by 18. That gives me the result 8.3333333. That's just a bit more than 8 boxes. So I would actually need 9 boxes. If I only had 8 boxes there would be some calculators which couldn't be fitted in, although the calculator answer doesn't actually tell me how many. The process involved in the reasoning here is an example of mathematical modelling. This process is summarised in Figure 3.2.

A problem in the real world is translated into a problem expressed in mathematical symbols. So, in this example, the real-world problem about buying boxes to hold calculators is modelled by the mathematical expression '150 ÷ 18'.

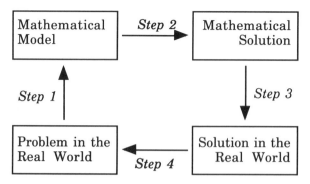

Figure 3.2   The process of mathematical modelling

The mathematical symbols are then manipulated in some way – this could be by means of a mental or written calculation or, as on this occasion, by pressing keys on a calculator – in order to obtain a mathematical solution, i.e. 8.3333333. This must then be interpreted back in the real world – for example, by saying that this means '8 boxes and a bit of a box'. The final step is, of course, to compare the result with the reality of the original situation. In this case, by considering the real situation and recognising that 8 boxes would leave some calculators not in a box, the appropriate conclusion is that we actually need 9 boxes.

So in this process there are basically four steps:

1. Set up the mathematical model.
2. Obtain the mathematical solution.
3. Interpret the mathematical solution back in the real world.
4. Compare the solution with the reality of the original situation.

There is potentially a fifth step, of course: if the solution does not make sense when compared with the reality of the original problem, then I may have to go round the cycle again, checking each stage of the process to determine what has gone wrong. Now it is important to note that the calculator does only the second of the steps in the process of mathematical modelling. I have done all the others. My contribution is significant mathematics. In a technological age, in which most calculations are done by machines, it surely cannot be disputed that knowing which calculation to do is more important than being able to do the calculation. As will be seen in Chapters 4, 6, 8 and 10, recognising which operations correspond to various real-world situations (step 1 above) is not always straightforward. These chapters indicate the range of categories of problems which pupils should learn to model with addition, subtraction, multiplication and division.

Is there much to learn about the interpretation of a calculator result?
The interpretation of the calculator result is far from being an insignificant aspect of the process. For example, in the problem above, the interpretation of the result 8.3333333 required a decision about what to do with all the figures after the decimal point.

When we carry out a calculation on a calculator in order to solve a practical problem, particularly those modelled by division, we can get three kinds of answer:

- An exact, appropriate answer.
- An exact but inappropriate answer.
- An answer which has been *truncated*.

In the last two cases, we normally have to round the answer in some way to make it appropriate to the real-world situation (rounding is considered in more detail in Chapter 12). For example, consider these three problems, all with the same identical mathematical structure:

1. How many apples at 15p each can I buy with 90p?
2. How many apples at 24p each can I buy with 90p?
3. How many apples at 21p each can I buy with 90p?

For problem (1) we might enter '90 ÷ 15 =' on to a calculator and obtain the result '6'. In this case there is no difficulty in interpreting this result back in the real world. The answer to the problem is indeed exactly 6 apples. The calculator result is both exact and appropriate.

For problem (2) we might enter '90 ÷ 24 =' and obtain the result '3.75'. This is the exact answer to the calculation which was entered on the calculator, i.e. the solution to the mathematical problem which we used to model the real-world problem, and is correctly interpreted as '3.75 apples'. But, since greengrocers sell only whole apples, clearly the answer is not appropriate. In the final step of the modelling process – comparing the solution with reality – clearly the 3.75 apples must be rounded to a whole number of apples. In this case we would conclude that we can actually afford only 3 apples.

For problem (3) we might enter '90 ÷ 21 =' on to the calculator and find that we get the result '4.2857142'. This is not an exact answer. Dividing 90 by 21 actually produces a *recurring decimal*, namely, 4.285714285714 . . . , with the '285714' repeating over and over again without ever coming to an end. Since a simple calculator can display only eight digits, it *truncates* the result, by throwing away all the extra digits. Of course, in this case, the bits that are thrown away are relatively tiny and the error involved in this truncation process is fairly insignificant. We can interpret the result displayed on the calculator as 'about 4.2857142 apples'. But again, when we compare this with the real-world situation, we must recognise the constraints of purchasing fruit and round the answer in some way to give a whole number of apples. The obvious conclusion is that we can afford only 4 apples.

Another problem arises when the calculator result in a money problem gives only one figure after the decimal point. For example, here is a problem in the real world: how much for 24 marker pens at £1.15 each? We might model this with the mathematical expression, '24 × 1.15' (step 1). Handing over the donkey work (step 2) to a calculator gives the result 27.6. Primary children have to be taught how to interpret this (step 3) as £27.60, in order to draw the conclusion (step 4) that this will be the total cost of the 24 marker pens.

Self-assessment questions

3.1: How much altogether for three books costing £4.95, £5.90 and £9.95? Use a calculator to answer this question, then identify the steps in the process of mathematical modelling in what you have done.

3.2: What does each person pay if three people share a restaurant bill for £27.90? Use a calculator to answer this question. Is the calculator result a) an exact, appropriate answer; b) an exact but inappropriate answer; or c) an answer which has been truncated? Identify the steps in the process of mathematical modelling in what you have done.

3.3: Repeat Question 3.2 with a bill for £39.70.

3.4: John was given £50 for his birthday and thought he might spend it all on his favourite chocolate bars. They cost 32p each. He wondered how many he might get. What is the mathematical model of this problem? Obtain the mathematical solution, using a calculator. Interpret the mathematical solution back in the real world. Is the calculator result a) an exact, appropriate answer; b) an exact but inappropriate answer; or c) an answer which has been truncated?

3.5: How many months will it take me to save up £500 if I save £35 a month? Use a calculator to answer this question. Is the calculator result a) an exact, appropriate answer; b) an exact but inappropriate answer; or c) an answer which has been truncated? Identify the steps in the process of mathematical modelling in what you have done.

Summary of teaching points

1. Recognise the validity of the three ways of doing calculations: algorithms, adhocorithms and calculators.
2. Provide pupils with plenty of opportunities to work through the process of mathematical modelling, emphasising the four steps in the process.
3. Recognise that all the steps are important and that step 2 (doing the calculation) is not actually as important as the other three steps.
4. Allow pupils to use a calculator when the calculations associated with a real-life problem are too difficult, so that they can still engage in the modelling process and learn to choose the right operation, to interpret the result and to compare it with reality.
5. Discuss with pupils real-life problems, particularly in the context of money, which produce calculator answers which require different kinds of interpretation, including those with a) an exact, appropriate answer; b) an exact but inappropriate answer; and c) an answer which has been *truncated*.
6. Explain truncation to primary pupils, but use informal language: 'When the calculator answer has a decimal point and fills up all the available spaces, then there are probably lots more figures to come after the ones we can see. Because the calculator does not have room for these it throws them away. This does not usually matter because they represent very small quantities.'

4

Addition Structures

Pupils should be taught to: understand the operation of addition, . . . and recognise situations to which it applies.

In this chapter there are explanations of

- two different structures of real-life problems modelled by addition; and
- the situations in which pupils will meet these structures.

What are the different kinds of situation which primary pupils might encounter to which the operation of addition applies?

There are two basic categories of real-life problems which are modelled by the mathematical operation we call addition. The problems in each of these categories may vary in terms of their content and context, but they all have the same basic structure. I refer to the structures in these two categories of problems as

- the aggregation structure; and
- the augmentation structure.

Aggregation refers to a situation in which two or more quantities are combined into a single quantity and the operation of addition is used to determine the

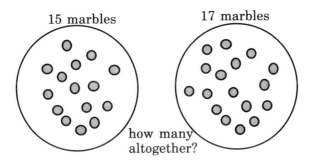

Figure 4.1   Addition as aggregation

total. For example, there are 15 marbles in one circle and 17 in another: how many marbles altogether? This idea of 'how many (or how much) altogether' is the central notion in the aggregation structure (see Figure 4.1).

Augmentation refers to a situation where a quantity is increased by some amount and the operation of addition is required in order to find the augmented or increased value. For example, the price of a bicycle costing £149 is increased by £25: what is the new price? The important language in augmentation therefore includes phrases like 'increased by' and 'goes up by'. This is the addition structure which lies behind the idea of counting-on along a number line which we might use with young children for experiencing simple additions such as, say, '7 + 5': 'start at 7 and count on 5' (see Figure 4.2).

start at 7...... count on 5

Figure 4.2   Addition as augmentation

It should just be mentioned at this stage that if the number which is added is a negative number, then the addition will not result in an increase, but in a *decrease*. This extension of the augmentation structure to negative numbers is discussed in Chapter 15, which deals with positive and negative integers.

Distinguishing between these two addition structures is not always easy, nor is it necessarily helpful to try to do so. But I find it is useful in teaching to have them in mind to ensure that pupils have opportunities to experience the full range of situations and the associated language which they have to learn to connect with addition.

What are some of the contexts in which pupils will meet addition in the aggregation structure?

First and most simply, pupils will encounter this structure whenever they are putting together two sets of objects into a single set, to find the total number. For example, combining two discrete sets of pupils (e.g. 25 boys and 29 girls, how many altogether?); combining two separate piles of counters (e.g. 46 red counters, 28 blue counters, how many altogether?).

Secondly, and, in terms of relevance, most importantly, pupils will encounter the aggregation structure in the context of money. This might be, for example, finding the total cost of two or more purchases, or the total bill for a number of services. The question will be, 'How much altogether?'

Then we also have to recognise addition in situations of aggregation in the contexts of measurements, such as length and distance, mass, capacity and liquid volume, and time. For example, addition would be the operation required to find the total distance for a journey made up of two stages of 48 miles and 63 miles, and also to find the total time for the journey if the first stage takes 65 minutes and the second stage takes 85 minutes.

What are some of the contexts in which pupils will meet addition in the augmentation structure?

The most important and relevant context for this structure is again that of money, particularly the idea of increases in price or cost, wage or salary. The key idea which signals the operation of addition is that of 'increasing'. This idea may also be encountered occasionally, but not often, in other measurement contexts, such as length (e.g. stretching a length of elastic by so much), mass (e.g. putting on so many pounds over Christmas) and time (e.g. increasing the length of the lunch break by so many minutes).

Self-assessment questions

4.1: Make up a problem which corresponds to the addition '5.95 + 6.99' using the aggregation structure in the context of shopping.

4.2: Make up a problem which corresponds to the addition '9750 + 145' using the augmentation structure in the context of salaries.

4.3: Make up a problem which corresponds to the addition '250 + 125' using the aggregation structure and liquid volume in the context of cooking.

4.4: Make up a problem which corresponds to the addition '15 + 25 + 55 + 20 + 65' using the aggregation structure in the context of time.

Summary of teaching points

1. Pupils should learn to connect the operation of addition with a range of problems, including situations using the idea of aggregation and those using the idea of augmentation.

2. The key language to be developed in the aggregation structure includes: *how many altogether, how much altogether, the total.*

3. The key language to be developed in the augmentation structure includes: *count on, increased by, goes up by.*

4. Pupils should experience these addition structures in a range of relevant contexts, including, especially, money (shopping, bills, wages and salaries) and various aspects of measurement.

5

Addition Calculations

Pupils should be taught to: use their understanding of place value to develop methods of computation; develop a variety of mental methods of computation; extend mental methods to develop a range of non-calculator methods of computation that involve addition . . . of whole numbers.

In this chapter there are explanations of:

- the idea of 'carrying' in the addition algorithm; and
- various informal, *ad hoc* ways of doing additions.

I can remember how to do the process of addition, but I don't really understand what's going on when you 'carry one'

The key to understanding the process for adding two or more numbers is a good grasp of the principle of *place value*, in particular the idea that when you have ten in one column they can be exchanged for one in the next column to the left. 'Ten of these can be exchanged for one of those' is the key phrase for teachers explaining the process to pupils.

Understanding the things we do with numbers often involves connecting the manipulation of the symbols with appropriate language and concrete materials. To explain addition, then, I will use £1, 10p and 1p coins, which will be referred to as 'hundreds', 'tens' and 'ones'. (Some teachers prefer to refer to the 'ones' as 'units'. I have no strong views about this and tend to switch freely between the two words.) Clearly the principle that 'ten of these can be exchanged for one of those' applies to the ones and the tens, and to the tens and the hundreds. The process could (and with children, should) equally well be experienced with base-ten blocks.

So to take an example: 356 + 267. The sum is set out with coins as shown in Figure 5.1, with 356 interpreted as 3 hundreds, 5 tens and 6 ones, and 267 interpreted as 2 hundreds, 6 tens and 7 ones.

The two numbers now have to be combined to find the total. So where do you start? There is an interesting phenomenon here. The standard algorithm involves working from right to left, i.e. starting with the ones. This seems a

24

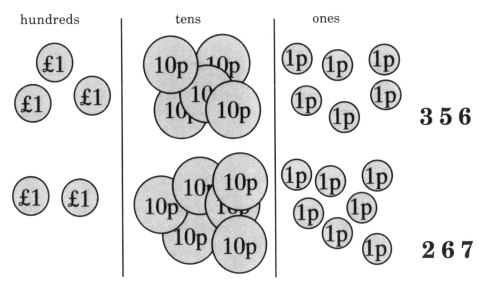

Figure 5.1 '356 + 267' set out with coins

little unnatural since the obvious thing would be to start with the biggest-value coins on the left. In fact, most people who can cope with this level of addition mentally do just that. They might reason something like this: 'Three hundred and two hundred make five hundred; sixty plus fifty is a hundred and ten, so that's six hundred and ten so far; six and seven give another thirteen, making six hundred and twenty-three in all.'

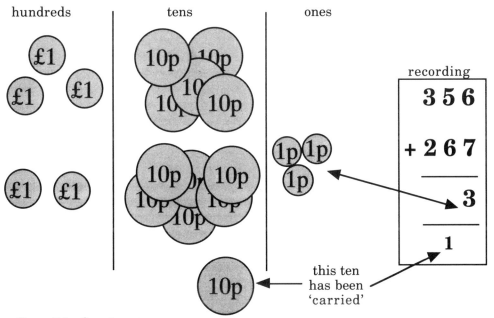

Figure 5.2 Carrying a ten

When it comes to using the standard addition algorithm, all I can say is that with experience you find that it's easier to be systematic and to avoid getting in a muddle if you work from right to left. But it really does not matter as long as you remember and apply correctly the principle that 'ten of these can be exchanged for one of those'.

So, in Figure 5.1, we first of all put together all the ones, making thirteen in all. Ten of these can then be exchanged at the bank for a ten. Since this ten is literally 'carried' from the bank and placed in the tens column, the language of 'carrying one' is very appropriate – provided it is clear that we are carrying 'one of these' and not carrying 'a one'. The coins at this stage are arranged as shown in Figure 5.2. This also shows the recording so far, in which there is direct relationship between what is done with the symbols and what has been done with coins. The 3 written in the ones column corresponds to the three remaining one-penny coins. The 1 written below the line in the tens column corresponds to the one ten which has been carried from the bank in exchange for ten ones.

Next all the tens are combined: that's the 5 tens in the top row, plus the 6 tens in the next row, plus the 1 ten which has been carried. This gives a total of 12 tens. Ten of these are then exchanged for a hundred. So once again we are 'carrying one', but this time, of course, it is 'one hundred'. Figure 5.3 shows the situation at this stage and, once again, the direct correspondence between the recording in symbols and the manipulation of the coins.

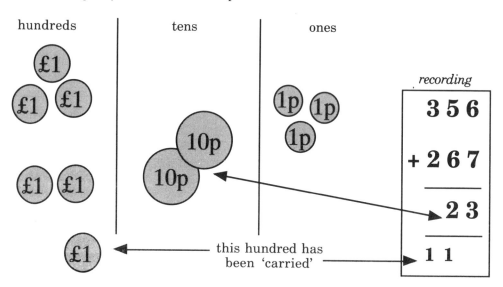

Figure 5.3   Carrying a hundred

The final stage in this calculation is to combine the hundreds: that's the 3 hundreds in the top row, plus the 2 hundreds in the next row, plus the 1 hundred which has been carried, giving a total of 6 hundreds. Figure 5.4 shows the final arrangement of the coins, with the 6 hundreds, 2 tens and 3 ones corresponding to the answer to the sum, namely 623.

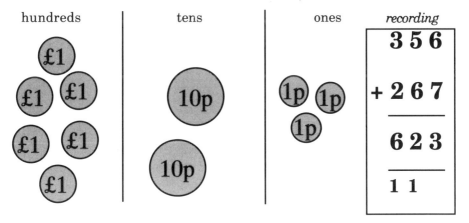

Figure 5.4   The result of adding 356 and 267

Are there any informal, *ad hoc* methods of doing additions which should be discussed with pupils in primary school?

Certainly. I have already mentioned above that it is perfectly acceptable to work from left to right, if you are able to keep track of where you are. Many people use this 'front-end' approach when doing arithmetic mentally or even informally on paper. The point about addition is that each number is made up of so many hundreds, tens and ones and you can combine these in any order you like. So, for example, given '457 + 359', we might be attracted first to the two fifties, because they combine nicely to make a hundred. Adding these to the other hundreds gives 800. Then we can add on the 7 and the 9 to get the answer 816.

In other cases you can convert the question into an easier question by temporarily adding or subtracting an appropriate small number. For example, many people would evaluate '673 + 99' by adding 1 temporarily to the 99, so the question becomes '673 + 100'. This gives 773. Now take off the extra 1, to get the answer 772.

Thirdly, there is the simple process of breaking up one of the numbers into appropriate bits which can be added to the other number a bit at a time. For example, to work out '307 + 424', I might think of the 307 as '300 + 6 + 1'. I can then add to 424, first the 6 (making 430), then the 300 (giving 730), and finally the 1 (to get 731).

There is a great neglect of open discussion of methods such as these in many of our primary schools. Greater sharing of these informal methods, whether mental or written, or a combination of the two, would undoubtedly lead to greater confidence with number.

Self-assessment questions

5.1: Using the same kind of explanation with coins as that given above, work through the addition of 208, 156 and 97.

5.2: Find the answer to '538 + 294' by the 'front-end' approach, i.e. starting with the hundreds and working from left to right.

5.3: Suggest some informal, *ad hoc* ways of evaluating a) '423 + 98'; b) '297 + 314'; and c) '309 + 492'.

Summary of teaching points

1. Important language used in the addition algorithm includes: *hundreds, tens, ones (units)*, *'ten of these can be exchanged for one of those'*, *carrying*.

2. The two most effective concrete embodiments of the place-value principle with which the addition algorithm can be explained to pupils and experienced by them are coins (hundreds, tens and ones) and base-ten blocks.

3. To develop their understanding of the addition algorithm, pupils should have opportunities to connect the manipulation of the materials (both coins and blocks) with the manipulation of the symbols and the corresponding language.

4. Discuss with pupils and encourage informal, *ad hoc* ways of doing addition calculations, both mental and written, or a combination of the two, including the 'front-end' approach.

6

Subtraction Structures

Pupils should be taught to: understand the operation of subtraction as taking away and comparison, and the relationship between addition and subtraction; recognise situations to which subtraction applies.

In this chapter there are explanations of

- four different structures of real-life problems modelled by subtraction; and
- the situations in which pupils will meet these structures.

What are the different kinds of situation which primary pupils might encounter to which the operation of subtraction applies?

There is, in fact, a daunting range of situations in which we have to learn to recognise that the appropriate operation is subtraction. I find it helpful to categorise these into the following four structures:

- The partitioning structure.
- The reduction structure.
- The comparison structure.
- The inverse-of-addition structure.

It helps us to connect these mathematical structures with the operation of subtraction if we ask ourselves the question: What is the calculation I would enter on a calculator in order to solve this problem? In each case the answer will involve using the subtraction key. It is one of the baffling aspects of mathematics that the same symbol, as we shall see with the example of the subtraction symbol, can have so many different meanings.

The *partitioning* structure refers to a situation in which a quantity is partitioned off in some way or other and subtraction is required to calculate how many or how much remains. For example, there are 17 marbles in the box, 5 are removed, how many are left? (See Figure 6.1.) The calculation to be entered on a calculator to correspond to this situation is '17 – 5'. This is the structure which teachers most frequently connect with subtraction and is strongly associated with the language 'take away' and 'how many (or how much) left'.

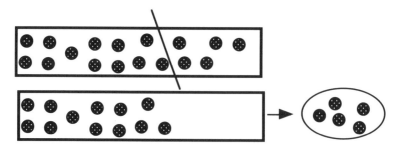

Figure 6.1   Subtraction as partitioning

The *reduction* structure is simply the reverse process of the augmentation structure of addition (see Chapter 4). It refers to a situation in which a quantity is reduced by some amount and the operation of subtraction is required to find the reduced value. For example, the price of a bicycle costing £149 is reduced by £25, what is the new price? The calculation which must be entered on a calculator to solve this problem is '149 – 25'. The important language in this structure includes phrases such as 'reduced by' and 'goes down by'. This is the subtraction structure which lies behind the idea of counting back along a number line, as shown in Figure 6.2.

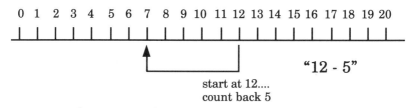

Figure 6.2   Subtraction as reduction

The *comparison* structure refers to a completely different set of situations, namely, those where subtraction is required to make a comparison between two quantities, as for example in Figure 6.3. How many more blue cubes are there than red cubes? The calculation to be entered on a calculator to correspond to this situation is '12 – 7'. Subtraction of the smaller number from the greater enables us to determine the *difference*, or to find out *how much greater* or *how much smaller* one quantity is than the other. Because making comparisons is such a fundamental process, with so many practical and social applications, the ability to recognise this subtraction structure and the confidence to handle the associated language patterns are particularly important.

The *inverse-of-addition* structure refers to situations where we have to determine what must be added to a given quantity in order to reach some target. The phrase 'inverse-of-addition' underlines the idea that subtraction and addition are *inverse* processes. This means, for example, that since '28 + 52' comes to 80, then '80 – 52' must be 28. The subtraction of 52 'undoes' the effect of adding 52. Hence to solve a problem of the form 'what must be added to X to give Y?' we subtract X from Y. For example: the entrance fee is

Figure 6.3   Subtraction as comparison

80p, but I have only 52p, how much more do I need? The calculation which must be entered on a calculator to solve this problem is the subtraction, '80 – 52'. Figure 6.4 shows how this subtraction structure is interpreted as an action on the number line: starting at 52 we have to determine what must be added to get to 80.

Figure 6.4   Subtraction as inverse-of-addition

What are some of the contexts in which pupils will meet the partitioning subtraction structure?

First of all this structure is encountered whenever we start with a given number of things in a set and a subset is taken away (removed, destroyed, eaten, killed, blown up, lost or whatever). In each case the question being asked is 'how many are left?' It also includes situations where a subset is identified as possessing some particular attribute and the question asked is, 'how many are not?' or 'how many do not?' For instance, there might be 58 children from a year group of 92 going on a field trip. The question, 'how many are not going?' has to be associated with the subtraction '92 – 58'.

Then the structure has a number of significant occurrences in the context of money and shopping. For example, we might spend £72 from our savings of £240 and need to work out how much is left (i.e. carry out the subtraction '240 – 72'). Or we might need to calculate the amount of change from a £10 note if our bill in the shop comes to £6.75 (i.e. carry out the subtraction '10 – 6.75').

Finally, there are a number of practical situations in the context of measurement where we encounter the partitioning subtraction structure. For example, when we have a given length of some material, cut off a length of it and wish to calculate how much is left; or where we have some cooking ingredients measured by mass or volume, we use a certain amount in a recipe and wish to calculate how much is left.

What are some of the contexts in which pupils will meet subtraction in the reduction structure?

Realistic examples of the reduction structure mainly occur in the context of money. The key idea which signals the operation of subtraction is that of 'reducing', for example, reducing prices and costs, cutting wages and salaries. For example, if a person's council tax of £625 is cut by £59, the reduced tax is determined by the subtraction, '625 – 59'. The structure may also be encountered occasionally in other measurement contexts, such as reduction in mass or temperatures falling.

What are some of the contexts in which pupils will meet subtraction in the comparison structure?

Almost any context! Wherever two numbers occur we will often find ourselves wanting to compare them, to determine the difference or to find out how much greater or smaller one is than the other. So we might wish to compare the numbers of items in two sets (e.g. the numbers of marbles in two bags, the numbers of cards in two packs, the numbers of children in two classes, the numbers of counters in two piles, the numbers of pages in two books, and so on). To do this we have to connect the situation and the associated language of 'difference', 'how many more', 'how many less (or fewer)' with the operation of subtraction.

Then in the context of money we would encounter this subtraction structure whenever we are comparing the prices of articles or the costs of services. If holiday package A costs £716 and package B costs £589, then we would ask questions such as: 'How much more expensive is A?' 'How much cheaper is B?' 'How much dearer is A?' 'How much more does A cost than B?' 'How much less does B cost than A?' In each case the question is answered by the subtraction, '716 – 589'. Also, we might use subtraction to compare salaries and wages: for example, how much more does a police officer earn than a teacher?

Finally, the process of comparison is a central idea in all measurement contexts. If we measure the heights of two pupils we would need a subtraction to compare them, to determine how much taller or shorter one pupil is than another. If we measure the masses of two articles we would compare them by asking 'how much heavier' or 'how much lighter' – and again subtraction is involved.

The language of comparison in the contexts of measurement is extensive. For example, we might ask: how much longer, taller, higher, further, wider, shorter, nearer, narrower, in the context of length; how much heavier, lighter, in the context of weighing; holds how much more or how much less, in the context of capacity; how much longer or shorter in time taken, how much sooner, earlier, later, younger, older, in the context of time; how much hotter, colder, in the context of temperature; how much faster, slower, in the context of speed. The development of this range of language is crucial to an understanding of the measurement concepts, as well as being important in building up confidence in recognising situations to be connected with subtraction.

What are some of the contexts in which pupils will meet subtraction in the inverse-of-addition structure?

This subtraction structure is often the most difficult to recognise for primary pupils because the language associated with it, such as 'how much more is needed?' and 'what must be added?', signals the idea of addition rather than subtraction.

There are many commonplace situations where we encounter this structure: for example, any situation where we have a number of objects or a number of individuals and we require some more in order to reach a target. The most convincing example for many will be in the contexts of sport. For example, if I have scored 180 in darts how many more do I need to reach 401? This corresponds to the subtraction, '401 – 180'. If we are chasing a score of 235 in cricket and we have scored 186 with eight overs remaining, how many more runs do we need? The calculation to be entered on a calculator to answer this is '235 – 186'.

Perhaps the most relevant instances of the inverse-of-addition subtraction structure occur in the context of money. For example, if we have saved up £485 towards a holiday costing £716, we would need to do the subtraction, '716 – 485', in order to calculate how much more we need to save. Again, if the reader is uncertain about the assertion that this situation is an example of subtraction, it will help to ask: What is the calculation you would enter on a calculator to work this out?

Other examples of the inverse-of-addition structure occur in the context of measurement, such as: how much further do you have to drive to complete a journey of 345 miles if you have so far driven 196 miles?

Self-assessment questions

6.1: An important event is planned for 1 January 2050. On 1 January 1996 how many years are there to wait? What is the calculation to be entered on a calculator to answer this? Of what subtraction structure is this an example?

6.2: There are 256 pages in my book. I have so far read 178 of them. How many more pages do I have to read? What is the calculation to be entered on a calculator to answer this? Of what subtraction structure is this an example?

6.3: I am 52 and my daughter is 25. How many years younger than me is she? What is the calculation to be entered on a calculator to answer this? Of what subtraction structure is this an example?

6.4: I have collected 565 points from my local service station, but I need 750 points to get the decanter from the free-gift catalogue: how many more points do I need? What is the calculation to be entered on a calculator to answer this? Of what subtraction structure is this an example?

6.5: Make up a problem which corresponds to the subtraction '3.95 – 2.99' using the comparison structure in the context of shopping.

6.6: Make up a problem which corresponds to the subtraction '25 – (–6)' using the comparison subtraction structure in the context of temperatures.

6.7: Make up a problem which corresponds to the subtraction '250 – 159' using the partitioning structure and the phrase 'how many do not . . . ?'.

6.8: Make up a problem in the context of shopping, which uses the inverse-of-addition structure, corresponding to '489 – 350'.

Summary of teaching points

1. Pupils should learn to connect the operation of subtraction with a wide range of problems, including situations using the ideas of partitioning, reduction, comparison and inverse-of-addition.
2. Pupils should experience these subtraction structures in a range of practical and relevant contexts, including especially money (shopping, bills, wages and salaries) and various aspects of measurement.
3. The key language to be developed in the partitioning structure includes: *Take away, how many left? How many are not? How many do not?*
4. Subtraction is not just 'take away'. Partitioning is only one subtraction structure. Teachers should not overemphasise the language of 'take away, how many left' at the expense of all the other important language which has to be associated with subtraction.
5. The key language to be developed in the reduction structure includes: *reduced by, cut by, count back.*
6. The key language to be developed in the comparison structure includes: *Difference, how many more? How many less (or fewer)? How much greater, smaller, longer, taller, higher, further, wider, shorter, nearer, narrower, heavier, lighter, longer or shorter in time taken, sooner, earlier, later, younger, older, hotter, colder, faster, slower? Holds how much more, how much less?*
7. The key language to be developed in the inverse-of-addition structure includes: *What must be added? How many (much) more needed?*
8. The language of problems with the inverse-of-addition structure often signals addition rather than subtraction, so that many pupils will automatically add the two numbers in the question. They will need specific help to recognise the need for a subtraction.
9. Asking the question, 'what is the calculation to be entered on a calculator to solve this problem?', helps to focus the pupil's thinking on the underlying mathematical structure of the situation.

7

Subtraction Calculations

Pupils should be taught to: use their understanding of place value to develop methods of computation; develop a variety of mental methods of computation; extend mental methods to develop a range of non-calculator methods of computation that involve . . . subtraction of whole numbers.

In this chapter there are explanations of

- the decomposition method for doing subtraction calculations;
- the equal additions method for subtraction;
- how the two methods differ and why decomposition is preferred;
- the problem with zeros in the top number in a subtraction calculation; and
- an *ad hoc* approach to subtraction based on the principles of equal additions and equal subtractions.

Children in school don't seem to use the same method for doing subtractions as I learnt when I was at school. I find it a bit confusing

Subtractions are straightforward when each digit in the first number is greater than the corresponding digit in the second, as, for example, in '576 – 324': we just take the 3 hundreds away from the 5 hundreds, the 2 tens away from the 7 tens, and the 4 units away from the 6 units, to get the answer 252. The problem with subtraction calculations is that we have to have some way of proceeding when one of the digits in the first number is smaller than the corresponding digit in the second number. For example, when working out '443 – 267', when we look at the units column we might find ourselves saying something like, 'Three take away seven, you can't do that'. Historically, in Britain, there have been essentially two ways of dealing with this.

Nowadays, nearly all primary schools, if they teach pupils a subtraction algorithm, use the method known as *subtraction by decomposition*. This has more or less completely ousted the method which most people of my age were taught at school, namely the method of *equal additions*. Even in the late 1990s I still find a significant proportion of student-teachers who have grown up using this method.

Do primary-school teachers have to be fluent in both methods?

No. The bad news for any readers who were brought up on equal additions is that they will definitely have to become fluent in using the method of decomposition. On the other hand, those who use decomposition already have no need to try to master the method of equal additions, although they may find it interesting to try to understand it.

Why has decomposition become the favoured method?

The reason for the shift towards decomposition is that it is much easier to *understand*, in the sense of making connections between the manipulation of concrete materials, the manipulations of the symbols and the corresponding language. Subtraction by equal additions can only really be taught to children by rote, as a procedure to be followed blindly with little real understanding of what is going on. The shift towards decomposition therefore coincided with a greater emphasis in teaching on learning mathematics with understanding.

So how does subtraction by decomposition work?

As with addition calculations, the key to explaining the method is a sound grasp of *place value* and the use of some appropriate concrete embodiments of number, such as coins or base-ten blocks.

I will explain the method of decomposition with base-ten blocks, using the example of '443 – 267'. First the 443 is set out with base-ten blocks, as shown in Figure 7.1: 4 hundreds, 4 tens and 3 units. The task is to take 267 away from this collection of blocks, i.e. to remove 2 hundreds, 6 tens and 7 units.

As with addition, the natural place to start might be to take away the biggest blocks first, i.e. working from left to right, and this is how many people would deal with a calculation of this kind if doing it mentally. Something like this:

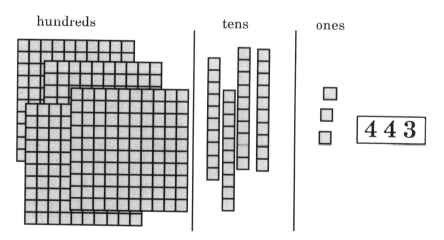

Figure 7.1   The number 443 set out with base-ten blocks

'443 take away 200, leaves 243; 243 take away 60, leaves 183; 183 take away 7, leaves 176.'

But again the standard written algorithm actually works from right to left. This is not essential, but it is simply tidier to do it this way. So we start by trying to remove 7 units from the collection of blocks in Figure 7.1. Since there are only 3 units there we cannot do this – yet. So we take one of the tens (i.e. take it to the box of blocks) and exchange it for ten units. Figure 7.2 shows the

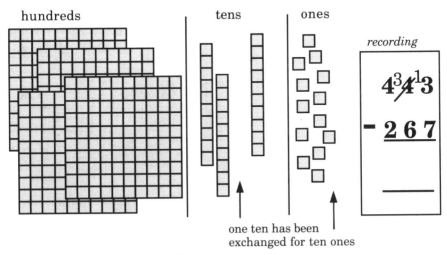

Figure 7.2   *Exchanging one ten for ten ones*

situation at this stage and the corresponding recording. Notice how the recording in symbols corresponds precisely to the manipulation of the materials. We have crossed out the 4 tens in the top number and replaced it by 3, because one of these tens has been exchanged for units and we do indeed now have 3 tens in our collection. The little '1' placed beside the 3 units in the top number is to

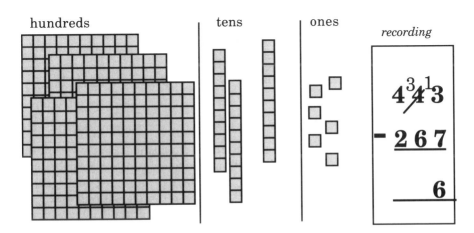

Figure 7.3   *After 7 units have been taken away*

indicate that we now have 13 units. We are now in a position to take away the 7 units as required, leaving 6 units. This is recorded as in Figure 7.3.

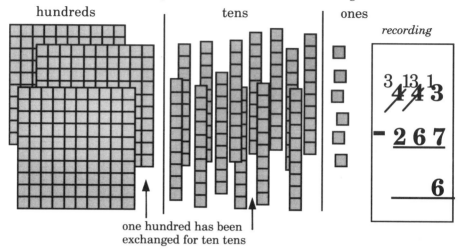

Figure 7.4   Exchanging one hundred for 10 tens

The next step is to deal with the problem of removing 6 tens when we have only 3 of them. So we take one of the hundreds and exchange it for 10 tens, producing the situation shown in Figure 7.4. The recording indicates that after the exchanging process we now have 3 hundreds and 13 tens. We can now complete the subtraction, taking away first the 6 tens and then the 2 hundreds. Figure 7.5 shows the final arrangement of the blocks, with the remaining 1 hundred, 7 tens and 6 units corresponding to the result of the subtraction, namely 176.

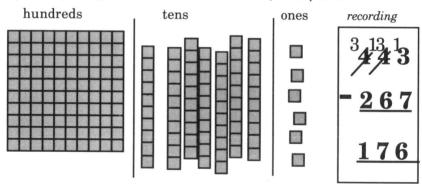

Figure 7.5   The result of subtracting 267 from 443

There are three important points to note about this method. First there is the quite natural idea of exchanging a block in one column for ten in the next column to the right when necessary. Secondly, there is the strong connection between the manipulation of the materials and the recording in symbols, supported by appropriate language. Notice, thirdly, that all the action in the recording takes place in the top line, i.e. in the number you are working on, not the number you are taking away.

How does the method of equal additions differ from this?

The method of equal additions differs in all three of these respects. It does not use the principle of exchange, it is not naturally rooted in the manipulation of materials and the method involves working on both numbers simultaneously. Although the method is not normally taught these days it will actually prove to be quite useful to 'explain' it. My explanation will be merely in terms of numbers, without the support of coins or blocks, simply because the method is not easily understood in these terms.

The method is based on the comparison structure of subtraction (see Chapter 6) and uses the principle that the difference between two numbers remains the same if you add the same number to each one. For example, the difference between your height and my height is the still same if we stand together on a table rather than on the floor! Faced with the subtraction '443 – 267', the person using equal additions would manipulate the symbols as shown in Figure 7.6.

$$
\begin{array}{c c c c}
\begin{array}{r} 4\ 4\ 3 \\ -2\ 6\ 7 \\ \hline \\ \end{array}
&
\begin{array}{r} 4\ 4\ {}^1 3 \\ -2\ 7\!\!\!/6\ 7 \\ \hline 6 \end{array}
&
\begin{array}{r} 4\ {}^1 4\ {}^1 3 \\ -{}^3 2\!\!\!/7\!\!\!/6\ 7 \\ \hline 6 \end{array}
&
\begin{array}{r} 4\ {}^1 4\ {}^1 3 \\ -{}^3 2\!\!\!/7\!\!\!/6\ 7 \\ \hline 1\ 7\ 6 \end{array}
\\
(a) & (b) & (c) & (d)
\end{array}
$$

Figure 7.6   The method of equal additions

Unable to deal with '3 take away 7', we add ten to both numbers, as shown in Figure 7.6a. In the top number this ten is added to the units digit, increasing the 3 to 13. This is shown by writing the little '1' in front of the three. In the bottom number the ten is added to the tens column, increasing the 6 to 7. I show this by striking through the 6 and writing 7, whereas some people indicate this by writing a little 1 somewhere in the tens column: various systems of recording are used for this step, but the principle of adding ten to both numbers is the same.

In Figure 7.6b we can now deal with the units, writing in 6 in the answer, but are faced with the problem of '4 subtract 7' in the tens column. We apply the same principle of adding the same thing to both numbers, but this time we actually add 100, as shown in Figure 7.6c. This appears as 10 tens in the top number, increasing the number of tens from 4 to 14. Simultaneously, in the bottom number we add one to the hundreds digit, increasing it from 2 to 3. We are then able to complete the subtraction as shown in Figure 7.6d. The reader may be encouraged to note that both methods produce the same answer.

What was meant by 'borrow one and pay it back'?

I really don't know. When we did equal additions we were taught to say, 'Borrow one and pay it back'. I have never understood this phrase, since it is not at all clear from whom we were borrowing or even whether we were paying it back to the same source. I have therefore come to the conclusion that it was merely something to say to yourself, with no meaning, simply as a reminder that there were two things to do. We could equally well have said, 'Pick one up and put one down'. The intriguing thing is, though, that this language of 'borrowing' has actually survived the demise of the method for which it was invented! It is still commonplace to hear teachers talking about 'borrowing one' when explaining the method of decomposition to children. I find this unhelpful. We are not 'borrowing one' in decomposition, we are '*exchanging* one of these for ten of those'.

Of course, in practice no one ever thought consciously that what they were doing, for example, was adding ten or a hundred to both numbers: they were simply 'borrowing one and paying it back'! Thus subtraction by equal additions was always taught by rote, with no real attempt to understand what was going on. This is the real advantage of decomposition: that there is the potential in the method for pupils to understand it in terms of concrete experiences of coins or blocks, supported by meaningful language.

So, why did not everyone always teach the method of decomposition?

The reason is that unfortunately there is sometimes a slight problem in using the decomposition method when there is a zero in the top number. A modification in the process of decomposition is required, whereas with equal additions zeros in the top number make no difference to the routine. However, the modification is a natural process, still easily understood if related strongly to concrete materials and the appropriate language of exchange.

What is the problem in decomposition with a zero in the top number?

Figure 7.7 shows the steps involved in tackling '802 – 247' by decomposition. In Figure 7.7a the person doing the calculation is faced with the problem of '2 subtract 7'. The decomposition method requires a ten to be exchanged for ten units, but in the 802 the zero indicates that there are no tens. This is the problem! However, it is not difficult to see that the thing to do is to go across to the hundreds column and exchange this for 10 tens, as shown in Figure 7.7b, then to take one of these and exchange it for ten units, as shown in Figure 7.7c. The subtraction can then be completed, as in Figure 7.7d. Of course, all

Figure 7.7   The problem of a zero in the top number

this can be carried out and understood easily in terms of base-ten blocks or coins, representing hundreds, tens and ones (units).

Is the idea of equal additions in subtraction totally redundant?

Surprisingly, in view of what I have said above, no. The principle of equal additions is actually an important tool in the collection of techniques which we might use for mental or informal methods of doing subtraction calculations. But it does not have to be ten or a hundred that you add. For instance, to work out '87 – 48' we could simply add 2 to both numbers and change it to '89 – 50', thus converting it into a much easier calculation. This 'adhocorithm' can almost be developed into an 'algorithm' which some pupils might find more to their liking than the formal method of decomposition.

So, for example, returning to '443 – 267', we could argue like this:

The problem is	'443 – 267'
Add 3 to both numbers, to give	'446 – 270' (that makes it a bit easier)
Add 30 to both numbers, to give	'476 – 300' (that makes it really easy!)
So the answer is	176

This approach can be combined where appropriate with 'subtracting the same thing from both numbers'. For example:

The problem is	'918 – 436' (no problem with the units . . .)
So, subtract 6 from both numbers	'912 – 430'
Now add 70 to both numbers	'982 – 500' (that makes it really easy!)
So the answer is	482

With a bit of practice, this method of converting the second number into a round number of tens or hundreds by adding the same thing to both numbers, or subtracting the same thing from both numbers, can become extremely efficient and just as quick as any other.

Self-assessment questions

7.1: Practise the explanation of the process of subtraction by decomposition using coins (1p, 10p and £1 to represents ones, tens and hundreds) and appropriate examples, such as '623 – 471'.

7.2: Practise the explanation of the process of decomposition using base-ten blocks to represent units, tens, hundreds and thousands, with examples with zero in the first number, such as '2006 – 438'.

7.3: Find the answer to '721 – 458' by converting it to an easier subtraction, by adding the same thing to both numbers.

7.4: Suggest some informal, *ad hoc* ways of working out these subtractions: a) '1000 – 458'; b) '819 – 523'; and c) '605 – 206'.

Summary of teaching points

1. For those pupils who need a formal method for subtraction and who can master it, teach the method of decomposition.

2. Explain the method in a way which encourages understanding of the process, not just as a recipe without meaning.
3. Provide pupils with plenty of opportunity to connect the manipulation of coins (1p, 10p and £1) and base-ten blocks with the manipulation of the symbols in the process of subtraction by decomposition, supported by the appropriate language.
4. Don't use the language of 'borrowing' when explaining subtraction by decomposition. It has no place there. Emphasise the idea of 'exchanging'.
5. Encourage pupils to set out written subtraction calculations generously, to give themselves plenty of room for their crossings-out and writing of little 1s, and so on.
6. Be alert to the possibility of parents and grandparents confusing children by trying to teach them the method of equal additions.
7. Discuss with pupils how the principle of adding the same thing to both numbers (or subtracting the same thing from both) can convert a subtraction question into an easier calculation.
8. Encourage pupils to share different ideas for working out subtraction calculations by informal, *ad hoc* methods.

8

Multiplication Structures

Pupils should be taught to: understand multiplication as repeated addition . . . use associated language and recognise situations to which multiplication applies.

In this chapter there are explanations of

- two different structures of real-life problems modelled by multiplication;
- the situations in which pupils will meet these structures;
- the commutative property of multiplication; and
- the idea of a rectangular array associated with multiplication.

What are the different kinds of situation which primary pupils might encounter to which the operation of multiplication applies?

There are essentially two categories of situation which have a structure that corresponds to the mathematical operation represented by the symbol for multiplication. They are

- the repeated aggregation structure; and
- the scaling structure.

These two structures are extensions of the two structures of addition, discussed in Chapter 4.

Repeated aggregation is the elementary idea that multiplication means 'so many sets of' or 'so many lots of'. If I have '10 sets of 3 counters' then the

Figure 8.1   Multiplication as repeated aggregation, 3 × 10

question, 'how many counters altogether?', is associated with the multiplication, '3 × 10' (see Figure 8.1). This structure is simply an extension of the aggregation structure of addition, with, for example, the repeated addition, '3 + 3 + 3 + 3 + 3 + 3 + 3 + 3 + 3 + 3', becoming the multiplication, '3 × 10'.

The *scaling* structure is a rather more difficult idea. It is an extension of the augmentation structure of addition. That structure referred to addition as meaning that we increase a quantity by a certain amount. With multiplication we also increase a quantity, but we increase it by a *scale factor*. So multiplication by 10 would be interpreted in this structure as scaling a quantity by a factor of 10, as illustrated in Figure 8.2.

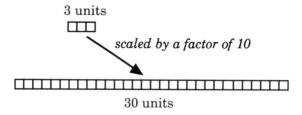

Figure 8.2   Multiplication as scaling, 3 × 10

It should perhaps be mentioned here that multiplication by a number less than 1 would correspond to a scaling which *reduces* the size of the quantity, not increases it. For example, scaling 3 by a factor of 0.5 would reduce it to 1.5, corresponding to the multiplication, '3 × 0.5 = 1.5'. (There is a parallel here with the addition of a negative number, which also results in a reduction rather than an increase – see Chapter 15.)

I'm not sure whether '3 × 5' means '3 lots of 5' or '5 lots of 3'

Which of the pictures in Figure 8.3 would we connect with '3 × 5'? If I were to be really pedantic, I suppose I would have to say that, strictly speaking, '3 × 5' means '5 lots of 3'. You start with 3, and multiply it by 5, i.e. reproduce the three, five times in all, as illustrated in Figure 8.3a. But I would prefer to let the meaning of the symbol be determined by how it is used. It seems to me that, in

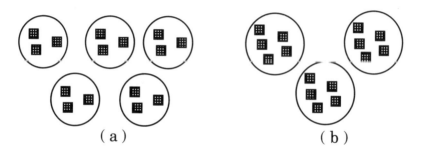

Figure 8.3   a) 5 sets of 3; b) 3 sets of 5

practice, people use the symbols '3 × 5' to mean both '3 lots of 5' and '5 lots of 3', i.e. both the examples shown in Figure 8.3a and b. I am happy therefore to let '3 × 5' refer to either (a) or (b). And the same goes for '5 × 3'. One symbol having more than one meaning is something we have to learn to live with in mathematics – as well as being a feature which makes mathematical symbols so powerful in their application.

The underlying mathematical principle here is what is called the *commutative property* of multiplication. This refers to the fact that when you are multiplying two numbers together the order in which you write them down does not make any difference. Addition also has this property. We recognise this commutative property formally by the following two generalisations, which are true whatever the numbers *a* and *b*:

$$a + b = b + a \quad \text{and} \quad b \times a = a \times b$$

The significance of this property is twofold. First of all it is important to realise that the other two basic number operations, subtraction and division, do *not* have this commutative property. For example, '10 – 5' is not equal to '5 – 10', and '10 ÷ 5' is not equal to '5 ÷ 10'. Secondly, particularly in multiplication, use of the commutative property enables us to simplify some calculations. For example, many of us would evaluate 'five lots of fourteen' by changing the question to the equivalent, 'fourteen lots of five' – because fives are much easier to handle than fourteens! Finally, grasping the principle of commutativity cuts down significantly the number of different results we have to memorise from the multiplication tables: if I know 'seven fives', for example, then I know 'five sevens'.

I find it difficult to bring to mind some kind of image of what multiplication is all about: is there a picture which can usefully be associated with this symbol?

It is interesting to note first that the commutative property of multiplication is by no means obvious. Other than by counting the numbers in each picture, we would not immediately recognise that (a) and (b) in Figure 8.3 have the same number of counters. So this picture is not especially helpful.

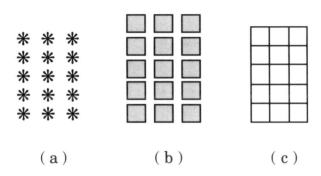

(a) (b) (c)

Figure 8.4   Examples of rectangular arrays for '3 × 5'

But there is one very significant picture of multiplication which does make this commutative property obvious. This is the association of multiplication with the image of a *rectangular array*. Figure 8.4 shows some examples of rectangular arrays which correspond to '3 × 5' (or '5 × 3').

This is the image of multiplication which we should carry round in our heads, particularly when we want to talk to children about multiplication and to illustrate our discussions with diagrams. This picture really does make the commutative property transparently obvious. We can actually see that '3 sets of 5' and '5 sets of 3' come to the same thing, because the array can be thought of as '3 rows of 5', using vertical rows, or '5 rows of 3', using horizontal rows.

There are other good reasons for strongly associating this image of a rectangular array with multiplication. For example, this idea leads on naturally to the use of multiplication for determining the area of a rectangle. In example (c) in Figure 8.4, '3 × 5' gives the number of square units in the rectangle and therefore determines its area. We can also extend this idea to develop an effective method for multiplying together larger numbers (see Chapter 9).

Apart from 'so many sets of so many,' are there other contexts in which pupils will meet multiplication in the repeated aggregation structure?

Any situation in which we aggregate a certain number of portions of a given quantity, such as mass, liquid volume, length and time, provides an application of this multiplication structure. For example: finding the total mileage for 42 journeys of 38 miles each (42 × 38); finding the total volume of drink required to fill 32 glasses if each holds 225 ml (32 × 225); finding the total time required for 12 events each lasting 25 minutes (12 × 25).

But, not surprisingly, the most important context will be shopping, particularly where we have to find the cost of a number of items given the *unit cost*. Two important words here are *each* and *per*. For example, we might need to find the cost of 25 cans of drink at 39p each (25 × 39). Or we might purchase 25 tickets at £3.50 per ticket (25 × 3.50). In both cases we have to associate the language and the structure of the example with the operation of multiplication.

Then there are important situations where we encounter repeated aggregation in the context of *cost per unit of measurement*. For example, if we purchase 28 litres of petrol at £0.56 per litre, we should recognise that a multiplication (25 × 0.56) is required to determine the total cost, although, of course, in practice the petrol pump will do it for us! Likewise, we should connect multiplication with situations such as finding the cost of so many metres of material given the cost per metre, or someone's earnings for so many hours of work given the rate of pay per hour, and so on.

What are some of the contexts in which pupils will meet multiplication in the scaling structure?

Most obviously, this structure is associated with scale models and scale drawings. For example, if a scale model is built using a scale factor of '1 to 10', then each linear measurement in the actual object is 10 times the corresponding measurement in the model. Similarly, if we have a plan of the classroom made using a scale factor '1 to 100' and the width of the chalkboard in the drawing is 2 cm, then the width of the actual chalkboard will be 200 cm, i.e. '2 × 100'.

This is also the multiplication structure which lies behind the idea of a *pro rata* increase. For example, if we all get a 13% increase in our salary, then all our salaries get multiplied by the same scale factor, namely 1.13 (see Chapter 18 for an explanation of percentage increases). The simplest experience of this structure is when we talk about *doubling* or *trebling* a given quantity: this is simply increasing the given quantity by applying the scale factors 2 or 3 respectively.

Then we also sometimes use this multiplication structure in order to express a comparison between two numbers or amounts, where we make statements using phrases 'so many times as much (or as many)' or 'so many times bigger (longer, heavier, etc. . . .)'. For example, '125 × 3' would be the calculation corresponding to this situation: John earns £125 a week, but his brother earns three times as much; how much does his brother earn? The phrase *three times as much* is what should prompt the association with multiplication by 3.

Self-assessment questions

8.1: Give two problems associated with the multiplication '29 × 12', one using the idea of '29 lots of 12' and the other using '12 lots of 29'.

8.2: Make up a problem using the repeated aggregation structure and the word *per*, in the context of shopping, corresponding to the multiplication, '12 × 25'.

8.3: A box of yoghurts consists of 4 rows of 6 cartons arranged in a rectangular array. How would you use this as an example to illustrate the commutative property of multiplication?

8.4: A model of an aeroplane is built on a scale of 1 to 25. Make up a question about the model and the actual aeroplane, using the scaling structure.

8.5: A headteacher earning £1827 a month gets a 12% pay rise. Model this situation with a multiplication by a scale factor and use a calculator to find her new monthly salary.

Summary of teaching points

1. Primary-school pupils' main experience of multiplication will be through the structure of repeated aggregation, although they may also meet some examples of multiplication used for scaling.

2. There is no need to make a fuss about whether '*a* × *b*' means '*a* lots of *b*' or '*b* lots of *a*'.

3. The key language to be developed in the repeated aggregation structure includes: *so many lots (sets) of so many, how many (how much) altogether, per, each*.

4. Give special attention to helping pupils to use the word *per* with confidence and to associate the practical problems about unit cost and cost per unit of measurement with the corresponding multiplications.

5. The key language to be developed in the scaling structure includes: *scaling, scale factor, so many times bigger (longer, heavier, etc. . . .), so many times as much (or as many)*.

6. Work hard with your pupils to establish the commutative principle in multiplication and encourage them to use it in recalling results from the multiplication tables.

7. Use rectangular arrays frequently to illustrate and to support your explanations about multiplication, particularly for reinforcing the commutative principle.

9

Multiplication Calculations

Pupils should be taught to: multiply by powers of 10; develop a variety of mental methods of computation; extend mental methods to develop a range of non-calculator methods of computation . . . , progressing to methods for multiplication of up to three-digit by two-digit whole numbers.

In this chapter there are explanations of

- the long multiplication algorithm;
- the distributive law and its relationship to long multiplication;
- a simpler method for multiplication using areas of rectangles; and
- a number of informal, *ad hoc* approaches to multiplication calculations.

I can't remember how to do long multiplication. I don't think I ever understood it anyway

The standard algorithm for multiplying together two numbers with two or more digits is usually called *long multiplication*. Figure 9.1 shows how the method might be set out for calculating '26 × 34'.

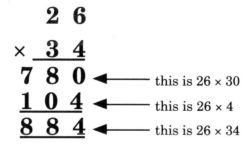

Figure 9.1   Long multiplication, 26 × 34

The method is based on what is called the *distributive law*. Formally, written out as an algebraic statement, this law of arithmetic looks like this:

$$A \times (B + C) = (A \times B) + (A \times C)$$

In words, what this means is that if I have to multiply the sum of two numbers, *B* and *C*, by another number, *A*, then I can multiply *B* and *C* separately by *A* and then add together the results. For example, using some actual numbers:

$$3 \times (6 + 4) = (3 \times 6) + (3 \times 4)$$

The left-hand side is 3 multiplied by 10, which comes to 30. The right-hand side is 18 plus 12, which also comes to 30. Applying this principle to '26 × 34', we can think of it as '26 × (30 + 4)' and get the answer by multiplying the 26 first by the 30 and then by the 4, and then adding up the results. This is precisely what goes on in long multiplication, as shown in Figure 9.1. But the problem with the method is that multiplications like '26 × 30' and '26 × 4' are themselves quite difficult calculations and there is consequently some potential for errors and confusion.

So is there a simpler method for multiplication of two-digit numbers which is easier to understand?

Yes, there is a simpler method. It is based on the idea of splitting up both the numbers being multiplied into their tens and units. So the 26 becomes '20 + 6' and the 34 becomes '30 + 4'. Then we have to multiply the 20 by the 30, the 20 by the 4, the 6 by the 30 and the 6 by the 4. To make sense of this we can visualise the multiplication as a question of finding the number of counters in a rectangular array of 26 by 34 (see Chapter 8), as shown in Figure 9.2. Thinking of the 26 and the 34 as '20 + 6' and '30 + 4' respectively suggests that we can split the array up into four separate arrays, representing '20 × 30', '20 × 4', '6 × 30' and '6 × 4'.

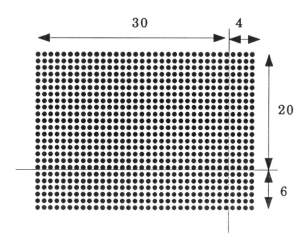

Figure 9.2   A simpler approach for '26 × 34'

Drawing pictures with hundreds of counters in them, like Figure 9.2, helps to explain the method, but it's very tedious. A more efficient picture, therefore, uses the idea, suggested in Chapter 8, that we can extend the notion of a rectangular array into that of the area of a rectangle. We can then explain '26 × 34' very simply using the diagrams shown in Figure 9.3.

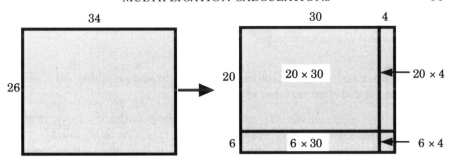

Figure 9.3 Using area to interpret '26 × 34'

The answer to the multiplication is then obtained by working out the areas of the four separate rectangles and adding them up. The actual calculation can be written out as follows:

$$
\begin{array}{rcl}
20 \times 30 &=& 600 \\
6 \times 30 &=& 180 \\
20 \times 4 &=& 80 \\
6 \times 4 &=& 24 \\
\hline
\text{so} \dots \quad 26 \times 34 &=& 884
\end{array}
$$

Can this method be used with three-digit numbers?

The method extends quite easily to multiplications involving three-digit numbers. Figure 9.4 shows a rough sketch which might be used to visualise '348 × 25'. (The rectangles in the diagram are not intended to be drawn to scale.) Clearly, in this example, there are now six bits to deal with separately, then to be added up. This leads to the calculation being set out, for example, as follows:

$$
\begin{array}{rcl}
300 \times 20 &=& 6000 \\
40 \times 20 &=& 800 \\
8 \times 20 &=& 160 \\
300 \times 5 &=& 1500 \\
40 \times 5 &=& 200 \\
8 \times 5 &=& 40 \\
\hline
\text{so} \dots \quad 348 \times 25 &=& 8700
\end{array}
$$

Figure 9.4 The area approach applied to '348 × 25'

Multiplications of this level of difficulty are about as far as most primary-school children would need to go.

You still have to be very confident with multiplications like '20 × 30', don't you, in order to use this method?

Yes. The first prerequisite for using the method outlined above is that you know thoroughly all the results in the multiplication tables up to '10 × 10'. Secondly, you should be able to derive from any one of these results a whole series of results for multiplications involving multiples of 10 and 100. For example, knowing '7 × 8 = 56', we should be able to deduce the following:

$$
\begin{array}{rcr}
70 \times 8 &=& 560 \\
7 \times 80 &=& 560 \\
70 \times 80 &=& 5600 \\
7 \times 800 &=& 5600 \\
700 \times 8 &=& 5600 \\
70 \times 800 &=& 56\,000 \\
700 \times 80 &=& 56\,000
\end{array}
$$

It helps enormously just to notice that the total number of zeros written in the numbers on the left-hand side of each of these results is the same as the extra number of zeros written after the 56 on the right-hand side. To help understand this, using the example '700 × 80', we can think of the 700 as '7 × 100' and think of the 80 as '8 × 10'. Then the whole calculation becomes: '7 × 100 × 8 × 10'. Rearranging this as '7 × 8 × 100 × 10' leads to '56 × 1000' and hence to 56 000.

Are there informal, *ad hoc* ways of doing multiplications?

Of course! As with all calculations we can always make use of those number facts and relationships with which we are confident to find our own individual approaches that make sense to us. Again there is great value in encouraging pupils, even in primary schools, to build on their growing confidence with number in order to develop their own approaches and to share different approaches to the same calculation.

For instance, here are two *ad hoc* ways of evaluating '26 × 34'. First, by breaking up the 26 into 10 + 10 + 2 + 2 + 2, on the basis that I am confident in multiplying by 10 and by 2

$$
\begin{array}{rcr}
10 \times 34 &=& 340 \\
10 \times 34 &=& 340 \\
2 \times 34 &=& 68 \\
2 \times 34 &=& 68 \\
2 \times 34 &=& 68 \\
\hline
26 \times 34 &=& 884
\end{array}
$$

adding up the numbers on the right . . .

Figure 9.5   An even simpler approach to '26 × 34'

Visually, this method is represented by the diagram in Figure 9.5. The trick in this kind of approach is to make sure you only ever multiply by easy numbers, like 1, 2, 5 and 10.

A second *ad hoc* approach to this calculation notices that 26 is quite close to 25, so we can make use of the handy piece of knowledge that '25 × 4 = 100':

$$25 \times 4 = 100, \text{ so } 25 \times 8 = 200, \text{ so } 25 \times 16 = 800, \text{ and } 25 \times 32 = 800$$

This is 32 twenty-fives, but we need 34. Adding on another two 25s (50) gives '25 × 34 = 850'. But we're after '26 × 34', so we need another 34, to get '26 × 34 = 884'.

Self-assessment questions

9.1: Use the method of Figure 9.3 to find '42 × 37'.

9.2: Deduce eight other multiplication results, involving 4, 40, 400, 9, 90 and 900, from the result '4 × 9 = 36'.

9.3: Use the method of Figure 9.4 to find '345 × 17'.

9.4: Use informal, *ad hoc* methods, based on your own level of confidence with number, to find a) 248 × 25; and b) 72 × 16.

Summary of teaching points

1. Make sure pupils have learnt thoroughly their multiplication tables up to '10 × 10' before they embark on multiplying bigger numbers.

2. Teach pupils how to multiply simple multiples of 10, such as '20 × 3', '2 × 30' and '20 × 30', before going on to multiplication with two-digit numbers.

3. Teach pupils how to multiply simple multiples of 10 and 100, such as '2 × 300' and '20 × 300', before going on to multiplication with three-digit numbers.

4. If primary-school pupils are to be taught a method for multiplying together two two-digit numbers, encourage the method based on the areas of four rectangles, splitting each of the two numbers into tens and units (as shown in Figure 9.3).

5. Some pupils in primary schools may be able to go on to extend this approach to multiply together a three-digit number and a two-digit number (as shown in Figure 9.4).

6. Value and encourage informal, *ad hoc* methods of tackling multiplications which build on the pupil's personal confidence with number and number relationships.

7. Show pupils how, by breaking down one of the numbers in the multiplication into smaller numbers, you can always get away with multiplying only by easy numbers such as 1, 2, 5 and 10.

10

Division Structures

Pupils should be taught to: understand . . . division as sharing and repeated subtraction; use associated language and recognise situations to which division applies; understand and use the relationships between the four operations, including inverses.

In this chapter there are explanations of

- three different structures of real-life problems modelled by division; and
- the situations in which pupils will meet these structures.

What are the different kinds of situation which primary pupils might encounter to which the operation of division applies?

There is a wide range of situations in which we have to learn to recognise that the appropriate operation is division. These can be categorised into at least the following three structures:

- The equal-sharing structure.
- The inverse-of-multiplication structure.
- The ratio structure.

As with the other operations analysed in earlier chapters, it helps us to connect these mathematical structures with the operation of division if we ask ourselves the question: What is the calculation I would enter on a calculator in order to solve this problem? In each case the answer will involve using the division key on the calculator. As we saw earlier, particularly with subtraction in Chapter 6, one of the difficulties in understanding the meanings of the symbols we use in mathematics is that one symbol, such as here the division symbol, can have a number of strikingly different meanings.

The *equal-sharing* structure refers to a situation in which a quantity is shared out equally into a given number of portions and we are asked to determine how many or how much there is in each portion. For example, 20 marbles might be shared equally between 4 pupils in a game, as shown in Figure 10.1. The calculation to be entered on a calculator to correspond to this situation is '20 ÷ 4'. This is the structure which teachers most naturally connect

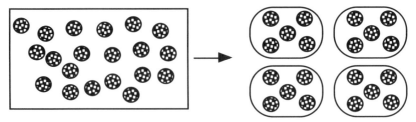

Figure 10.1   Division as equal sharing, '20 ÷ 4'

with division and is strongly associated with the language 'sharing' and 'how many (or how much) each?'

The *inverse-of-multiplication* structure, however, interprets '20 ÷ 4' in a completely different way, as shown in Figure 10.2. Now the question being asked is: 'How many groups of 4 marbles are there in the set of 20 marbles?'

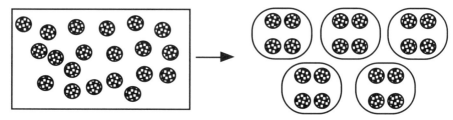

Figure 10.2   Division as inverse-of-multiplication, '20 ÷ 4'

Both Figures 10.1 and 10.2 are equally valid interpretations of the division, '20 ÷ 4', even though they are answering two different questions:

• Share 20 equally into 4 groups: how many in each group? (Figure 10.1.)
• Share 20 into groups of 4: how many groups? (Figure 10.2.)

The phrase 'inverse-of-multiplication' underlines the idea that division and multiplication are *inverse* processes. This means, for example, that since '6 × 9' comes to 54, then '54 ÷ 9' must be 6. The division by 9 'undoes' the effect of multiplying by 9. Hence to solve a problem of the form 'what must X be multiplied by to give Y?' we divide Y by X. For example: How many tickets costing £1.50 each do I need to sell to raise £90? The calculation which must be entered on a calculator to solve this problem is the division, '90 ÷ 1.50'.

The actual practical problems with this inverse-of-multiplication structure can often be further subdivided. There are problems which incorporate the notion of *repeated subtraction from a given quantity*, such as 'how many sets of 4 can I get from a set of 20?' And there are those which incorporate the idea of *repeated addition to reach a target*, such as 'how many sets of 4 do you need to get a set of 20?' First, the process of sharing out the 20 marbles in the above example can be thought of as *repeatedly subtracting* 4 marbles from the set of 20 until there are none left, counting the number of groups as you do this. But the problem might also be based on the idea of repeated addition to reach a target. The question, 'how many groups of 4 marbles are there in a set of 20 marbles?' could mean, in practical terms, *repeatedly adding* sets of 4 marbles until the target of 20 is achieved, counting the number of sets required as you do this. In Chapter 12 we shall see that this distinction between the repeated subtraction idea and the repeated addition idea in the inverse-of-multiplication structure is particularly significant when the answer to the division is not a whole number.

The *ratio* division structure refers to situations where we use division to compare two quantities. As has already been discussed in Chapter 6, in a situation where a comparison has to be made between two numbers, sums of money or measurements of some kind, we can make the comparison by subtraction, focusing on the difference between the quantities. For example, if A earns £300 a week and B earns £900 a week, one way of comparing them is to state that B earns £600 more than A, or A earns £600 less than B. The '600' is arrived at by the subtraction, '900 – 300'. But we could also compare A's and B's earnings by looking at their ratio, stating, for example, that B earns three times more than A. The 'three' is obtained by the division, '900 ÷ 300'. This process is simply the inverse of the scaling structure of multiplication described in Chapter 8, since what we are doing here is finding the scale factor by which one quantity must be increased in order to match the other; i.e., in the above example, by what factor must 300 be multiplied to give 900?

The reader may have noticed that all the examples of division used in this chapter so far have had whole-number answers and no remainders. The problems of remainders and rounding are dealt with in Chapter 12.

What are some of the contexts in which pupils will meet division in the equal-sharing structure?

At first sight we might think that 'sharing' is a very familiar experience for pupils: sharing sweets, sharing pencils, sharing books, sharing toys, and so on. But this idea of sharing a set into subsets corresponds to division only under certain conditions. First, the set must be shared into *equal* subsets, which is certainly not always the case in children's experience of sharing. Secondly, it is important to note that the language is *sharing between* rather than *sharing with*. Children's normal experience is to share sets of things *with* a number of friends. Division requires sharing them *between* a number of people. The division '12 ÷ 3' does not correspond to 'I have 12 marbles and I share them with my 3 friends'. The situation required is: 'Share 12 marbles equally between 3 people'. This is a somewhat artificial process and may not be encountered as often in the pupil's experience as we might imagine at first sight. So, sharing does not always correspond to division: it must be not just 'sharing', nor just 'sharing equally', but 'sharing equally between'.

In the context of measurement, similarly, it is not difficult to come up with imaginary situations where we might share a given quantity into a number of equal portions. Cutting up a 750-cm length of wood into 6 equal lengths, or pouring out 750 ml of wine equally into 6 glasses, or sharing out 750 g of chocolate equally between 6 children, for example, all correspond to the division '750 ÷ 6'. But these problems tend to feel like situations contrived for mathematics lessons rather than genuine problems.

The context of money does, however, provide some of the more natural examples in real life for this structure of the operation. For example, a group of people might share a prize in a lottery, or share a bill in a restaurant: in both cases it is likely that we would 'share equally between' the number of people in the group. An important class of everyday situations is where items are sold in multiple packs: a familiar requirement is to want to know the price per item. So, for example, if a shop is selling a pack of 9 audiocassettes for £7.92, the cost per cassette, in pence, is found by the division '792 ÷ 9'. We can think to ourselves that the 792 pence are being shared equally between the 9 cassettes.

This then extends naturally to the idea of price per unit of measurement. For example, to find the cost per litre of a 6-litre flagon of milk costing 210p, we should recognise that the calculation to be entered on a calculator is the division, '210 ÷ 6'. It is as though the 210 pence are being shared out equally between the 6 litres, giving 35p for each litre. Once again the word 'per', meaning 'for each', plays an important part in our understanding of this kind of situation.

This idea of 'per' turns up in numerous other situations in everyday life. For example, when calculating for a purchase how many or how much we get per penny or per pound, when finding miles per litre, determining how much someone earns per hour, an average speed in miles per hour, the number of words typed per minute, and so on: all these situations would correspond to the operation of division using the equal-sharing structure.

What are some of the contexts in which pupils will meet division in the inverse-of-multiplication structure?

There are many practical situations in which a set is to be sorted out into subsets of a given size and the question to be answered is, 'how many subsets are there?' For example, a school with 240 pupils may wish to organise them into classes of 30 children. How many classes do we need? This is modelled by '240 ÷ 30', i.e. 'how many 30s make 240?' Then the teacher with a class of 30 children may wish to organise them into groups of 5 children and ask: How many groups? This is modelled by '30 ÷ 5', i.e. 'how many 5s in 30?'

The structure extends quite naturally into the context of money. A familiar question is: How many of these can I afford? This kind of question incorporates the idea of *repeated subtraction from a given quantity*. For example, how many items costing £6 each can I buy with £150? The question is basically 'how many 6s can I get out of 150? We could imagine repeatedly spending (subtracting) £6 until all the £150 is used up. Similar situations occur in the context of measurement. For instance, the question, 'how many 150-ml servings of wine from a 750-ml bottle?' is an example of the inverse-of-multiplication division structure, in the context of liquid volume and capacity, corresponding to the calculation, '750 ÷ 150', i.e. 'how many 150s make 750?' Again the notion of repeated subtraction from a given quantity is evident here. We can imagine repeatedly pouring out (subtracting) 150 ml servings, until the 750 ml is used up.

Then there are problems in the context of money and measurement which ask the question: How many do we need? This kind of question incorporates the idea of *repeated addition to reach a target*. For example, how many items priced at £6 each must I sell to raise £150? We could imagine repeatedly adding £6 to our takings until we reach the target of £150. In spite of the language used, the problem is modelled by the division, '150 ÷ 6'.

The word 'per' turns up again in this division structure. For example, if we know the price per kg of potatoes is 50p, then we might find ourselves asking a question like, 'how many kilograms can I get for £10 (i.e. 1000p)?' Similarly, if I save 50p per week, I might ask the question, 'how long will it take to save £10?' Or, if the price of petrol is 50p per litre, the question might be, 'how many litres can I get for £10?' Each of these is, of course, another instance of 'how many 50s make 1000?', so they are again examples of the inverse-of-multiplication structure, corresponding in these cases to the division, '1000 ÷ 50'.

Exactly the same mathematical structure occurs in finding the time for a journey given the average speed. For example, the question, 'how long will it take me to drive 1000 miles, if I average 50 miles per hour?', is equivalent again to the question, 'how many 50s make 1000?', and hence, using the inverse-of-multiplication structure, to the division, '1000 ÷ 50'.

What about situations using the ratio division structure?

Many primary-school pupils can learn to recognise the need to use division in order to compare two quantities by ratio. Situations where comparisons could be made between numbers in sets, between amounts of money or between measurements of various kinds are readily available. The problem is, however, that in practice, unless the questions are contrived carefully, the answers tend to be quite difficult to interpret. It's easy enough to deal with, say, comparing two children's journeys to school of 10 minutes and 30 minutes, and, using division ('30 ÷ 10'), making the statement that one pupil's journey is three times longer than the other. But it's a huge step from interpreting a statement like that with whole numbers to making sense of, say, comparing the heights of two pupils, 125 cm and 145 cm, using a calculator to do the division ('145 ÷ 125 = 1.16'), and concluding that one pupil is 1.16 times taller than the other.

Self-assessment questions

10.1: The real car is 300 cm long and the model car is 15 cm long: how many times longer is the real car? (i.e. what is the scale factor?). What is the calculation to be entered on a calculator to answer this? Of what division structure is this an example?

10.2: A sack of apples weighing 28 pounds costs £7: what is the price per pound-weight of apples? What is the calculation to be entered on a calculator to answer this? Of what structure of division is this an example?

10.3: How many CDs costing £12.50 each can I afford to buy with £100? What is the calculation to be entered on a calculator to answer this? Of what division structure is this an example?

10.4: How many months do I need to save up £300 if I save £12 a month? What is the calculation to be entered on a calculator to answer this? Of what division structure is this an example?

10.5: Make up a problem which corresponds to the division, '60 ÷ 4', using the equal-sharing structure in the context of shopping.

10.6: Make up a problem which corresponds to the division, '60 ÷ 4', using the inverse-of-multiplication structure, incorporating the idea of repeated subtraction from a given quantity, in the context of shopping.

10.7: Make up a problem using the ratio structure in the context of salaries. Use a calculator to answer your own problem.

Summary of teaching points

1. Pupils should learn to connect the operation of division with a wide range of problems, including situations with the structures of equal-sharing, inverse-of-multiplication (including both repeated subtraction from a given quantity and repeated addition to reach a target) and, possibly, ratio.

2. Pupils should experience these division structures in a range of practical and relevant contexts, including especially shopping, rates of pay and the many kinds of problems associated with the word *per*, such as 'price per unit'.

3. The key idea in the equal-sharing structure is: *sharing equally between*.

4. Division is not just 'sharing'. Equal sharing is only one division structure. Teachers should not overemphasise the language and imagery of 'sharing' at the expense of the other important language and imagery which has to be associated with division, particularly inverse-of-multiplication.

5. Two key ideas in the inverse-of-multiplication structure are: *how many Bs make A?* (repeated addition to reach a target), *how many times can B be taken away from A until there's nothing left?* (repeated subtraction from a given quantity). Both these have to be connected with the division, '*A ÷ B*'.

6. Particularly important are division problems with questions such as 'how many can I afford?', which incorporate the idea of repeated subtraction from a given quantity, and 'how many do I need?', which incorporate the idea of repeated addition to reach a target.

7. Primary pupils can be introduced to the idea of using division to find the ratio between two quantities in order to compare them, but the results are difficult to interpret if they are not whole numbers.

8. Asking the question, 'what is the calculation to be entered on a calculator to solve this problem?', helps to focus the pupil's thinking on the underlying mathematical structure of the situation and hence to make the connection with division.

11

Division Calculations

Pupils should be taught to: divide by powers of 10; develop a variety of mental methods of computation; extend mental methods to develop a range of non-calculator methods of computation . . . , progressing to methods for division of up to three-digit by two-digit whole numbers.

In this chapter there are explanations of

- dividend and divisor;
- the *ad hoc* repeated subtraction method of doing division calculations;
- the algorithm known as short division;
- a number of informal, *ad hoc* approaches to division calculations; and
- the use of the distributive law in division calculations.

I could never master long division. Is there a simpler alternative that makes more sense?

Since, with the ready availability of calculators, we do not need to be able to do complicated divisions by paper-and-pencil methods, I would encourage the use of a more *ad hoc* method described below. It works very well with problems up to the level of difficulty with which we might hope most people would be able to cope, i.e. dividing a three-digit number by a two-digit number. The approach builds on the individual's personal confidence with multiplication and the process is easily understood. This contrasts with the conventional algorithm, known as long division, which can involve some tricky multiplications and is, to say the least, not easy to make sense of. I do not intend therefore to explain 'long division'. In my view, it is a method which could well be laid to rest as we approach the end of the twentieth century.

So, take as an example the division, '648 ÷ 24'. The first number in the division (i.e. 648, in this case) is technically called the *dividend* and the second number (i.e. 24) is called the *divisor*. The method uses the inverse-of-multiplication structure and the idea of repeated subtraction, outlined in Chapter 10. Hence the question is: How many 24s make 648? We approach this step by step, using whatever multiplications we are confident with and repeatedly subtracting from the dividend various numbers of the divisor, in an *ad hoc* manner.

```
      (a)              (b)              (c)              (d)
   |648 ÷ 24       |648 ÷ 24       |648 ÷ 24       |648 ÷ 24
10 |240         10 |240         10 |240         10 |240
   |408            |408            |408            |408
                10 |240         10 |240         10 |240
                   |168            |168            |168
                                 2 | 48          2 | 48
                                   |120            |120
                                                 2 | 48
                                                   | 72
                                                 2 | 48
                                                   | 24
                                                 1 | 24
                                                27 |  0
```

Figure 11.1: Ad hoc *repeated subtraction approach to '648 ÷ 24'*

For example, we should know easily that ten 24s make 240. We subtract this 240 from the 648. That leaves us with 408 to find. At this stage our working might be as shown in Figure 11.1a. Try another ten 24s. That's a further 240, leaving us with 168, as shown in Figure 11.1b. We do not have enough for another ten 24s, so we might try two 24s (or one 24, if we prefer it, or whatever we are confident to do mentally). This gives us the situation shown in Figure 11.1c. And so we proceed, until we've used up all the 648, as shown in Figure 11.1d. Totting up the numbers of 24s we've used down the left-hand side gives us the answer to the calculation: 10 + 10 + 2 + 2 + 2 + 1 = 27. Someone with greater confidence with multiplication might get to the result more quickly, as shown in Figure 11.2. Here I have gone straight in with twenty 24s (20 × 24 = 480), followed this up with five 24s (5 × 24 = 120) and finished off with two 24s (2 × 24 = 48). We should note that you will not get far with this method for division by a two-digit number if you are not fluent in subtraction.

```
        |648 ÷ 24
     20 |480
        |168
      5 |120
        | 48
      2 | 48
     27 |  0
```

Figure 11.2 '648 ÷ 24' with fewer steps

Does this method work when there's a remainder?

Yes. Take as an example '437 ÷ 18' (Figure 11.3). This time I have started with twenty 18s, because I can do that in my head easily (20 × 18 = 360), then followed it up with two 18s and a further two 18s. At this stage I'm left with 5. Since this is less than the divisor, 18, I can go no further. The answer to the question is therefore '24 remainder 5'. The meaning of this answer will, of course, depend on the actual practical situation which gave rise to the calculation. Remainders in various division situations are discussed in Chapter 12.

```
         |4 3 7 ÷ 1 8
      20 |3 6 0
         |  7 7
       2 |  3 6
         |  4 1
       2 |  3 6
      24 |rem 5
```

Figure 11.3   An example with a remainder, '437 ÷ 18'

Since this approach to division is likely to be unfamiliar to many readers I have provided some further examples of the method in use in Figure 11.4. It should be noted that we can be very efficient with this approach simply by being very confident in multiplying by 1, 2, 5, 10, 20 and 50.

```
     |4 7 5 ÷ 2 5        |6 6 9 ÷ 1 2        |8 0 6 ÷ 3 1
  10 |2 5 0           50 |6 0 0           20 |6 2 0
     |2 2 5              |  6 9              |1 8 6
   1 |  2 5            5 |  6 0            2 |  6 2
     |2 0 0           55 |rem 9              |1 2 4
   4 |1 0 0                                2 |  6 2
     |1 0 0                                  |  6 2
   4 |1 0 0                                2 |  6 2
  19 |    0                               26 |    0
```

Figure 11.4   Further examples of the ad hoc repeated subtraction method of division

What about short division? How does that work? Should we use it?

Short division is the standard algorithm often used for dividing by a single-digit number. It can be demonstrated clearly using the equal-sharing structure for division and either coins (1p, 10p and £1) or base-ten blocks to represent the numbers. For example, Figure 11.5 shows the division, '75 ÷ 5', interpreted with 10p and 1p coins. The 7 tens and 5 ones in the dividend are to be shared equally between five recipients.

In Figure 11.6, 1 ten has been given to each of the five recipients and the remaining 2 tens have been exchanged for 20 ones. There is therefore a total of

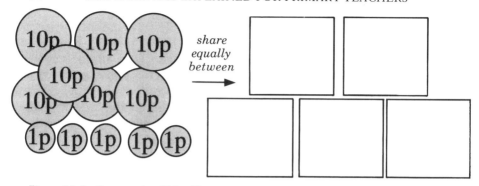

Figure 11.5   Interpreting '75 ÷ 5'

25 ones still to be shared out. When this is done each recipient gets 1 ten and 5 ones. Hence the answer is clearly 15.

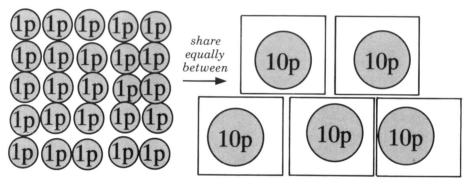

Figure 11.6   Dealing with the tens for '75 ÷ 5'

One of the standard ways of recording this process is shown in Figure 11.7. The little 2 represents the 2 tens which have been exchanged for 20 ones; written in front of the 5, it indicates that at that stage there are 25 ones to be shared out. The 15 written above the line represents the 1 ten and 5 ones which each of the recipients gets when 75 is shared between five.

$$\frac{1\ 5}{5\,\lvert\,7\ ^2 5}$$

Figure 11.7   Short division, '75 ÷ 5'

The problem with this explanation is that, in practice, when using the short division algorithm, particularly with bigger numbers, you probably do not use the equal-sharing structure consistently, but switch between this and the inverse-of-multiplication structure. So, for example, in Figure 11.8a, tackling '438 ÷ 6', the first question I find myself asking might be: Can I share 4 (hundreds) between 6? Since the answer is 'no', I exchange these 4 hundreds for 40 tens, giving a total of 43 tens, and so I am now looking at '43 tens to be shared between 6'. I now find myself saying: How many 6s in 43? I have switched from sharing to inverse-of-multiplication. The answer is 7 with 1 (ten) remaining, which is exchanged for 10 ones, giving a total of 18 ones still to be shared out. Again, I will probably switch to inverse-of-multiplication and think: how many 6s in 18? The calculation is completed as shown in Figure 11.8. But the explanation gets unwieldy and wordy.

$$6\overline{\smash{)}\,4\ 3\ 8}$$

(a)

$$6\overline{\smash{)}\,4\ 3\,{}^{1}8}\quad 7\ 3$$

(b)

Figure 11.8   Short division, '438 ÷ 6'

On balance, I prefer to introduce with division by single-digit numbers the rather *ad hoc* repeated subtraction approach I have outlined above for dividing by a two-digit number, rather than plump for the standard short division algorithm. Figure 11.9 shows this repeated subtraction method applied to the two examples just considered, namely, '75 ÷ 5' and '438 ÷ 6'. Clearly, the method gets easier the more fluent we are with mental multiplication. It therefore encourages us to handle calculations like '50 × 6' and '20 × 6' mentally.

```
        |75 ÷ 5            |438 ÷ 6
   10   |5 0          50   |3 0 0
        |2 5               |1 3 8
    5   |2 5          20   |1 2 0
   15   |  0               |  1 8
                       3   |  1 8
                      73   |    0
```

Figure 11.9   The ad hoc *repeated subtraction alternative to short division*

Are there other informal, *ad hoc* approaches to division calculations?

As ever with calculations we can call on whatever number knowledge and relationships we are confident with to devise our own *ad hoc* approaches to various division questions. In the classroom there is a great deal of value in getting pupils to share their different ways of arriving at the results. Here are some examples.

First, we can use this important principle: that we do not change the answer to a division calculation if we multiply both the numbers by the same thing. This is the equivalent of the 'equal additions' principle in subtraction (see Chapter 7). To understand this it might help to think of the division in terms of the ratio structure: if both quantities are scaled by the same factor, then their ratio does not change – just as when you add the same thing to two numbers their difference does not change. For instance, all these divisions give the same result as '6 ÷ 2':

'60 ÷ 20'   (multiply both numbers by 10)
'12 ÷ 4'   (multiply both numbers by 2)
'30 ÷ 10'   (multiply both numbers by 5)
'6000 ÷ 2000' (multiply both numbers by 1000)

One of the calculations done above by short division was '75 ÷ 5'. This can be used to illustrate the application of this principle. Multiply both numbers by 2 and the question becomes: '150 ÷ 10'. So the answer is clearly 15.

You can also use the reverse principle: that we do not change the answer to a division calculation if we *divide* both the numbers by the same thing. I would use this principle if I was dealing with, for example, the first question in this chapter, '648 ÷ 24', as follows:

'648 ÷ 24' is the same as '324 ÷ 12' (dividing both numbers by 2)
'324 ÷ 12' is the same as '108 ÷ 4' (dividing both numbers by 3)
'108 ÷ 4' is the same as '54 ÷ 2' (dividing both numbers by 2), which is 27

These two principles can be combined, as in this example: '225 ÷ 15'. Multiply both numbers by 2: '450 ÷ 30'. That makes it an easier question. Why? Because, by dividing both numbers by 10, '450 ÷ 30' is immediately changed to '45 ÷ 3', which gives the answer, 15.

In Chapter 9, I explained how the *distributive law* applied to multiplication. It also applies to division. Written formally as an algebraic generalisation it looks like this:

$$(A + B) ÷ C = (A ÷ C) + (B ÷ C)$$

Informally this means that if the dividend can be thought of as the sum of two numbers (A and B), then you can divide each of A and B separately by the divisor (C) and add up the results. We can often employ this principle to simplify division questions. For example, since $45 = 30 + 15$, you can think of '45 ÷ 3' as '$(30 + 15) ÷ 3$', which, using the distributive law, can be split up into '30 ÷ 3' and '15 ÷ 3'. This is, of course, the same as what happens when you evaluate '45 ÷ 3' using the short division algorithm, where, by exchanging one of the 4 tens for 10 ones, effectively all you are doing is changing 45 into '30 + 15'. The difference is that you can transform the 45 into '30 + 15' before you do any division, being guided by your awareness that with a divisor of 3, numbers like 30 and 15 are highly desirable.

That's the trick in using the distributive law in an *ad hoc* approach: look for numbers that are easy to handle with the particular divisor. So, tackling '145 ÷ 11', I might make use of the fact that 99 is a good number to have around with 11, and think of 145 as '99 + 46' as follows:

$145 ÷ 11 = (99 + 46) ÷ 11 = (99 ÷ 11) + (46 ÷ 11) = 9 + 4$, with remainder 2 . . . = 13 remainder 2

Of course, there's no need to set out the working as formally as I have done here. It will probably be done mainly mentally with a few numbers written down to keep track of where you are.

One last suggestion: you can sometimes make the division much easier by adding on a bit to make the dividend into a nice, convenient number. For example, if you've got your wits about you, given '638 ÷ 32' you might spot that it would have been much nicer if the question had been '640 ÷ 32' (answer 20). So the 638 is just 2 short of being twenty 32s: hence, the answer is '19 with remainder 30'.

So these are just a few of the numerous ways that division questions can be tackled. I hope by now the reader is convinced that no one really needs to learn the standard long division algorithm.

Self-assessment questions

11.1: A carton holds 6 bottles of squash. I have 288 bottles to put in cartons: How many cartons will I need? In the division calculation corresponding to this problem, which number is the dividend and which the divisor?

11.2: Write down the values of: 7 × 3, 7 × 5, 7 × 10. Now find '126 ÷ 7', using the method of *ad hoc* repeated subtraction.

11.3: Write down the values of: 23 × 2, 23 × 5, 23 × 10, 23 × 20. Now find '851 ÷ 23', using the method of *ad hoc* repeated subtraction.

11.4: Write down the values of: 8 × 5, 8 × 10, 8 × 50. Now find '529 ÷ 8', using the method of *ad hoc* repeated subtraction.

11.5: Use the distributive law and the fact that '154 = 88 + 66' to find the answer to '154 ÷ 22'.

11.6: Find informal, *ad hoc* ways of evaluating; a) '385 ÷ 55'; and b) '419 ÷ 21'.

Summary of teaching points

1. Teach pupils the *ad hoc* repeated subtraction method for dividing first by single-digit numbers and then by two-digit numbers.
2. You might wish to teach short division as a method for dividing by a single-digit number, explaining it with coins or base-ten blocks. The conventional long division algorithm, as a method for dividing by a two-digit number, is not to be recommended.
3. Provide pupils with plenty of practice in mental multiplication by 1, 2, 5, 10, 20 and 50: this is all that is required by way of multiplication to be efficient in doing divisions by the *ad hoc* repeated subtraction method.
4. Another prerequisite for success with this approach is fluency in subtraction.
5. Share and encourage informal, *ad hoc* approaches to various division questions.
6. Make explicit the principle that you do not change the ratio if you multiply or divide two numbers by the same thing, and use this principle in various examples.

12

Remainders and Rounding

Pupils should be taught to: understand and use the features of a basic calculator, interpreting the display in the context of the problem, including rounding and remainders; approximate numbers to the nearest 10 or 100.

In this chapter there are explanations of
- the different interpretations required for the results of division calculations done on a calculator and those done by methods which produce a remainder;
- the relationship between the answer with a remainder and the calculator answer;
- the way in which the context determines whether to round a result up or down;
- the idea of rounding to the nearest something; and
- how to give answers to so many decimal places or significant figures.

I get confused between the figures after the decimal point in a calculator answer to a division calculation and the remainder

Consider the problem of seating 250 pupils in coaches which hold 60 pupils each. Using the process of mathematical modelling (see Chapter 3), we would model this problem with the division, '250 ÷ 60'. It is interesting to contrast the kind of reasoning involved in interpreting the answer to this division calculation when we do it with or without a calculator. If we divide 250 by 60, using whatever mental or written procedure we are confident with, we might get to the result '4 remainder 10'. To interpret this result we should note that the 'remainder 10' does not stand for 10 coaches; it represents the 10 pupils who would be left out if you ordered only 4 coaches. When we do the calculation on a calculator, however, and get the result 4.1666666, the .1666666 represents a bit of a coach, not a bit of a pupil. So, in this example, the figures after the decimal point represent a bit of a coach, whereas the remainder represents a number of pupils. They are certainly not the same thing. This is a very significant observation, requiring careful explanation to pupils, through discussion of a variety of examples. The way we interpret back in the real world the mathematical solution to a calculation involving a division actually depends on: a) whether the manipulation of the symbols has led to an answer with a remainder or an answer with figures after the decimal point; and b) whether the problem giving rise to the division is an *equal-sharing* structure or an *inverse-of-multiplication* structure (see Chapter 10).

How does the interpretation of the results differ for the different division structures?

Consider the division, '150 ÷ 18'. If I do this by mental or written methods I may get to the result '8 remainder 6'. But if I do it on a calculator I get '8.3333333'.

First of all we will analyse how these results are interpreted if the problem giving rise to the calculation is an *equal-sharing* structure, of the form '150 things shared between 18'. For example, if I share 150 pencils equally between 18 people, how many do they each get? In interpreting the answer '8 remainder 6', the remainder represents the 6 pencils left over after you have done the sharing, giving 8 pencils to each person. But the figures after the decimal point in the calculator answer (the .3333333 part of 8.3333333) represent the portion of a pencil which each person would get if you were able to share out the remainder equally. This would, of course, involve cutting up the pencils into bits. So both the remainder and the figures after the decimal point in this example refer to pencils, although the first refers to pencils left over and the second to portions of pencils received if the left-overs are shared out. Whether or not you can actually share out the remainder will, of course, depend on what you are dealing with. For example, people and pencils are not usually cut up into smaller bits, so the answer with the remainder is actually more useful. But lengths, areas, weights and volumes can be further subdivided into smaller units, so the calculator answer might make more sense in examples in measurement contexts.

Now consider the interpretation of the two results if the problem giving rise to '150 ÷ 18' is an *inverse-of-multiplication* structure, i.e. of the form: 'How many sets of 18 can you get from 150 things?' For example, how many boxes which hold 18 pencils each do you need to store 150 pencils? Now we notice that the remainder 6 represents the surplus of pencils after you have filled up 8 boxes of 18. The figures after the decimal point in the calculator answer (the .3333333 part of 8.3333333) then represent what fraction this surplus is of a full set of 18. In our example, the .3333333 means the fraction of a box which would be taken up by the 6 remaining pencils. So the *remainder* in this division problem represents surplus pencils, but the *figures after the decimal point* represent 'a bit of a box'. In simple language, we might say either 'we need eight boxes and there will be six pencils left over', referring to the answer with the remainder, or 'we need eight boxes and a bit of a box', referring to the answer with figures after the decimal point.

How can you get from the calculator answer to the remainder, and vice versa?

We will compare the calculator answer for a division question with the answer with a remainder obtained by some written or mental method:

- Calculator: 100 ÷ 7 = 14.285714.
- Written or mental method: 14 remainder 2.

Note that the calculator answer is truncated (see Chapter 3) and would actually continue 14.2857142857142857 . . . , if the calculator were able to display more than eight digits.

Now, the 14 is common to both answers. The question is, how does the .285714 in the first answer relate to the remainder 2 in the second? The easiest way to see this is to imagine that the division is modelling a problem with an equal-sharing structure in a measuring context; for example, sharing 100 cl (i.e. a litre) of wine equally between 7 glasses (for reference, a centilitre is one-hundredth of a litre). The 14 represents 14 whole centilitres of wine in each portion, and the remainder 2 represents 2 centilitres of wine left over. If this 2 cl is also shared out between the 7 glasses, then each glass will get a further portion of wine corresponding to the answer to the division, '2 ÷ 7'. Doing this on the calculator gives the result .28571428, which is clearly the same as the bit after the decimal point in the calculator answer to the original question, allowing for the calculator's truncation of the result. So the figures after the decimal point are the result of dividing the remainder by the divisor.

This means, of course, that, since multiplication and division are inverse processes, the remainder should be the result of multiplying the bit after the decimal point by the divisor. Checking this with the above example, we would multiply .285714 by 7 and expect to get the remainder, 2. What we actually get is 1.999998, which is *nearly* equal to 2, but not quite. The discrepancy is due, of course, to the tiny bit of the answer to '100 ÷ 7' which the calculator discarded when it truncated the result.

Another way of getting from the calculator answer (14.285714) to the remainder (2) is simply to multiply the whole number part of the calculator answer (14) by the divisor (7) and subtract the result (98) from the dividend (100). The reasoning here is that the 14 represents the 14 whole centilitres in each glass. Since there are 7 glasses, this amounts to 98 cl (since 14 × 7 = 98). Taking this 98 cl away from the original 100 cl leaves the remainder of 2 cl.

So, in summary, allowing for small errors resulting from truncation:

- The figures after the decimal point are the result of dividing the remainder by the divisor.
- The remainder is the result of multiplying the figures after the decimal point by the divisor.
- The remainder is also obtained by multiplying the whole number part of the calculator answer by the divisor and subtracting the result from the dividend.

What about rounding?

Numbers obtained from measurements or as the results of calculations in practical situations often have to be rounded in some way in order to make sense and to be of any use to us. Sometimes we round up and sometimes we round down. The first consideration must always be the *context* which gives rise to the numbers. For example, when buying wallpaper most people find it helpful to round *up* in their calculation of how many rolls to purchase, to be on the safe side. On the other hand if we were planning to catch the 8.48 train we might well decide to round this *down* to 'about a quarter to nine', since rounding this time *up* to 'about ten to nine' would result in our missing the train. So sometimes the context requires us to round *down* in our calculations and sometimes to round *up*. This consideration of the context is much more important than any rule we might remember from school about digits being greater or smaller than five.

Are there particular kinds of division problems which can be given to pupils where the context requires that you have to round up or round down?

Consider these two examples, both of which are problems modelled by '44 ÷ 6', with the inverse-of-multiplication structure, i.e. of the form 'how many sixes make 44?':

(a) You can fit six children on a bench. How many benches do we need if we have 44 children to be seated?
(b) A pencil costs 6p. How many pencils can I buy with 44p?

For each problem I might enter '44 ÷ 6 =' on my calculator and get the result '7.3333333' displayed. The answer is a recurring decimal which has been truncated by the calculator to show just eight figures and is interpreted as 'about 7.3333333 benches'.

Clearly, in problem (a), we cannot bring in 7.3333333 benches, so, since seven benches would not be enough for everyone to get a seat, we conclude that eight benches are needed. In this case the context determines that we round the 7.3333333 *up* to 8.

Then, in example (b), obviously we can only purchase whole pencils, so the answer 'about 7.3333333 pencils' must again be rounded. In this case, however, the context determines that we round the answer *down*. We can clearly afford only 7 pencils.

In explaining what is going on to pupils, we could talk about the '.3333333' in example (a) as representing 'a bit of a bench'. We need 7 benches and a bit of a bench: so we must get 8 benches, otherwise some people will be left standing. Similarly, the '.3333333' in example (b) represents 'a bit of a pencil': we can afford 7 pencils and a bit of a pencil, but we will only be able to buy 7 pencils.

These two examples illustrate the point noted in Chapter 10 that a division problem with the inverse-of-multiplication structure often takes one of two forms. First, there are those which incorporate the idea of *repeated addition to reach a target*, such as problems which use the question, 'how many do we need?' Problems of this kind, such as problem (a) above, require a calculator answer with superfluous figures to be rounded *up*. Then there are those which incorporate the idea of *repeated subtraction from a given quantity*, such as problems which use the question, 'how many can we afford?'. Problems of this kind, such as problem (b) above, require a calculator answer with superfluous figures to be rounded *down*.

This framework is useful for teachers generating division problems for pupils, to ensure that they get examples of both kinds and therefore experience a range of situations where the contexts require both rounding up and rounding down.

What about the rule of rounding up when the next figure is 5 or more?

In practice it is the context which most often determines that we should round up or that we should round down. In some situations, however, there is a convention that we should round an answer to the nearest something. In fact, such situations are fairly rare in practice, since there is more often than not a contextual reason for rounding up or down, particularly when dealing with money. One situation where 'rounding to the nearest something' is sometimes employed is in recording measurements.

Think of examples from everyday life where measurements are recorded in some form. It is very possible that the measurement is actually recorded to the nearest something. For example, when the petrol pump says that I have put 15.8 litres in my tank this presumably means that the amount of petrol I have taken is really 15.8 litres to the nearest tenth of a litre. So it could actually be slightly more than that or slightly less. When I stand on the bathroom scales and record my weight as 12 stone 7 pounds, I am actually recording my weight to the nearest pound: I sometimes have to decide whether the pointer on the scales is nearer to, say, 7 pounds or 8 pounds. When I read that someone has run 100 metres in 9.84 seconds, the time is presumably rounded to the nearest one-hundredth of a second. In all these examples the measurement is recorded to the nearest something. The reason for this is sometimes the limitations of the measuring device and sometimes simply that no practical purpose would be served by having a more accurate measurement.

It is in the handling of statistical data that the convention of rounding to the nearest something is employed most frequently. For example, you may well need to round your answer in this way when calculating averages (means). If my scores one cricket season are 50, 34, 0, 12, 0 and 43, I would calculate my average score by adding these up and dividing by 6 (see Chapter 20 for a discussion of averages). Doing this on a calculator I get the result 23.166666. Normally I would not wish to record all these figures, so I might round my average score to the nearest whole number, which would be 23, or possibly to the nearest tenth, which would be 23.2.

So how does the process of rounding to the nearest something work?

It is helpful to note that the concept of 'nearest' is essentially a spatial one, so it helps in this process to imagine the position of the number concerned on a number line, as shown in Figure 12.1. Clearly the decision to round down or up is determined by whether the number is less or more than halfway along the line between two marks on the scale. The crucial questions in this process are always: 1) what number would be halfway?; and 2) is my number less or more than this? So, to express 23.166666 to the nearest whole number, we have to

Figure 12.1 *Rounding to the nearest something*

decide between 23 and 24. The number halfway between 23 and 24 is 23.5, so we round *down* to 23, because our number is *less* than 23.5. But to express 23.166666 to the nearest tenth we have to decide between 23.1 and 23.2. The number halfway between 23.1 and 23.2 is 23.15, so we round *up* to 23.2, because our number is more than 23.15.

This is just the same principle as when you are rounding to the nearest ten, the nearest hundred, the nearest thousand, and so on. For example, imagine I had worked out the estimated cost for renovating a classroom to be £8357. In discussions with the governors I might find it appropriate to round this figure to the nearest hundred, or even the nearest thousand. To the nearest hundred I have to choose between £8300 and £8400. Halfway between these two figures is £8350. My figure of £8357 is more than this, so I would round *up* and say that we estimate the cost to be about £8400. But if it is sufficient to discuss the cost to the nearest thousand, then I now have to choose between £8000 and £9000. Once again I ask what is halfway between these two figures. The answer is clearly £8500 and, since my estimated cost of £8357 is less than this, we would round *down* and say that the cost is going to be about £8000, to the nearest thousand.

But what do you do if the number you are dealing with is exactly halfway between your two marks on the scale?

Someone always asks this question. My answer is normally not to do anything. There really isn't much point, for example, in pretending to round a figure like £8500 to the nearest thousand. Just give it as £8500 and leave it at that. If I normally work my batting average out to the nearest whole number and one year it happens to come out exactly as 23.5, well, I think I will just leave it like that: at least I will be able to deduce from my records that I did a bit better than last year when my average to the nearest whole number was 23.

What about rounding to so many decimal places and significant figures?

When we are rounding a number like 23.166666, it is unnecessarily complex to talk about rounding it to the nearest tenth, hundredth, thousandth, ten thousandth, and so on. Apart from anything else, most of us find it difficult to articulate a word like 'thousandth' in a way which distinguishes it from 'thousand'. It is much easier therefore to talk about rounding *to so many decimal places*. For example, 23.166666, is

> 23, when rounded to the nearest whole number
> 23.2, when rounded to one decimal place
> 23.17, when rounded to two decimal places
> 23.167, when rounded to three decimal places
> 23.1667, when rounded to four decimal places.

A bit trickier, but often more appropriate, is the idea of rounding *to so many significant figures*. A full consideration of this is properly beyond the scope of this book, but for the sake of completeness I will try to clarify the main idea. The point is that in many practical situations we are really only interested in the approximate size of an answer to a calculation, and just the first two or three figures are normally enough.

If you are applying for a new job, you are not going to get terribly concerned about whether the salary offered is £17437 or £17431. In either case, the salary is about £17400. When you are talking about thousands of pounds the choice between an additional £37 or £31 is not likely to be particularly significant. If, however, I am buying a pair of trousers then the difference between £37 and £31 becomes quite significant. It is this kind of reasoning which is the basis of the practice of rounding to a certain number of significant figures.

Giving the salaries above as 'about £17400' in either case is the result of rounding them to three significant figures. The first significant figure, indeed the most significant figure, is the '1', since this represents the largest part of the salary, namely, ten thousand pounds. Then the '7' and the '4' are the second and third significant figures respectively. This might be all we want to know, since we would reckon that the figures in the tens and units columns are relatively insignificant.

Here are some simple examples of rounding to significant figures:

On my monthly trip to the supermarket I spend £270.96. When I get home my wife asks me how big the bill was.
Exact statement: *The bill came to £270.96.*
Using just one significant figure: *The bill came to about £300.*
(This is to the nearest hundred pounds.)
Using two significant figures: *The bill came to about £270.*
(This is to the nearest ten pounds.)
Using three significant figures: *The bill came to about £271.*
(This is to the nearest pound.)

A rich man left £270 550 to be shared equally between four children.
Mathematical model: 270 550 ÷ 4 = 67 637.5.
Exact solution: *They each inherit £67 637.50.*
To two significant figures we say: *They each inherit about £68 000.*
(In this case, this is the same as giving the figure to the nearest thousand pounds.)

To three significant figures we say: *They each inherit about £67 600.*
(This is the same as giving the figure to the nearest hundred pounds.)
To four significant figures we say: *They each inherit about £67 640.*
(This is the same as giving the figure to the nearest ten pounds.)

In most practical situations it is rarely useful to give approximate answers to more than three significant figures.

Self-assessment questions

12.1: A teacher wants to order 124 copies of a mathematics book costing £5.95. She must report the total cost of the order to the year-group meeting. What is the mathematical model of this problem? Obtain the mathematical solution, using a calculator. Interpret the mathematical solution as an exact statement back in the real world. What would the teacher say if she reports the total cost to the nearest ten pounds? What would the teacher say if she reports the total cost to three significant figures?

12.2: Jackie knows there are 365 days in a year and 7 days in a week. She wants to work out how many weeks in a year. What is the mathematical model of Jackie's problem? Use a non-calculator method to solve the mathematical problem, giving the answer with a remainder. What is the answer to Jackie's question? What is the meaning of the remainder? Now obtain the mathematical solution using a calculator. Is this calculator answer: a) an exact, appropriate answer; b) an exact but inappropriate answer; or c) an answer which has been truncated? (See Chapter 3.) What do the figures after the decimal point in the calculator answer represent?

12.3: Would you round your calculator answers up or down in the following situations? a) There are 327 children on a school trip and a coach can hold 40. How many coaches are needed? ($327 \div 40 = \ldots$); b) how many cakes costing 65p each can I buy with £5? ($500 \div 65 = \ldots$).

12.4: What is the average (mean) height, *to the nearest centimetre*, of 9 pupils with heights, 114 cm, 121 cm, 122 cm, 130 cm, 131 cm, 136 cm, 139 cm, 146 cm, 148 cm? (See Chapter 20: use a calculator, add up the heights, divide by 9.)

12.5: There was a total of 1459 goals in 462 matches in a football league one season. How many goals is this per match, on average? ($1459 \div 462 = \ldots$) Do this on a calculator and give the answer: a) rounded to the nearest whole number; b) rounded to one decimal place; and c) rounded to two decimal places.

12.6: A batch of 3500 books is to be shared equally between 17 shops. Using a calculator, I get '$3500 \div 17 = 205.88235$'. How many books are there for each shop? What is the remainder?

Summary of teaching points

1. Explicitly discuss with pupils the difference in meaning between the remainder in a division problem and the figures after the decimal point in the calculator answer.

2. Use the phrase 'a bit of a . . .' to explain informally the figures after the decimal point.

3. Provide pupils with a range of examples of real-life division problems, including those with the equal-sharing structure and those with the inverse-of-multiplication structure, to be done both by a method producing a remainder and on a calculator, and each time discuss what the remainder means and what the figures after the decimal point mean.

4. Explain, with examples of equal-sharing in measurement contexts, the relationship between the calculator answer to a division problem and the answer with the remainder.

5. When considering practical division problems with the inverse-of-multiplication structure which do not work out exactly when done on a calculator, discuss from the context whether to round up or to round down.

6. Use problems which incorporate both the ideas of repeated addition, such as those which ask 'how many do we need?', and repeated subtraction, such as those which ask 'how many can we afford?'

7. Emphasise the idea of recording measurements 'to the nearest something' when doing practical measuring tasks.

8. Use a number-line explanation of rounding to the nearest something, making use of the crucial questions in this process, i.e.: a) what number would be halfway?; and b) is my number less or more than this? Emphasise that we do not always use this process, and that it is most important that we first consider the context of the calculation to decide whether we should round up, round down or round to the nearest something.

13

Multiples, Factors and Primes

Pupils should be taught to: use some properties of numbers, including multiples, factors, . . . extending to primes.

In this chapter there are explanations of

- natural numbers;
- multiples;
- some ways of spotting multiples of various numbers;
- digital sums and digital roots;
- factors;
- the transitive property of multiples and factors; and
- prime numbers and composite (rectangular) numbers.

What are multiples?

First it should be made clear that in this chapter we will deal only with what are called the *natural numbers*, i.e. the numbers we use for counting: 1, 2, 3, 4, 5, 6, and so on, *ad infinitum*. So when you read the word 'number' in this chapter it refers to one of these; we are therefore excluding zero, negative numbers and anything other than positive whole numbers.

The *multiples* of any given number are obtained by multiplying the number in turn by each of the natural numbers, 1, 2, 3, 4, 5, 6, and so on. For example

- multiples of 3 are: 3, 6, 9, 12, 15, 18, 21, 24, 27, 30, 33, 36, 39, 42, 45, . . . etc.;
- multiples of 7 are: 7, 14, 21, 28, 35, 42, 49, 56, 63, 70, 77, 84, 91, 98, . . . etc.; and
- multiples of 37 are: 37, 74, 111, 148, 185, 222, 259, 296, 333, 370, . . . etc.

You can easily generate the multiples of a given number using a simple calculator with a constant facility (most have this). Enter the number, for example, 37, on to the calculator, press '+', then repeatedly press the equals button. The calculator responds by repeatedly adding 37 to itself and thus produces on display the multiples of 37.

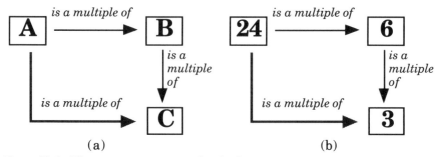

Figure 13.1   The transitive property of multiples

The mathematical relationship 'is a multiple of' applied to numbers possesses what is called the *transitive property*. Formally, this means that if *A* is a multiple of *B* and *B* is a multiple of *C* then it follows that *A* is a multiple of *C*. This is illustrated in general terms in Figure 13.1a. Figure 13.1b gives an example: any number which is a multiple of 6, such as 24, must also be a multiple of 3, because 6 itself is a multiple of 3. Applying this principle, we can deduce that all multiples of 6 are multiples of 3 (but not vice versa). Similarly, all multiples of 28 must be multiples of 7, because 28 is itself a multiple of 7.

Is there anything else to know about multiples?

Being able to recognise multiples and having an awareness of some of the patterns and relationships within them helps to develop a high level of confidence and pleasure in working with numbers. For example, this pattern in the multiples of 37 may appeal to some readers:

$$3 \times 37 = 111$$
$$6 \times 37 = 222$$
$$9 \times 37 = 333$$
$$12 \times 37 = 444 \ldots \text{and so on}$$

The pattern in the multiples of 9, with the tens digit increasing by one and the units digit decreasing by one each time, is a useful aid for learning the nine-times table:

$$1 \times 9 = 09$$
$$2 \times 9 = 18$$
$$3 \times 9 = 27$$
$$4 \times 9 = 36$$
$$5 \times 9 = 45 \ldots \text{and so on}$$

There are a number of ways of spotting certain multiples. For example, you will surely be able to tell at a glance that all these numbers are multiples of ten: 20, 450, 980, 7620. That's using a very obvious pattern, namely, that all multiples of ten end with the digit zero. Similarly, you probably know that all multiples of two (even numbers) end in 0, 2, 4, 6 or 8; and that all multiples of five end in 0 or 5.

There's a simple way to spot whether a number greater than 100 is a multiple of 4. Since 100 is a multiple of 4, then any multiple of 100 is a multiple of 4. So, given, for example, 4528, we can think of it as '4500 + 28'. We know that the 4500 is a multiple of 4, because it's a multiple of 100. So all we need to decide is whether the 28 is a multiple of 4, which it is. So if you have a number with three or more digits you need only look at the last two digits to determine whether or not you are dealing with a multiple of 4.

Would you spot immediately that all these are multiples of nine: 18, 72, 315, 567, 4986? If so, you may be making use of the *digital sum* for each number. This is the number you get if you add up the digits in the given number. If you then add up the digits in the digital sum, and keep going with this process of adding the digits until a single-digit answer is obtained, the number you get is called the *digital root*. For example, 4986 has a digital sum of 27. This is itself a multiple of nine! This is true for any multiple of 9: the digital sum is itself a multiple of 9. If you then add up the digits of this digital sum (i.e. 2 + 7) you get the single-digit number, 9, which is therefore the digital root. Fascinatingly, the digital root of a multiple of 9 is always 9.

Here is a summary of some useful tricks for spotting various multiples:

- Every natural number is a multiple of 1.
- Multiples of 2 are even numbers and end in 0, 2, 4, 6 or 8.
- The digital sum of a multiple of 3 is always a multiple of 3; and the digital root is always 3, 6 or 9.
- The last two digits of a multiple of 4 are themselves a multiple of 4.
- Multiples of 5 always end in 0 or 5.
- Multiples of 6 are multiples of 2 *and* multiples of 3; so they must end in 0, 2, 4, 6 or 8 *and* have a digital root of 3, 6 or 9.
- The last three digits of a multiple of 8 must be a multiple of 8.
- The digital sum of a multiple of 9 is always a multiple of 9; and the digital root is always 9.
- Multiples of 10 always end in zero.

What is a 'lowest common multiple'?

If we list all the multiples of each of two numbers, then inevitably there will be some multiples common to the two sets. For example, with 6 and 10, we obtain the following sets of multiples:

- Multiples of 6: 6, 12, 18, 24, 30, 36, 42, 48, 54, 60, 66, . . . etc.
- Multiples of 10: 10, 20, 30, 40, 50, 60, 70, . . . etc.

The numbers common to the two sets are: 30, 60, 90, 120, and so on. The smallest of these (i.e. 30) is known sometimes as *the lowest common multiple*. The lowest common multiple of 6 and 10 is therefore the smallest number which can be split up into groups of 6 and into groups of 10. This concept occurs in a number of practical situations. For example, a class of 30 children is the smallest size which can be organised into groups of 6 children for mathematics and teams of 10 for games. Or if I have to feed one plant every six days and another plant every ten days, then the lowest common multiple indicates the first day on which both plants have to be fed, i.e. the 30th day. Or if I can only buy a certain kind of biscuit in packets of 10 and I want to share the biscuits equally between 6 people, the number of biscuits I buy must be a multiple of both 6 and 10; so the smallest number I can purchase is the lowest common multiple, i.e. 30 biscuits.

What is a factor?

The concept of *factor* is simply the reverse of multiple. If *A* is a multiple of *B* then *B* is a factor of *A*. For example, 24 is a multiple of 6, so 6 is a factor of 24. Colloquially, we say '6 goes into 24'. So the factors of 24 are all those natural numbers by which 24 can be divided exactly: 1, 2, 3, 4, 6, 8, 12 and 24. Notice that 1 and 24 are included as factors of 24. Of course, 1 is a factor of all numbers and every number is a factor of itself. Recognising quickly all the factors of a given number is, of course, very useful. For example, with a set of 24 people we can know instantly that they can be put into groups of 2, 3, 4, 6 or 12. This makes a number like 24, with lots of factors, much more useful for many practical purposes than a number like 23, which has no factors other than 1 and itself.

```
× × × × × × × × × × × × × × × × × × × × × × × ×          × × × ×
                                                        × × × ×
               1 by 24                                  × × × ×

                              × × × × × × × ×            × × × ×
× × × × × × × × × × × ×        × × × × × × × ×            × × × ×
× × × × × × × × × × × ×        × × × × × × × ×            × × × ×
        2 by 12                     3 by 8               4 by 6
```

Figure 13.2   Factors of 24 shown in rectangular arrays

The idea of a *rectangular array*, introduced in Chapter 8, provides a good illustration of the concept of a factor. Figure 13.2 shows all the different rectangular arrays possible with a set of 24 crosses. The dimensions of these arrays are all the factors of 24: i.e. 1 and 24, 2 and 12, 3 and 8, 4 and 6. A calculator can be used to determine whether or not a number is a factor of a given number. Divide the given number by the possible factor: if the answer is a whole number it is a factor, otherwise it is not. For example, is 23 a factor of

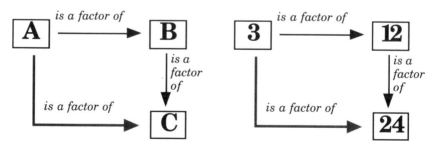

Figure 13.3   The transitive property of factors

1955? Using a calculator, I get '1955 ÷ 23 = 85', so 23 *is* a factor of 1955. Is 15 a factor of 1955? Using a calculator, I get '1955 ÷ 15 = 130.33333', so 15 is *not* a factor of 1955.

The mathematical relationship, 'is a factor of', also possesses the transitive property as illustrated in Figure 13.3. So, for example, any factor of 12 must be a factor of 24, because 12 is a factor of 24.

What about the 'highest common factor'?

This is a similar idea to the lowest common multiple. If we list all the factors of two numbers, the two sets of factors may have some numbers in common. (Since 1 is a factor of all numbers they must at least have this number in common!) The largest of these common factors is sometimes called the *highest common factor*. For example, with 24 and 30 we have the following two sets of factors:

- Factors of 24: 1, 2, 3, 4, 6, 8, 12, 24.
- Factors of 30: 1, 2, 3, 5, 6, 10, 15, 30.

The factors in common are 1, 2, 3 and 6. So the highest common factor is 6. This concept occurs in many practical situations. For example, imagine that two classes in a year group have 24 and 30 children respectively, and that we wish to divide them up into a number of groups, with each class of children shared equally between the groups. The number of groups must clearly be a factor of both 24 and 30. The largest possible number of groups is therefore 6, since this is the highest common factor.

The idea of the highest common factor can be illustrated with a rectangular array. The geometric problem would be to arrange, say, 24 crosses and 30 noughts in a rectangular array, with the same combination of noughts and crosses in each row. It's possible to achieve this with 1 row, 2 rows, 3 rows or 6 rows. So the highest common factor, 6, is the greatest number of rows possible. This is shown in Figure 13.4, where the 24 crosses and 30 noughts have been arranged in 6 rows: with 4 crosses and 5 noughts in each row.

```
× × × × O O O O O
× × × × O O O O O
× × × × O O O O O
× × × × O O O O O
× × × × O O O O O
× × × × O O O O O
```

Figure 13.4   The highest common factor of 24 and 30 shown in a rectangular array

What is a prime number?

Any number which has precisely two factors, and no more than two, is called a *prime number*. This is the strict mathematical definition. In practice we think of a prime number as a number which cannot be divided exactly by any number apart from 1 and itself. So, for example, 7 is a prime number because it has precisely two factors, namely 1 and 7. But 10 is not a prime number because it has four factors, namely 1, 2, 5 and 10. A number, such as 10, with more than two factors is sometimes called a *composite number*, or, because it can be arranged as a rectangular array with more than one row (see Figure 13.5), a *rectangular number*. Prime numbers cannot be arranged as rectangular arrays, other than with a single row. The first twenty prime numbers are: 2, 3, 5, 7, 11, 13, 17, 19, 23, 29, 31, 37, 41, 43, 47, 53, 59, 61, 67 and 71.

(a) 10   (b) 7

Figure 13.5   a) 10 is a composite number   b) 7 is a prime number

Notice that according to the strict mathematical definition, the number 1 is *not* a prime number since, uniquely, it has only one factor (itself). So 1 is the only number which is neither prime nor composite. The exclusion of 1 from the set of prime numbers often puzzles students of mathematics. The reason is related to the most important property of prime numbers: given any composite number whatsoever, there is only one combination of prime numbers which multiplied together give the number. I will illustrate this with the number 24. This number can be obtained by multiplying together various combinations of numbers, such as: 2×12, $2 \times 2 \times 6$, $1 \times 2 \times 3 \times 4$, and so on. If, however, we stipulate that only *prime* numbers can be used, there's only one combination which will produce 24: namely, $2 \times 2 \times 2 \times 3$. (This is called the *prime factorisation* of 24.) This is such a powerful property of prime numbers that it would be a pity to mess it up by allowing 1 to be a prime number! If we did, then the prime factorisation of 24, for example, would not be unique, because we could also get to 24 with $1 \times 2 \times 2 \times 2 \times 3$, or $1 \times 1 \times 2 \times 2 \times 2 \times 3$, and so on.

The study of primes is a fascinating branch of number theory. Computers have been employed to search for very large numbers which are prime. At the time of writing, the largest known prime number is '$2^{859433} - 1$'. (This means 859 433 twos multiplied together, minus 1: this produces a number with over a quarter of a million digits!) However, this is definitely not the largest prime number because, as the Greek mathematician, Euclid, proved, as long ago as 300 BC, there is no largest prime number! The really annoying facet of prime numbers is that there is no pattern or formula which will generate the set of prime numbers.

What is the point of learning about multiples, factors and primes?

I recall once, in response to this question, asking a student whether she felt differently about the numbers 47 and 48. I was surprised to be told that she did not! To me, 48 seems such a friendly number, flexible and amenable. If I have 48 in a group there are so many ways I can reorganise them: 6 sets of 8, 3 sets of 16, 4 sets of 12, and so on. By contrast, 47 is such an awkward number! The difference, of course, is that 47 is prime, but 48 has lots of factors. This is all part of what is sometimes called 'having a feel for number'. Our confidence in responding to numbers in the everyday situations where they occur will be improved enormously by having this kind of feel for numbers; by being aware of the significant relationships between them; and by recognising at a glance which properties they possess and which they do not. And the more we are aware of properties like multiples, factors and primes, the more we learn to delight in the pattern and fascination of number. Being able to spot at a glance which car registration numbers are multiples of eleven, or how many of the hymn numbers in church on Sunday morning are prime, is of no immediate practical use, but it all leads to yet greater confidence when we have to respond to numerical situations that do matter. Whether the reader is convinced or not by this argument will, no doubt, be evident in the level of enthusiasm with which they tackle the self-assessment questions which follow.

Self-assessment questions

13.1: Continue the pattern shown earlier in this chapter for certain multiples of 37, until the pattern breaks down.

13.2: Multiply each of these numbers by 9 (use a calculator) and check that the digital root in each case is 9: a) 47; b) 172; and c) 9 876 543.

13.3: Use some of the methods for spotting multiples to decide whether the following numbers are multiples of 2, 3, 4, 5, 6, 8, or 9: a) 2652; b) 6570; and c) 2401.

13.4: These car registration numbers are all multiples of 11: a) 561; b) 594; c) 418; d) 979; and e) 330. Add up the two outside digits and subtract the middle one. Do this with a few more three-digit multiples of 11. Can you state a rule?

13.5: What is the smallest number of people that can be split up equally into groups of 8 and groups of 12? What mathematical concept is used in solving this problem?

13.6: Find all the factors of a) 95; b) 96; and c) 97. Which of these two numbers would be most flexible as a year-group size for breaking up into smaller-sized groups for various activities?

13.7: List all the factors of 48 and 80. What are the common factors? If there are 48 blue chairs and 80 red chairs to be arranged in rows, with the same combination of reds and blues in each row, how can this be done?

13.8: List all the prime numbers between 70 and 100.

13.9: By trying each prime number in turn, using a calculator to help you, find the prime numbers which multiply together to give 4403.

13.10: Starting with 1, add 4, add 2, add 4, add 2, and continue this sequence until you pass 60. How many of the answers are prime?

13.11: A famous unproven theorem, called Goldbach's conjecture (Christian Goldbach, 1690–1764), states that every even number greater than 2 is the sum of two primes. For example, $52 = 5 + 47$. Test this conjecture with all the even numbers from 4 to 30.

13.12: Find a number which is a multiple of all the numbers from 1 to 10 inclusive.

Summary of teaching points

1. Encourage pupils to be fascinated by number and patterns in number.
2. Build up pupils' confidence in responding to numerical situations by exploring the concepts and properties of multiples, factors and prime numbers.
3. Share with pupils some of the ways of testing for various multiples.
4. Use calculators to explore factors, multiples and primes.
5. Use rectangular arrays to illustrate the concepts of factor, prime number and composite (rectangular) number.

14

Squares, Cubes and Number Shapes

Pupils should be taught to: explore number sequences, explaining patterns and using simple relationships; use some properties of numbers, including . . . squares, . . . cubes, and square roots.

In this chapter there are explanations of

- square numbers;
- cube numbers;
- square roots and cube roots;
- the trial and improvement method for finding square roots and cube roots using a calculator;
- the relationship between sequences of geometric patterns and sets of numbers; and
- triangle numbers.

Why are some numbers called squares? A square is a shape, isn't it?

Connecting pictures with number concepts helps to build up our understanding and confidence, as was seen in the previous chapter with concepts like 'factor' and 'multiple'. In particular we saw that a prime number, like 7, could be represented as a rectangle of dots only with one row, whereas a composite (rectangular) number, like 10, could be be shown as a rectangular array with more than one row (see Figure 13.5). Now some rectangles have equal sides: these are the ones called squares. So numbers, such as 1, 4, 9, 16, 25, and so on, which can be represented by square arrays, as shown in Figure 14.1, are called *square numbers*. If we use an array of small squares, called square units, as in Figure 14.1b, rather than just dots, as in Figure 14.1a, then the number of squares in the array also corresponds to the total area. For example, the area of the 5 by 5 square grid is 25 square units. Of course, square numbers are also composite (rectangular) numbers, just as squares are rectangles. (Strictly speaking, there is one exception: the number 1 is considered a square number but, as we saw in the previous chapter, it is usually considered to be neither prime nor composite.)

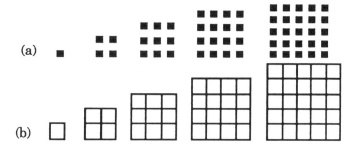

Figure 14.1   Pictures of square numbers; a) using dots; b) using a square grid

This explains the geometric idea of square numbers. The arithmetic idea which corresponds to this is that a square number is any number which is obtained by multiplying a number by itself. The number 16 is represented in Figure 14.1 by 4 rows of 4 dots, or 4 rows of 4 squares, which, of course, corresponds to the multiplication '4 × 4'. Likewise, the representation of 25 as a square corresponds to '5 × 5'. There is a special mathematical notation which can be used as a shorthand for writing '5 × 5'. This is '5^2', which means simply that there are two fives to be multiplied together. This is read as 'five squared' or 'five to the power two' (see the discussion about powers of 10 in Chapter 2). The square numbers can be obtained easily using a calculator. For example, to find six squared, just enter '6, ×, ='. This is the numerical pattern for the set of square numbers:

$$1 \times 1 = 1^2 = \ 1$$
$$2 \times 2 = 2^2 = \ 4$$
$$3 \times 3 = 3^2 = \ 9$$
$$4 \times 4 = 4^2 = 16$$
$$5 \times 5 = 5^2 = 25$$
$$6 \times 6 = 6^2 = 36 \ \ldots \text{ and so on}$$

What about cube numbers?

Just as some numbers can be represented by square arrays, there are those, such as 1, 8 and 27, which can be represented by arrangements in the shape of a cube. Figure 14.2 shows how the first three cube numbers are constructed from small cubes, called cubic units. The first three cube numbers are made from 1 cubic unit, from 8 cubic units and from 27 cubic units, respectively. The 27, for example, is produced by 3 layers of cubes, with 3 rows of 3 cubes in each layer, and is therefore equal to '3 × 3 × 3'. The number of cubic units in the whole construction corresponds to the total volume of the cube. For example, the volume of the 3 by 3 by 3 cube is 27 cubic units. It is difficult, of course, to represent these cubic constructions in a two-dimensional picture, and readers are encouraged to build various-sized cubes from cubic units and to generate these cube numbers for themselves. The same kind of notation is used for cube numbers as square numbers: '3 × 3 × 3' is abbreviated to 3^3 and

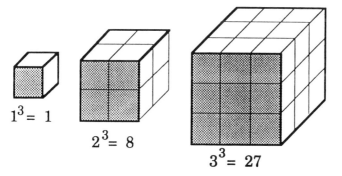

Figure 14.2   Examples of cube numbers

read as 'three cubed' or 'three to the power three'. Again, it is easy to generate cube numbers using a simple calculator; for example, to obtain six cubed, simply enter: '6, ×, =, ='. By analogy with the square numbers above, we can construct the following pattern for the cube numbers:

$$1 \times 1 \times 1 = 1^3 = \quad 1$$
$$2 \times 2 \times 2 = 2^3 = \quad 8$$
$$3 \times 3 \times 3 = 3^3 = \quad 27$$
$$4 \times 4 \times 4 = 4^3 = \quad 64$$
$$5 \times 5 \times 5 = 5^3 = 125$$
$$6 \times 6 \times 6 = 6^3 = 216 \ldots \text{and so on}$$

What are square roots and cube roots?

What is the length of the side of a square which has an area of 729 square units? Another way of asking the same question is: Which number when multiplied by itself gives 729? Or which number has a square equal to 729? The answer (27) is called the *square root* of 729. (Strictly speaking, 27 is the *positive* square root of 729; you can also get 729 by multiplying the negative number, '–27', by itself, but we are not concerned with negative numbers in this chapter.) The mathematical abbreviation for 'the (positive) square root of' is '$\sqrt{\ }$'. So we could write, for example, $\sqrt{729} = 27$. Finding a square root is the *inverse* process of finding a square. This means that one process undoes the effect of the other, for example:

$$2^2 = \quad 4 \text{ so } \sqrt{4} = 2$$
$$3^2 = \quad 9 \text{ so } \sqrt{9} = 3$$
$$4^2 = \quad 16 \text{ so } \sqrt{16} = 4$$
$$27^2 = 729 \text{ so } \sqrt{729} = 27$$

The idea of a *cube root* follows the same logic. In geometric terms the question would be: What is the length of the side of a cube with a total volume of 729 cubic units? Or, in arithmetic terms, what number has a cube equal to 729? The answer (9) is called the cube root of 729. As with square roots we can think in terms of an *inverse* process: finding the cube root is the inverse process of finding the cube. For example, the cube of 14 is 2744, so the cube root of 2744 is 14.

How can you find square roots and cube roots?

Using a basic calculator, finding a square root is very simple, since they usually have a square root key, with the symbol for square root ($\sqrt{\ }$) written on it. So, for example, to find the square root of 361, you simply enter: '361, $\sqrt{\ }$' and the calculator displays the answer, 19. It is actually quite instructive to try to find some square roots without using the square root key, since this introduces a mathematical process, sometimes called *trial and improvement*, which can then be applied to other problems. For example, the problem might be to find the side of a square with a total area of 3844 square units. Using a calculator, we simply try various numbers, square them and decide whether we are too high or too low, gradually refining our guesses so that we home in on the solution. Like this:

Try 50 . . . square it (enter 50, ×, =) . . . answer: 2500 . . . too low.
Try 60 . . . square it (enter 60, ×, =) . . . answer: 3600 . . . too low.
Try 70 . . . square it (enter 70, ×, =) . . . answer: 4900 . . . too high.
So, the answer lies between 60 and 70 . . .
Try 65 . . . square it (enter 65, ×, =) . . . answer: 4225 . . . too high.
Try 63 . . . square it (enter 63, ×, =) . . . answer: 3969 . . . too high.
Getting close!
Try 62 . . . square it (enter 62, ×, =) . . . answer: 3844 . . . got it.

So the square root of 3844 is 62.

This is really the only way to find a cube root using a simple calculator. For example, to find the cube root of 85 184:

Try 50 . . . cube it (enter 50, ×, =, =) . . . answer: 125 000 . . . too high.
Try 30 . . . cube it (enter 30, ×, =, =) . . . answer: 27 000 . . . too low.
Try 40 . . . cube it (enter 40, ×, =, =) . . . answer: 64 000 . . . too low.
Try 45 . . . cube it (enter 45, ×, =, =) . . . answer: 91 125 . . . too high.
Try 43 . . . cube it (enter 43, ×, =, =) . . . answer: 79 507 . . . too low
Try 44 . . . cube it (enter 44, ×, =, =) . . . answer: 85 184 . . . got it.

In the two examples above the numbers were chosen carefully so that there was an exact whole number which was the square root or the cube root. In real situations where a square root or cube root is required, this is unlikely to be the case. For example, if I want to build a square patio with an area of 200 square metres, the length of the side in metres must be the square root of 200. However, my calculator tells me that $14^2 = 196$ (too low) and $15^2 = 225$ (too high). So the answer lies between 14 and 15. There is, in fact, no number which I can enter on a calculator which is the exact square root of 200. But using the trial and improvement method, we can get an answer as close as we wish, by going into decimals. For example, since I find that $14.1^2 = 198.81$ (too low) and $14.2^2 = 201.64$ (too high), the answer must lie between 14.1 and 14.2. Readers confident in handling decimals may wish to pursue this in Questions 14.6 and 14.7 in the self-assessment questions which follow.

People with little experience of mathematics are often uneasy about this kind of approach, feeling that it is not respectable mathematics. So let me assure you that it is! There are many problems in advanced mathematics which were at one time, in practice, impossible to tackle, but which can now be solved by using numerical methods of this kind, employing a calculator or a computer to do the hard grind of the successive calculations involved.

Are there any other geometric shapes which describe numbers?

Almost any sequence of geometric shapes or patterns, such as those shown in Figure 14.3, can be used to generate a corresponding set of numbers. Exploring these kinds of sequences, trying to relate the geometric and numerical patterns, can produce some intriguing mathematics. For example, we might consider why the first sequence of patterns in Figure 14.3 generates the odd numbers: 1, 3, 5, 7, 9 and so on ; and why the second sequence generates the multiples of 3: 3, 6, 9, 12, and so on.

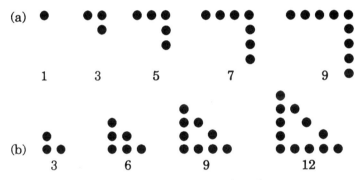

Figure 14.3   Geometric patterns generating sets of numbers

Some of these patterns turn out to be particularly interesting and are given special names. For example, you may come across the so-called *triangle numbers*. These are the numbers which correspond to the particular pattern of triangles of dots shown in Figure 14.4: 1, 3, 6, 10, 15, and so on. Notice that you get the 2nd triangle by adding 2 dots to the first; the 3rd by adding 3 dots to the 2nd; the 4th by adding 4 dots to the 3rd; and so on.

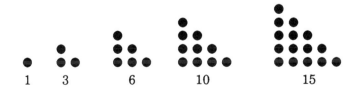

Figure 14.4   Triangle numbers

The geometric arrangements of dots show that these triangle numbers have the following numerical pattern:

$$1 = 1$$
$$3 = 1 + 2$$
$$6 = 1 + 2 + 3$$
$$10 = 1 + 2 + 3 + 4$$
$$15 = 1 + 2 + 3 + 4 + 5, \text{ and so on}$$

Self-assessment questions 14.3 and 14.8 below provide two examples of explaining patterns in number sequences by thinking about the geometric patterns to which they correspond.

Self-assessment questions

14.1: Drawing on the ideas of this and the previous chapter, find at least one interesting thing to say about each of the numbers from 20 to 29.

14.2: Find a triangle number which is also a square number.

14.3: Look at the sequence of square numbers: 1, 4, 9, 16, 25, 36, and so on. Find the differences between successive numbers in this sequence. What do you notice? Can you explain this in terms of patterns of dots?

14.4: Use a calculator. Choose a number. Square it, then cube the answer. Cube it, then square the answer. Are the results the same? Can you find a whole number less than 100 which is a cube number and a square number?

14.5: Use the trial and improvement method to find: a) the square root of 3249; and b) the cube root of 4913.

14.6: For those confident with decimals: continue with the trial and improvement method for finding the square root of 200, until you can give the length of the side of the square patio with area of 200 square metres to the nearest centimetre.

14.7: I wish to construct a cube with a volume of 500 cubic centimetres. What should be the length of the sides of this cube? Use a calculator and trial and improvement to answer this to a practical level of accuracy.

14.8: List all the triangle numbers less than 100. Find the sums of successive pairs of triangle numbers, e.g. 1 + 3 = 4, 3 + 6 = 9, 6 + 10 = 16, and so on. What do you notice about the answers? Can you explain this numerical pattern with the geometric patterns for these numbers?

Summary of teaching points

1. Use geometric pictures such as square arrays of dots and square grids to explain square numbers, and cubes constructed from cubic units to explain cube numbers.

2. Connect the square of a number with the area of a square grid, given by counting the number of square units in the grid.

3. Connect the cube of a number with the volume of a cube, given by counting the number of cubic units used to construct it.

4. Emphasise the idea of inverse processes when discussing squares and square roots: one process undoes the effect of the other.

5. Explicitly teach pupils the calculator key sequences for finding squares (number, ×, =) and cubes (number, ×, =, =).
6. Introduce primary pupils to the method of trial and improvement, using a calculator to find square roots (without using the square root key) and cube roots.
7. Encourage pupils to explore the relationships between sequences of geometric patterns of dots and the corresponding sequences of numbers.

15

Integers: Positive and Negative

Pupils should be taught to: extend their understanding of the number system to negative numbers in context; extend methods of computation to include addition and subtraction with negative numbers.

In this chapter there are explanations of

- integers;
- the cardinal and ordinal aspects of number;
- contexts for understanding positive and negative numbers;
- situations in the contexts of temperatures and bank balances which are modelled by the addition and subtraction of positive and negative numbers; and
- how to enter negative numbers on a basic calculator.

What are integers?

The mathematical word 'integer' is related to words such as 'integral' (forming a whole) and 'integrity' (wholeness). So integers are simply *whole numbers*. But this includes both positive and negative whole numbers, and zero. So the set of integers includes the set of *natural numbers* described in Chapter 13.

People have difficulty with the concept of a negative number, mainly because we overemphasise the idea that a number represents a set of things. So when a teacher wants to demonstrate to a young child, say, '3 + 4', the first thing they do is to put out a set of 3 things (counters, blocks, fingers, etc.) and a set of 4 things, and put the two sets together to form a new set. This is the so-called *cardinal aspect* of number. The problem is that we cannot conceive of a set of negative three things! But this does not mean that negative numbers are some kind of mysterious, abstract mathematical notion, because numbers are not just sets of things. For instance, the numeral '3' can also be thought of as representing a point on a number line, such as that shown in Figure 15.1, and the instruction, 'add 4', interpreted as moving 4 steps further along the number line. It is this *ordinal aspect* of number which extends our understanding of number quite naturally and simply to include negative numbers: the idea that numbers are also labels used for putting things in order. In Figure 15.1 the numbers are just that, i.e. labels for putting in order the particular points on the line which have been marked.

Figure 15.1   Numbers as points on a line

So, extending the number line, as shown in Figure 15.2, in the other direction, some symbols, i.e. those for negative numbers, are needed to label the points less than zero. This then produces the set of numbers called the integers: (. . . , –5, –4, –3, –2, –1, 0, +1, +2, +3, +4, +5, . . .), going on for ever in both directions. Note that we would not normally write, for example, '+4', for 'positive four', but would simply write '4', unless in the context it is particularly helpful to signal the distinction between the negative and the positive integers. Pupils can have fun generating the integers on a calculator. To produce the positive integers, just enter: +,1, =, =, =, =, . . . and continue pressing the equals sign as many times as you wish. To produce the negative integers, just enter: –, 1, =, =, =, =, . . . The reader should be warned, however, that various calculators have different ways of displaying negative numbers.

Figure 15.2   Extending the number line

The number line, either drawn left to right, as in Figures 15.1 and 15.2, or, preferably, drawn vertically with positive numbers going up and negative numbers going down, is the most straightforward image for us to associate with positive and negative integers. There are some other contexts which help us to make sense of negative numbers especially.

The most familiar is probably the context of temperature. Quite young children can grasp the idea of the temperature falling below zero, associating this with feeling cold and icy roads, and are often familiar with the use of negative numbers to describe this. One small point about different uses of language should be made here. Mathematicians might prefer to refer to the integer, '–5', as 'negative five' rather than 'minus five', using the word 'minus' as a synonym for the operation of subtraction. But weather-forecasters tend to say that the temperature is falling to 'minus five degrees'. Similarly, they might refer to a positive temperature as 'plus five' rather than 'positive five'. However, these are not serious difficulties and temperature is still one of the best contexts for experiencing positive and negative numbers.

We can also associate positive and negative integers with levels in, say, a multistorey car park or department store, with, for example, '1' being the first floor, '0' being ground level, '–1' being one floor below ground level, and '–2' being two floors below ground level, and so on. We have a department store locally which has the buttons in the lift labelled in this way. Then, the specification of heights of locations above and below sea level provides another application for positive and negative numbers. For some people the context of bank balances is one where negative numbers make real, if painful, sense. For example, being overdrawn by £5 at the bank can be represented by the negative number, '–5'. Finally, in football league tables we find another application of positive and negative integers. If two teams have the same number of points, their order in the table is determined by their goal difference, which is 'the number of goals-for subtract the number of goals-against'. So, for example, a team with 28 goals-for and 23 goals-against has a goal difference of '+5'. But a team with 23 goals-for and 28 goals-against has a goal difference of '–5'. Many pupils find this a relevant and realistic context for experiencing the process of putting in order a set of positive and negative numbers.

How do you explain addition of positive and negative integers?

The difficulty in making sense of the ways in which we manipulate positive and negative integers is that we really need to use different images to support different operations. With addition, we need contexts and problems which help us to make sense of such calculations as: a) '10 + (–2)'; b) '2 + (–7)'; (c) '(–3) + 4'; and d) '(–5) + (–3)'.

Let's try bank balances. Interpret the addition as follows: the first number represents your starting balance, the second number represents either a credit (a positive number) or a debit (a negative number). So with this interpretation each of the examples (a)–(d) above can be seen as a mathematical model (see Chapter 3) for a real-life situation, as follows. In example (a), we start with £10 and add a debit of £2: the result is a balance of eight pounds. The corresponding mathematical model is: $10 + (-2) = 8$. In example (b), we start with a balance of £2 and add a debit of £7: the result is a balance of £5 overdrawn. The corresponding mathematical model is: $2 + (-7) = -5$. In example (c), we start with a balance of £3 overdrawn and add a credit of £4: the result is a balance of £1. The corresponding mathematical model is: $(-3) + 4 = 1$. Then, in example (d), we start with a balance of £5 overdrawn and add a debit of £3: the result is a balance of £8 overdrawn. The corresponding mathematical model is: $(-5) + (-3) = -8$.

We could also interpret these collections of symbols in the context of temperatures, with the first number being a starting temperature and the second being either a rise or a fall in temperature; or, on the number line, which, of course, is just like the scale on a thermometer, with the first number being the starting point and the second number a move in either the positive or the negative direction. The reader is invited to construct problems of this kind in self-assessment question 15.3 below.

What about subtraction? Why do 'two minuses make a plus'?

The key to making sense of subtraction with positive and negative integers is to get out of our heads the idea of subtraction meaning 'take away'. This structure only applies to positive numbers: you cannot 'take away' a negative number. The calculation '6 – (–3)', for example, cannot model a problem about having a set of 6 things and 'taking away negative three things': the words here are just nonsense. We make sense of subtracting with negative numbers by drawing on situations which incorporate some of the other structures for subtraction, notably the comparison and the inverse-of-addition structures (see Chapter 6).

The kinds of calculations to which we need to give meaning through experience in context would include a) '6 – (–3)'; b) '(–3) – (–8)'; c) '6 – 9'; and d) '(–3) – 4'.

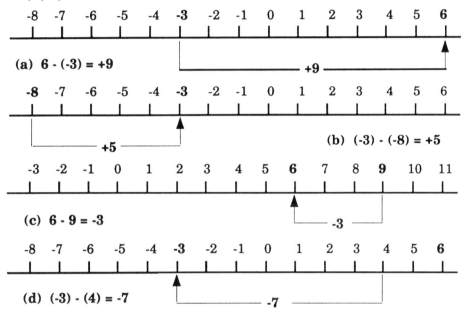

Figure 15.3   *Subtractions interpreted as comparison and inverse-of-addition*

Let's look at these in the context of temperatures. First we will think in terms of the comparison structure for subtraction. In this structure, the subtraction '*a* – *b*' models a question of the form, 'How much greater is *a* than *b*?' Problems which incorporate the comparison structure for subtraction would require us therefore to find how much hotter is the first temperature than the second. So, in example (a), the problem might be to find how much higher is a temperature of 6 degrees indoors than a temperature of –3 degrees outdoors. Reference to the number line in Figure 15.3a) makes it clear that the difference between the two temperatures is 9 degrees. The corresponding mathematical model is therefore: 6 – (–3) = 9. Then in example (b) we are comparing a temperature of –3 degrees in the morning with the overnight temperature of –8 degrees, deducing that the morning temperature is 5 degrees higher than the overnight. The corresponding mathematical model is therefore: (–3) – (–8) = 5.

This idea of comparison makes a lot of sense when we are using a subtraction to model a situation in which the first temperature is higher than the second. Personally, I would restrict primary-school pupils' experience of subtracting with negative numbers to problems of this kind, i.e. comparing two temperatures, one or both of which might be negative, to find the difference. This will always correspond then to a subtraction in which the first number is the higher temperature. In examples (c) and (d), as can be seen in Figure 15.3, the first temperature is *lower* than the second. Because of this the answers to the question, 'how much higher is the first temperature?', are negative numbers. This gets a bit confusing. So perhaps it is easier to relate these examples to problems with the inverse-of-addition structure. In this structure, the subtraction '$a - b$' models a question of the form, 'What must be added to b to give a?' So, in the context of temperatures, we are asking what change in temperature takes us from the *second* temperature to the *first*. Note the order here. So, in example (a) in Figure 15.3, the +9 could represent a rise of 9 degrees which has to be added to a temperature of –3 degrees to produce a temperature of 6 degrees. In (b), the +5 could represent a rise of 5 degrees which has to be added to a temperature of –8 degrees to produce a temperature of –3 degrees. Example (c) then is related to the question: What change in temperature takes you from 9 degrees to 6 degrees? Clearly this is a fall of 3 degrees, represented by –3. The corresponding mathematical model is therefore: $6 - 9 = -3$. Finally, in example (d), the question is: What change in temperature takes you from 4 degrees to –3 degrees? Clearly this is a fall of 7 degrees, represented by –7. The corresponding mathematical model is therefore: $(-3) - (4) = -7$.

Alternatively, it would be possible to pose exactly corresponding problems, modelled by these same subtractions, with a starting and a finishing bank balance, and then asking what credit or debit has been added. The reader is invited to construct problems of this kind in self-assessment question 15.4 below.

I hope that these illustrations make it clear that we do not need a nonsense rule like, 'two minuses make a plus'. Apart from anything else, to be just a little pedantic, in a question such as $6 - (-3)$, the first '–' is a minus sign, indicating subtraction, and the second is a negative sign, indicating a negative number. Simply interpret the subtraction as 'compare the first number with the second' or 'what must be added to the second to give the first?' and, by putting these questions into contexts such as temperatures and bank balances, there is some chance of actually understanding what is going on.

How do you put negative numbers on to a calculator?

Some calculators have a special key, usually labelled '+/–', which does this for you. To enter '–78', for example, you press this key sequence: 78, +/–. So to do a calculation such as, '184 – (–78)', you could use this key sequence: 184, – , 78, +/–, =. Many basic calculators do not have this special key. But most of them do have a memory and a key labelled something like 'M–' which allows you to subtract a number from whatever is in the memory. This enables us very easily to put a number like '–78' into the memory. First ensure the memory is clear (on my calculator I do this by pressing a key labelled MRC twice), then press: 78, M–. This subtracts 78 from the zero in the memory, to give –78. There is then a key on the calculator which enables you to recall what is in the memory. This is often the same key as the one which clears the memory, e.g. the MRC key. So to do a calculation such as, '184 – (–78)', you might use this key sequence: MRC, MRC (to clear the memory), 78, M–, (puts –78 in the memory), 184, –, MRC (recalls the –78 from the memory), =. The reader should try this on his or her own calculator: it is not nearly as complicated as it looks in print!

However, having explained all that, I should say that the context which gives rise to the problem will very often suggest that the actual calculation which you do makes no use of negative numbers whatsoever. For example, if the problem had been to find the difference in height between two points, one 184 metres above sea level and the other 78 metres below sea level, then the image formed in my mind by the context leads me simply to add 184 and 78.

My conclusion therefore is that we rarely need to use calculations with negative numbers to solve real-life problems; but we do need the real-life problems to help to explain the way we manipulate positive and negative numbers when we are doing abstract mathematical calculations!

Self-assessment questions

15.1: Which of these are integers: 6.8, 472, 0, –10, –5.5?

15.2: In a football league table, Arsenal, Blackburn and Chelsea all have the same number of points. Arsenal have 18 goals-for and 22 against, Blackburn have 32 for and 29 against, Chelsea have 25 for and 30 against. Work out the goal differences and put the teams in order in the table.

15.3: Make up situations about temperatures which are modelled by the additions: a) '4 + (–12)'; and b) '(–6) + 10'. Give the answers to the additions.

15.4: Give situations about bank balances which are modelled by the subtractions: a) '20 – (–5)'; b) '(–10) – (–15); and c) (–10) – 20. Give the answers to the subtractions.

15.5: Find how to enter the integer, –42, on your calculator, in the middle of a calculation. Note how your calculator displays this integer.

15.6: Yesterday I was overdrawn at the bank by £187.85. Someone paid a cheque into my account and this morning I am £458.64 in credit. Model this situation with a subtraction. Use a calculator to find out how much the cheque was that was paid in.

Summary of teaching points

1. Use the number line and the ordinal aspect of number (numbers as labels for putting things in order) to introduce the concept of negative integers.

2. Use contexts such as temperatures, multistorey buildings, heights above and below sea level and bank balances to give meaning to positive and negative numbers.

3. Use problems with temperatures to explain additions with positive and negative integers: with the first number representing a starting point and the second a rise or fall.

4. To experience subtractions with positive and negative integers, use problems about the comparison of two temperatures, finding how much higher is one temperature than another, or the difference in temperature.

5. If necessary, extend this experience to situations with the inverse-of-addition structure, finding the change (up or down) from one temperature to another .

6. Use parallel examples about bank balances, credits and debits to provide further experience of the same structures as in 3, 4 and 5.

7. Do not talk about 'taking away' a negative number.

8. Make sure pupils know how to enter negative numbers on the basic calculators used in their school and that they know how they are displayed.

16

Fractions

Pupils should be taught to: understand and use, in context, fractions . . . to estimate, describe and compare proportions of a whole; calculate fractions . . . of quantities, using a calculator where appropriate.

In this chapter there are explanations of

- the different meanings of the fraction notation;
- some of the traditional language of fractions;
- the important idea of equivalent fractions;
- how to compare two simple fractions; and
- how to find a simple fraction of a quantity.

I think of a fraction as representing a part of a whole – is there any more to it than that?

Once again we encounter the special difficulty presented by mathematical symbols: that one symbol can represent a number of different kinds of situation in the real world. The mathematical notation used for a fraction might, in fact, be used in at least four different ways:

- To represent a part of a whole or a unit.
- To represent a part of a set.
- To model a division problem.
- As a ratio.

Consider, for example, the fraction three-eighths, which can be written either as $\frac{3}{8}$ or, more conveniently for typesetting, ⅜. The commonest interpretation of these symbols is illustrated by the diagrams in Figure 16.1. I find the most useful everyday examples are chocolate bars (rectangles) and pizzas (circles). One thing (sometimes called the 'whole'), such as a bar of chocolate or a pizza, is somehow subdivided into eight equal sections, called 'eighths', and three of these, i.e. 'three-eighths', are then selected. Note that the word 'whole' does sound the same as 'hole'; this can be confusing for pupils in some situations. I recall one teacher tearing a sheet of paper into four quarters and then, in the

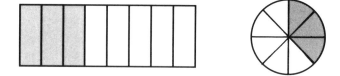

Figure 16.1   The shaded sections are three-eighths of the whole shape

course of her explanation, asking a child to show her 'the whole'; not surprisingly, the child kept pointing to the space in the middle. It's also acceptable colloquially to talk about 'a whole half', as in 'I ate a whole half of a pizza'. Because of all this I prefer to talk about 'fractions of a unit', and to use the word 'whole' only as an adjective, e.g. 'three-eighths of a whole pizza'.

This idea can then be extended to situations where a set of items is subdivided into eight equal subsets and three of these subsets are selected. For example, the set of 40 dots in Figure 16.2a has been subdivided into eight equal subsets (of 5 dots each) in Figure 16.2b. The 15 dots selected in Figure 16.2c can therefore be described as three-eighths of the set.

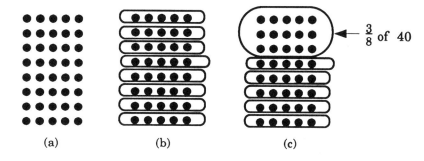

Figure 16.2   Three-eighths of a set of 40

But the fraction ⅜ can also be used to represent the division of 3 by 8. It might, for example, represent the result of sharing three bars of chocolate between eight people. Notice the marked difference here: in Figure 16.1, it was one bar of chocolate which was being subdivided; now we are talking about cutting up three bars. The actual process we would have to go through to solve this problem practically is not immediately obvious. One way of doing it is to lay the three bars side by side, as shown in Figure 16.3, and then to slice through all three bars simultaneously with a knife, cutting each bar into eight equal pieces. The pieces then form themselves nicely into eight equal portions. Figure 16.3 then shows that each of the eight people gets the equivalent of three-eighths of a whole bar of chocolate. (If you are doing this with pizzas you have to place them one on top of the other, rather than side by side, but otherwise the process is the same.) So what we see here is, first, that the symbols ⅜ can mean 'divide 3 units by 8' and, secondly, that the result of doing this division is 'three-eighths of a unit'. So the symbols ⅜ represent both an instruction to perform an operation *and* the result of performing it! We

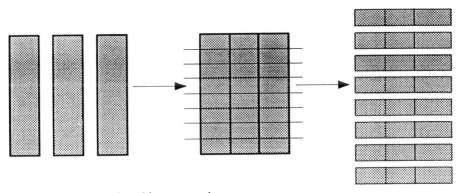

Figure 16.3   Three shared between eight

often need this idea that the fraction '*p/q*' means '*p* divided by *q*' in order to handle fractions on a calculator. Simply by entering '*p* ÷ *q*' we can express the fraction as a decimal.

We have seen in Chapter 10 that one of the categories of problems modelled by division is where two quantities are compared by means of ratio. So, because the symbols ⅜ can mean 'three divided by eight', we can extend the meanings of the symbols to include 'the ratio of three to eight'. This is written sometimes as '3:8'. For example, in Figure 16.4a, when comparing the set of circles with the set of squares, we could say that 'the ratio of circles to squares is three to eight'. This means that for every three circles there are eight squares. Arranging the squares and circles as shown in Figure 16.4b shows this to be the case. The reason why we also use the fraction notation (⅜) to represent the ratio (3:8) is simply that another way of expressing the comparison between the two sets is to say that the number of circles is three-eighths of the number of squares.

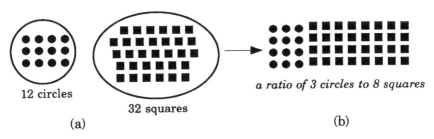

Figure 16.4   A ratio of three to eight

I can remember teachers talking about numerators, denominators, vulgar fractions, proper and improper fractions, mixed numbers, and so on. Do I have to understand all these terms?

These are all important ideas associated with learning about fractions but, in my view, it is quite acceptable to use more informal language to refer to them. For example, the *numerator* and the *denominator* are simply the top number and the bottom number in the fraction notation. So, for example, in the fraction ⅜ the numerator is 3 and the denominator is 8. I prefer to call them simply the top number and the bottom number. The phrase 'vulgar fraction', in which the word 'vulgar' actually means 'common' or 'ordinary', is certainly archaic. It was used to distinguish between the kinds of fractions discussed in this chapter, such as ⅜, written with a top number and a bottom number, and decimal fractions, such as 0.375, which are discussed in the next. (For those who are interested in the ways in which words shift their meaning, I have an arithmetic book dated 1886 in which the chapter on 'vulgar fractions' concludes with a set of 'promiscuous exercises'!)

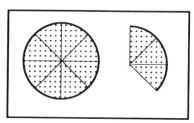

Figure 16.5   A fraction greater than 1

The fraction notation for parts of a unit can also be used in a situation such as that shown in Figure 16.5, where there is more than one whole unit to be represented. Here there are, altogether, eleven-eighths of a pizza, written ¹¹⁄₈. Since eight of these make a whole pizza this quantity can be written as '1 + ⅜', which is normally abbreviated to 1⅜. This is sometimes called a *mixed number*. A fraction in which the top number is smaller than the bottom number, such as ⅜, is sometimes called a *proper fraction*, with a fraction such as ¹¹⁄₈ being referred to as an *improper fraction*. Proper fractions are therefore those which are less than 1, with improper fractions being those greater than or equal to 1. We could refer to the latter more informally as 'top-heavy fractions'.

What are equivalent fractions?

The concept of equivalence is one of the key ideas for pupils to grasp when working with fractions. Using the first idea of a fraction above, i.e. that it represents a part of a unit, then it is immediately apparent from Figure 16.6, for example, that the fractions, three-quarters, six-eighths and nine-twelfths, all represent the same amount of chocolate bar. This kind of 'fraction chart' is an important teaching aid for explaining the idea of equivalence. Sequences of equivalent fractions follow a very straightforward pattern. For example, all these fractions are equivalent:

$$\frac{3}{5} \ \frac{6}{10} \ \frac{9}{15} \ \frac{12}{20} \ \frac{15}{25} \ \frac{18}{30} \ \frac{21}{35} \ \frac{24}{40} \ \ldots \text{ and so on}$$

The numbers on the top and bottom are simply the three-times and five-times tables, respectively. This means that, given a particular fraction, you can always generate an equivalent fraction by multiplying the top and the bottom by the same number; or, vice versa, by dividing by the same number. So, for example:

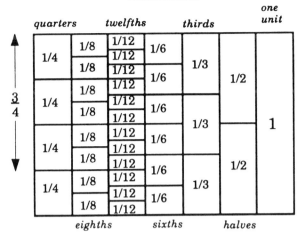

Figure 16.6 A fraction chart showing some equivalent fractions

⁴/₇ is equivalent to ³⁶/₆₃ (multiplying top and bottom by 9); and
⁴⁰/₇₀ is equivalent to ⁴/₇ (dividing top and bottom by 10).

If we remember that the fraction notation can also be interpreted as meaning division of the top number by the bottom number, the principle above is merely repeating what was said about informal methods of division in Chapter 11: that you do not change the answer to a division calculation if you multiply or divide both numbers by the same thing. The same applies to ratios, of course: that if you multiply or divide two numbers by the same thing then the ratio stays the same.

This is an important method for simplifying fractions and ratios. For example, if I am comparing the price of two articles costing £28 and £32 by looking at the ratio of the prices, then the ratio 28:32 can be simplified to the ratio of 7:8 (dividing both numbers by 4). This means that one price is ⁷/₈ (seven-eighths) of the other. Another example: if I am comparing a journey of 4.2 miles with one of 7 miles, then I could simplify the ratio, 4.2:7, by first multiplying both numbers by 10 (42:70) and then dividing both numbers by 14 (3:5), drawing the conclusion that one journey is ³/₅ (three-fifths) of the other.

How do you compare one fraction with another?

The first point to notice here is that when you increase the bottom number of a fraction you actually make the fraction smaller, and vice versa. For example, ½ is greater than ⅓, which is greater than ¼, which is greater than ⅕, and so on. This is very obvious if the symbols are interpreted in concrete terms, as bits of pizzas or chocolate bars, for example. It is possible to get this wrong, of course, if you simply look at the numbers involved in the fraction notation without thinking about what they mean.

Then, secondly, there is no difficulty in comparing two fractions with the same bottom number. Clearly, five-eighths of a pizza (⁵/₈) is more than three-eighths (³/₈), for example.

But, generally, to compare two fractions with *different* bottom numbers we may need to convert them to equivalent fractions with the *same* bottom number. This will have to be a common multiple of the two numbers. It might be (but does not have to be) the lowest common multiple (see Chapter 13). For example, which is greater, seven-tenths ($\frac{7}{10}$) of a chocolate bar or five-eighths ($\frac{5}{8}$)? The lowest common multiple of ten and eight is 40, so convert both fractions to fortieths:

$\frac{7}{10}$ is equivalent to $\frac{28}{40}$ (multiplying top and bottom by 4); and
$\frac{5}{8}$ is equivalent to $\frac{25}{40}$ (multiplying top and bottom by 5).

We can then see instantly that, provided you like chocolate, the seven-tenths is the better choice.

What calculations with fractions do we have to do in everyday life?

The commonest everyday situations involving calculations with fractions are those where we have to calculate a simple fraction of a set or a quantity. For example, we might say, 'three-fifths of my class of 30 are boys'. If we see an article priced at £45 offered with one-third off, then the reduced price must be 'two-thirds of £45'. Or we might encounter fractions in measurements such as 'three-quarters of a litre' or 'two-fifths of a metre' and want to change these to millilitres and centimetres respectively. The process of doing these calculations is straightforward. For example, to find '$\frac{3}{5}$ of 30', first divide by the 5 to find one-fifth of 30, then multiply by the 3 to obtain three-fifths:

$\frac{1}{5}$ of 30 is 6, so $\frac{3}{5}$ of 30 is 18.
$\frac{1}{3}$ of £45 is £15, so $\frac{2}{3}$ of £45 is £30.
$\frac{1}{4}$ of 1000 ml is 250 ml, so $\frac{3}{4}$ of 1000 ml (a litre) is 750 ml.
$\frac{1}{5}$ of 100 cm is 20 cm, so $\frac{2}{5}$ of 100 cm (a metre) is 40 cm.

If the division and multiplication involved are difficult a calculator can be used. For example, if I am due to get three-sevenths of a legacy of £4500, then the calculation is performed on a calculator by entering: 4500, ÷ 7, × 3, =. The calculator display of 1928.5714 indicates that my entitlement is £1928.57. There is probably no need to go further than this in calculations with fractions in the primary school.

Self-assessment questions

16.1: Give examples where '$\frac{4}{5}$' represents: a) a part of a whole or a unit; b) a part of a set; c) a division using the idea of sharing; and d) a ratio.

16.2: Find as many different examples of equivalent fractions illustrated in the fraction chart in Figure 16.6 as you can.

16.3: Assuming you like pizzas, which would you prefer, three-fifths of a pizza ($\frac{3}{5}$) or five-eighths (5/8)? (Convert both fractions to fortieths.)

16.4: $\frac{3}{4}$, $\frac{1}{6}$, $\frac{1}{3}$, $\frac{2}{3}$, $\frac{5}{12}$ . . . put these fractions in order, from the smallest to the largest.

16.5: Make up a problem about prices to which the answer is 'the price of A is three-fifths ($\frac{3}{5}$) of the price of B'.

16.6: Walking to work takes me 24 minutes, cycling takes me 9 minutes. Complete this sentence with an appropriate fraction: 'The time it takes to cycle is . . . of the time it takes to walk.'

16.7: Find: a) three-fifths of £100, without using a calculator; and b) five-eighths of £2500, using a calculator.

Summary of teaching points

1. Introduce fraction notation as meaning a number of equal parts of a unit, making particular use of pizzas (circles) and chocolate bars (rectangles) in the explanation. In this interpretation, the fraction 'p/q' means 'divide the unit into q equal parts and take p of these parts'.

2. When explaining fractions be careful about using 'the whole' as a noun: try to use it only as an adjective, e.g. 'a whole pizza'.

3. Extend the idea of a fraction as representing a number of equal parts of a unit to meaning a number of equal parts of a set, e.g. two-thirds of a set of 12.

4. It is quite acceptable to use informal language such as top number, bottom number and top-heavy fraction.

5. Emphasise very strongly the idea of equivalent fractions. Children should make fractions charts like Figure 16.6 and find various examples of equivalent fractions.

6. Help children to see the pattern in sequences of equivalent fractions and use this to establish the idea that you can change one fraction into an equivalent fraction by multiplying (or dividing) the top and bottom numbers by the same thing.

7. Using simple examples with sharing pizzas and chocolate bars, establish the idea that 'p/q' can also mean 'p divided by q'. For example, 'three pizzas shared between four people' is '3 divided by 4' and this results in ¾ of a pizza each.

8. Introduce children to the use of fractions to compare one quantity with another (i.e. finding the ratio) especially in the context of prices. For example, we can compare two prices of £9 and £12 by stating that one is three-quarters of the other.

9. Explain to children, with concrete illustrations, why making the bottom number larger makes the fraction smaller, and vice versa.

10. Introduce the procedure for finding which is the larger or which the smaller of two fractions, by changing them to equivalent fractions with the same bottom number.

11. Explain to children the procedure for finding a fraction of a quantity, by dividing by the bottom number and then multiplying by the top number, applying this procedure to a range of everyday, practical contexts, and using a calculator where necessary.

12. There is more than enough involved in the important ideas associated with fractions listed above to introduce to primary-school children. There is no need to go any further into more complex calculations with fractions, such as addition, subtraction, multiplication and division.

17

Calculations with Decimals

Pupils should be taught to: extend methods of computation to include . . . all four operations with decimals . . . using a calculator where appropriate.

In this chapter there are explanations of

- the procedures for addition and subtraction with decimal numbers;
- the contexts which might give rise to the need for calculations with decimals;
- multiplication and division of a decimal number by an integer, in real-life contexts;
- the results of repeatedly multiplying or dividing decimal numbers by 10;
- how to deal with multiplication of two decimals;
- some simple examples of division by a decimal; and
- converting fractions to decimals and, vice versa.

Is there anything different about the procedures for addition and subtraction with decimals from those with whole numbers?

The procedures are effectively the same. Difficulties would arise only if you were to forget about the principles of place value outlined in Chapter 2. Provided you remember which digits are units, tens and hundreds, or tenths, hundredths, and so on, then the algorithms (and adhocorithms) employed for whole numbers (see Chapters 5 and 7) work in an identical fashion for decimals, with the principle that 'one of these can be exchanged for ten of these' guiding the whole process. A useful tip with decimals, however, is to ensure that the two numbers in an addition or a subtraction have the same number of digits after the decimal point. If one has fewer than the other then fill up the empty places with zeros, acting as 'place-holders' (see Chapter 2). So, for example, '1.45 + 1.8' would be written as '1.45 + 1.80', '1.5 – 1.28' would be written as '1.50 – 1.28' and '10 – 4.25' would be written as '10.00 – 4.25'. This makes the standard algorithms for addition and subtraction look just the same as when working with whole numbers, but with the decimal points in the two numbers lined up, one above the other, as shown in Figure 17.1.

2.86	1.45	1.50	10.00
+4.04	+1.80	- 1.28	- 4.25

| (a) | (b) | (c) | (d) |

Figure 17.1   Additions and subtractions with decimals

In practice, additions and subtractions like these with decimals would usually be employed to model real-life situations related to money or measurement. In Chapter 2, I discussed the convention of putting two digits after the decimal point when recording money in pounds. We saw also that when dealing with measurements of length in centimetres and metres, with a hundred centimetres in a metre, it was a good idea to adopt the same convention, for example, writing 180 cm as 1.80 m, rather than 1.8 m. Similarly, when handling liquid volume and capacity, where we have 1000 millilitres in a litre, or mass, where we have 1000 grams in a kilogram, the convention would be to write measurements in litres or kilograms with three digits after the point. This means that, if this convention is followed, the decimal numbers will arrive for the calculation already written in the required form, i.e. with each of the two numbers in the addition or subtraction having the same number of digits after the point, with zeros used to fill up empty places.

For example, the four calculations shown in Figure 17.1 might be modelling the following real-life situations:

(a) Find the total cost of two articles, costing £2.86 and £4.04 respectively.
(b) Find the total length of wall space taken up by a cupboard which is 1.45 m wide and a bookshelf which is 1.80 m wide.
(c) What is the difference in height between a girl who is 1.50 m tall and a boy who is 1.28 m tall?
(d) What is the change from a ten-pound note (£10.00) if you spend £4.25?

What about multiplications and divisions involving decimals?

I will discuss first of all multiplying a decimal number by a whole number. Once again, the key point is to think about the practical contexts which would give rise to the need to do multiplications of this kind. In the context of money we might need to find the cost of a number of articles at a given price. For example, find the cost of 12 rolls of sticky tape at £1.35 per roll. This problem in the real world is modelled by the multiplication, '1.35 × 12'. On a calculator, we enter 1.35, ×, 12, =, read off the mathematical solution '16.2' and then interpret this as a total cost of £16.20.

But there is some potential to get in a muddle with the decimal point when doing this kind of calculation by non-calculator methods. So a useful tip is: avoid multiplying the decimal numbers altogether! In the example above this is easily achieved, simply by rephrasing the situation as 12 rolls at 135p per roll, i.e. writing the cost in pence rather than in pounds. We then multiply 135 by

12, by whatever methods we prefer (see Chapter 9), to get the answer 1620, interpret this as 1620p and finally write the answer as £16.20.

Almost all the multiplications involving decimals we have to do can be tackled like this. Here's another example: find the length of wall space required to display eight posters each 1.19 m wide. Rather than tackle '1.19 × 8', rewrite the length as 119 cm, calculate '119 × 8' and convert the result (952 cm) back to metres (9.52 m).

The same principle applies when dividing a decimal number by a whole number. The context from which the calculation has arisen will suggest a way of handling it without the use of decimals. For example, a calculation such as '3.45 ÷ 3' could have arisen from a problem about sharing £3.45 between 3 people. We can simply rewrite this as the problem of sharing 345p between 3 people and deal with it by whatever division process is appropriate (see Chapter 11), concluding that each person gets 115p each. The final step is to put this back into pounds notation, as £1.15.

How do you explain the business about moving the decimal point when you multiply and divide by 10 or 100 and so on?

On a basic calculator, enter the following key sequence and watch carefully the display: '10, ×, 1.2345678, =, =, =, =, =, =, ='. This procedure is making use of the constant facility, which is built into most basic calculators, to multiply repeatedly by 10. The results are shown in Figure 17.2a. It certainly looks on the calculator as though the decimal point is gradually moving along one place at a time to the right. Now, without clearing your calculator, enter: '÷, 10, =, =, =, =, =, =, ='. This procedure is repeatedly dividing by 10, thus undoing the effect of multiplying by 10 and sending the decimal point back to where it started, one place at a time. Because of this phenomenon we tend to think of the effect of multiplying a decimal number by 10 to be to move the decimal point one place to the right, and the effect of dividing by 10 to be to move the decimal point one place to the left. Since multiplying (dividing) by 100 is equivalent to multiplying (dividing) by 10 and by 10 again, this results in the

(a) Results as displayed on a calculator	(b) Results displayed on the basis of place value
1.2345678	1.2345678
12.345678	12.345678
123.45678	123.45678
1234.5678	1234.5678
12345.678	12345.678
123456.78	123456.78
1234567.8	1234567.8
12345678.	12345678

Figure 17.2   The results of repeatedly multiplying by 10

point moving two places. Similarly multiplying or dividing by 1000 will shift it three places, and so on, for other powers of 10.

However, to understand this phenomenon rather than just observing it, it is more helpful to suggest that it is not the decimal point which is moving, but the digits. This is shown by the results displayed on the basis of place value, as shown in Figure 17.2b. Each time we multiply by 10 the digits all move one place to the left – and the decimal point stays where it is! To understand why this happens, trace the progress of one of the digits, for example the '3'. In the original number it represents '3 hundredths'. When we multiply the number by 10, each hundredth becomes a tenth, because ten hundredths can be exchanged for a tenth. This is, once again, the principle that 'ten of these can be exchanged for one of these', as we move right to left. So the 3 hundredths become 3 tenths, i.e. the digit 3 moves from the hundredths position to the tenths position. Next time we multiply by 10, these 3 tenths become three whole units, and the 3 shifts to the units position. Next time we multiply by 10, these 3 units become 3 tens, and so on. Because the principle that 'ten of these can be exchanged for one of these' as you move from right to left applies to any position, each digit moves one place to the left every time we multiply by 10. Since dividing by 10 is the inverse of multiplying by 10 (i.e. one operation undoes the effect of the other), clearly the effect of dividing by 10 is to move each digit one place to the right.

How does all this help when you have to multiply together two decimal numbers?

Imagine we want to find the area in square metres of a rectangular lawn, 3.45 m wide and 4.50 m long. The calculation required is: '3.45 × 4.50'. For multiplications there is no particular value in carrying around surplus zeros, so we can rewrite the 4.50 as 4.5, giving us this calculation to complete: '3.45 × 4.5'. This is a pretty difficult calculation. In practice, most people would sensibly do this on a calculator and read off the answer as 15.525 square metres. But it may be instructive to look at how to tackle it without a calculator. There are three steps involved: 1) get rid of the decimals by multiplying each number by 10 as many times as necessary; 2) multiply together the two integers which result; and 3) divide the result by 10 as many times in total as you multiplied by 10 in step (1).

So the first step is to get rid of the decimals altogether, using our knowledge of multiplying decimals repeatedly by 10, as follows:

$$3.45 \times 10 = 34.5 \text{ then } 34.5 \times 10 = 345$$
$$4.5 \times 10 = 45$$

Hence, by doing '× 10' *three* times in total we have changed the multiplication into '345 × 45', a straightforward calculation with integers. The second step is to work this out, using whatever method is preferred (see Chapter 9), to get the result 15 525. Then finally, we simply undo the effect of multiplying by 10 three times, by dividing by 10 three times, shifting the digits three places to the right and producing the required result, 15.525.

To be honest, you don't actually have to think in terms of multiplying and dividing by 10 like this, when doing an actual calculation, although you will probably not understand what you are doing without the explanation above. We can simply notice that the total number of times we have to multiply by 10 is determined by the total number of digits after the decimal points in the numbers we are multiplying. For example, in '3.45 × 4.5', there are two digits after the point in the first number and one in the second, giving a total of three: so we have to apply '× 10' three times in total to produce a multiplication of whole numbers. Then when we apply '÷ 10' three times to our whole-number result, the effect is to shift three digits to positions after the decimal point. The upshot is that the total number of digits after the decimal points in the two numbers being multiplied is the same as the number of digits after the decimal point in the answer! So our procedure can be rewritten as follows: 1) count the total number of digits after the decimal points in the numbers being multiplied; 2) remove the decimal points from the two numbers and multiply them as though they were integers; and 3) put the decimal point back in the answer, ensuring that the number of digits after the point is the same as the total found in (1).

For example:

1. to calculate 0.04 × 3.6 (three digits in total after the decimal points);
2. 4 × 36 = 144 (dropping the decimal points altogether); so
3. 0.04 × 3.6 = 0.144 (with three digits after the decimal point).

Using this principle, Figure 17.3 shows how a whole collection of results can be deduced from one multiplication result with integers, using as examples: a) 4 × 36 = 144; and b) to show that the procedure works just the same when there is a zero in the result, 5 × 44 = 220. At an appropriate stage in the development of their work with decimals it can be instructive for pupils to use a calculator to compile various tables of this kind and to discuss the patterns which emerge.

×	36	3.6	0.36	0.036
4	144	14.4	1.44	0.144
0.4	14.4	1.44	0.144	0.0144
0.04	1.44	0.144	0.0144	0.00144
0.004	0.144	0.0144	0.00144	0.000144

×	44	4.4	0.44	0.044
5	220	22	2.2	0.22
0.5	22	2.2	0.22	0.022
0.05	2.2	0.22	0.022	0.0022
0.005	0.22	0.022	0.0022	0.00022

Figure 17.3   Multiplication tables for decimal numbers derived from a) 4 × 36 = 144; and b) 5 × 44 = 220

And what about dividing a decimal by a decimal?

The need to divide a decimal number by a decimal number might occur in a real-life situation with the inverse-of-multiplication division structure (see Chapter 10). This could be in the contexts of money or measurement. In these cases we can usually recast the problem in units which dispense with the need for decimals. For example, to find how many payments of £3.25 we need to make to reach a target of £52 (£52.00), we might at first be inclined to model the problem with the division, '52.00 ÷ 3.25'. This would be straightforward if using a calculator. However, without a calculator we might get in a muddle with the decimal points. So what we do is to rewrite the problem in pence and dispense with the decimal points altogether: how many payments of 325p do we need to reach 5200p? The mathematical model is now '5200 ÷ 325', which can then be solved by whatever method is appropriate. Similarly, to find how many portions of 0.125 litres we can pour from a 2.500-litre container, we could model the problem with the division, '2.500 ÷ 0.125'. But it's much less daunting if we change the measurements to millilitres, so that the calculation becomes '2500 ÷ 125', with no decimals involved at all.

In fact, what we are doing here, in changing, for example, '52.00 ÷ 3.25' into '5200 ÷ 325', is multiplying both numbers by 100. This is using the principle established in Chapter 11, that you do not change the result of a division calculation if you multiply both numbers by the same thing. We can use this principle whenever we have to divide by a decimal number. For example, to find '4 ÷ 0.8', simply multiply both numbers by 10, to get '40 ÷ 8': so the answer is 5. To find '2.4 ÷ 0.08', multiply both numbers by 100, to get '240 ÷ 8': so the answer is 30.

Any division calculations more difficult than the ones I have used in this section are either beyond the scope of primary-school mathematics or more appropriately done with a calculator.

I will conclude this section with one further observation about division by decimals: the smaller the number you divide by, the larger the answer. Notice the pattern in the results obtained when, for example, 10 is divided by 2, 0.2, 0.02, 0.002, and so on:

$$10 \div 2 \qquad = 5$$
$$10 \div 0.2 \qquad = 50$$
$$10 \div 0.02 \qquad = 500$$
$$10 \div 0.002 \quad = 5000$$
$$10 \div 0.0002 = 50\,000, \text{ etc.}$$

Each time the divisor gets ten times smaller the answer gets ten times bigger. This is such a significant property of division, which for some reason often surprises people, that it is worth drawing specific attention to it from time to time. It's easy enough to make sense of this property if you think of '$A \div B$' as meaning 'how many Bs make A?' Is it not obvious that the smaller the number B, the greater the number of Bs that you can get from A?

How do you change fractions into decimals, and vice versa?

Fractions such as tenths, hundredths and thousandths, where the bottom number is a power of ten, can be written directly as decimals. Here are some examples to show how this works:

$3/_{10}$ = 0.3   (0.3 means 3 tenths)
$23/_{10}$ = 2.3   (the 20 tenths make 2 whole units)
$3/_{100}$ = 0.03   (0.03 means 3 hundredths)
$23/_{100}$ = 0.23   (the 20 hundredths make 2 tenths)
$123/_{100}$ = 1.23   (the 100 hundredths make 1 whole unit)
$3/_{1000}$ = 0.003   (0.003 means 3 thousandths)
$23/_{1000}$ = 0.023   (the 20 thousandths make 2 hundredths)

Then there are those fractions which we can readily change into an equivalent fraction (see Chapter 16) with a bottom number of 10, 100 or 1000. For example, $1/_5$ is equivalent to $2/_{10}$ (multiplying top and bottom by 2), which, of course is written as a decimal fraction as 0.2. Similarly, $3/_{25}$ is equivalent to $12/_{100}$ (multiplying top and bottom by 4), which then becomes 0.12. Here are some further examples, many of which should be memorised, to show how this works:

$1/_2$ is equivalent to $5/_{10}$ which as a decimal is 0.5
$4/_5$ is equivalent to $8/_{10}$ which as a decimal is 0.8
$1/_4$ is equivalent to $25/_{100}$ which as a decimal is 0.25
$3/_4$ is equivalent to $75/_{100}$ which as a decimal is 0.75
$1/_{20}$ is equivalent to $5/_{100}$ which as a decimal is 0.5
$7/_{20}$ is equivalent to $35/_{100}$ which as a decimal is 0.35
$1/_{50}$ is equivalent to $2/_{100}$ which as a decimal is 0.02
$3/_{50}$ is equivalent to $6/_{100}$ which as a decimal is 0.06
$1/_{25}$ is equivalent to $4/_{100}$ which as a decimal is 0.04

Otherwise, to change a fraction into an equivalent decimal, recall that one of the meanings of the fraction notation is division (see Chapter 16). So all you have to do is to divide the top number by the bottom number, preferably using a calculator. Sometimes the result obtained will be an exact decimal, but often it will be a recurring decimal which has been truncated by the calculator (see Chapter 3).

The reverse process is to change a decimal into a fraction. First we recall that the decimal 0.3 means 'three-tenths', so it is clearly equivalent to the fraction $3/_{10}$. Likewise, 0.07 means 'seven-hundredths' and is equivalent to the fraction $7/_{100}$. Then to deal with, say, 0.37 (3 tenths and 7 hundredths), we have to recognise that the 3 tenths can be exchanged for 30 hundredths, which, together with the 7 hundredths, makes a total of 37 hundredths, i.e. the fraction $37/_{100}$. The only slight variation in all this is that sometimes the fraction obtained can be changed to an equivalent, simpler fraction, by dividing top and bottom numbers by the same number. Here are a few examples:

0.6 becomes $6/_{10}$ which is equivalent to $3/_5$ (dividing top and bottom by 2)
0.04 becomes $4/_{100}$ which is equivalent to $1/_{25}$ (dividing top and bottom by 4)
0.45 becomes $45/_{100}$which is equivalent to $9/_{20}$ (dividing top and bottom by 5)
0.44 becomes $44/_{100}$which is equivalent to $11/_{25}$ (dividing top and bottom by 25)

Self-assessment questions

17.1: Complete the solution of the problems (a), (b), (c) and (d) modelled by the additions and subtractions in Figure 17.1.

17.2: Remembering that there are 1000 millilitres in a litre and 1000 grams in a kilogram, suggest real-life questions which would be modelled by: a) '1.500 – 0.125', in the context of liquid volume and capacity; and b) '1.120 + 2.500', in the context of weighing. Answer your questions without using a calculator.

17.3: Pose a problem in the context of money, which is modelled by '3.99 × 4'. Solve your problem without using a calculator.

17.4: Pose a problem in the context of length which might be modelled by '4.40 ÷ 8'. Solve your problem without using a calculator.

17.5: Given that 4 × 46 = 184, find: a) 4 × 4.6; b) 0.4 × 46; c) 0.04 × 0.046.

17.6: Given that 4 × 45 = 180, find: a) 4 × 4.5; b) 0.4 × 45; and c) 0.04 × 0.045.

17.7: What is the value of $(0.01)^2$ (zero point zero one, squared)? Can you think of a question about area which might be modelled by this calculation?

17.8: Find: a) 2 ÷ 0.5 (hint: multiply both numbers by 10); and b) 5.5 ÷ 0.11 (hint: multiply both numbers by 100).

17.9: Express these fractions as equivalent decimals: a) $^{17}/_{100}$; b) $^{3}/_{5}$; c) $^{7}/_{20}$; d) $^{2}/_{3}$ (use a calculator); and e) $^{1}/_{7}$ (use a calculator).

17.10: Express these decimals as fractions: a) 0.09; b) 0.79; and c) 0.15.

Summary of teaching points

1. Always try to locate calculations with decimals in realistic contexts where the decimals represent money or measurements.

2. Emphasise the importance of having the same number of digits after the decimal point, when adding or subtracting money or measurements written in decimal notation. Explain to children about putting in extra zeros as place-holders where necessary.

3. Show how the principle of 'one of these can be exchanged for ten of these' works when adding or subtracting with decimals in the same way as when working with integers.

4. Realistic multiplication and division problems with decimals involving money or measurements can nearly always be recast into calculations with whole numbers by changing the units (e.g. pounds to pence, metres to centimetres). Teach children how to do this.

5. Base your explanation of multiplication and division of decimal numbers by 10 (and 100 and 1000) on the principle of place value. Talk about the digits moving, rather than the decimal point.

6. But allow pupils to explore repeated multiplications and divisions by 10 with a calculator, making use of the constant facility.

7. Not many primary pupils will get on to multiplying two decimal numbers together by non-calculator methods. For those who do, show how this can be done by getting rid of the decimal point and putting it back after the multiplication has been done. Explain the procedure in terms of multiplying repeatedly by 10, but teach them the trick of counting the digits after the points as well.

8. Show the more able pupils how to simplify divisions with decimals by multiplying both numbers by 10, 100, 1000, and so on, as appropriate.

9. Emphasise the principle that the smaller the number you divide by, the larger the answer, and let pupils explore this with sequences of divisions on a calculator.

10. Remember that in practice most people do calculations with decimals with a calculator, so be reasonable in the demands put upon pupils for non-calculator methods.

11. Pupils should explore equivalences between fractions and decimals, using calculators where necessary; encourage them to learn by heart some of the common equivalences, such as ½ = 0.5, ¼ = 0.25, ¾ = 0.75, ⅕ = 0.2, ⅖ = 0.4, and so on.

18

Percentages

Pupils should be taught to: understand and use, in context, . . . percentages to esti-mate, describe and compare proportions of a whole; calculate . . . percentages of quantities, using a calculator where appropriate.

In this chapter there are explanations of

- the meaning of the term *per cent*;
- the use of percentages to express proportions of a quantity or of a set;
- *ad hoc* and calculator methods for evaluating percentages;
- the usefulness of percentages for comparing proportions;
- equivalences between fractions, decimals and percentages;
- the meaning of percentages greater than 100; and
- how to calculate a percentage of a given quantity or number, using *ad hoc* and calculator methods.

What does 'per cent' mean?

The term *per cent* means 'for each hundred'. We are familiar, of course, with the Latin root *cent*, meaning 'a hundred', as it is used in many English words, such as 'century', 'centurion', 'centigrade' and 'centipede'. We use the concept of per cent first and foremost to describe a proportion of a quantity or of a set. So, for example, if there are 300 pupils in a school and 180 of them are girls, we might describe the proportion of girls as 'sixty per cent' (written as 60%) of the school population. This means simply that there are 60 girls for each 100 pupils. If on a car journey of 200 miles a total of 140 miles is single carriage-way, we could say that 70% (seventy per cent) of the journey is single car-riageway, meaning 70 miles for each 100 miles. What we are doing in these examples is exactly the same as we did with fractions in Chapter 16, when we used them to represent a part of a unit or of a set. The concept of a percentage is therefore no different from that of a fraction. It is simply a special case of a fraction, with 100 as the bottom number. So 60% is an abbreviation for $^{60}/_{100}$ and 70% for $^{70}/_{100}$.

How do you express a proportion as a percentage?

In the examples above it was very obvious how to express the proportions involved as 'so many per hundred'. This is not always the case. The following examples demonstrate a number of approaches to expressing a proportion as a percentage, using *ad hoc* methods, when the numbers can be related easily to 100. The trick is to find an equivalent proportion for a population of 100, by multiplying or dividing by appropriate numbers:

1. In a school population of 50, there are 30 girls. What percentage are girls? What percentage are boys?
   Reason as follows:
   30 girls out of 50 pupils is the same proportion as 60 out of 100.
   So, 60% of the population are girls.
   This means that 40% are boys. (Since the total population must be 100%.)

2. In a school population of 250, there are 130 girls. What percentage are girls? What percentage are boys?
   Reason as follows:
   130 girls out of 250 pupils is the same proportion as 260 out of 500.
   260 girls out of 500 pupils is the same as 52 per 100 (dividing 260 by 5).
   So, 52% of the population are girls.
   This means that 48% are boys. (52% + 48% = 100%)

3. In a school population of 75, there are 30 girls. What percentage are girls? What percentage are boys?
   Reason as follows:
   30 girls out of 75 pupils is the same proportion as 60 out of 150.
   60 girls out of 150 pupils is the same proportion as 120 out of 300.
   120 girls out of 300 pupils is the same as 40 per 100 (dividing 120 by 3).
   So, 40% of the population are girls, and therefore 60% are boys.

4. In a school population of 140, there are 77 girls. What percentage are girls?
   Reason as follows:
   77 girls out of 140 pupils is the same proportion as 11 out of 20 (dividing by 7).
   11 girls out of 20 pupils is the same proportion as 55 per 100 (multiply by 5).
   So, 55% of the population are girls, and therefore 45% are boys.

When the numbers do not relate so easily to 100 as in these examples, the procedure is more complicated and is best done with the aid of a calculator:

5. In a school population of 140, there are 73 girls. What percentage are girls? What percentage are boys?
   Reason as follows:
   73 girls out of 140 pupils means that $73/140$ are girls.
   The equivalent proportion for a population of 100 pupils is $73/140$ of 100.
   Work this out on a calculator. (Key sequence: 73, ÷, 140, ×, 100, =.)
   Interpret the display (52.14285): just over 52% of the population are girls.
   This means that just under 48% are boys.

Most calculators have a percentage key (labelled %) which enables this last example to be done without any complicated reasoning at all. On my calculator, for example, I could use the following key sequence: 73, ÷, 140, %. This really does make finding percentages with a calculator very easy indeed.

Why are percentages used so much?

They certainly are used extensively, in newspapers, in advertising, and so on. We are all familiar with claims such as '90% of cats prefer Kittymeat' and '20% of 7-year-olds cannot do subtraction'. There is certainly no shortage of material in the media for us to use with our pupils to make this topic relevant to everyday life. The convention of always relating everything to 100 enables us to make comparisons in a very straightforward manner. It is much easier, for example, to compare 45% with 40%, than to compare ⁴⁄₉ with ²⁄₅. This is why percentages are used so much: they provide us with a standard way of comparing various proportions.

Consider this example. School A spends £190 300 of its annual budget of £247 780 on teaching-staff salaries. School B is larger and spends £341 340 out of an annual budget of £450 700. It is very difficult to take in figures like these. The standard way of comparing these would be to express the proportions of the budget spent on teaching-staff salaries as percentages. Using a calculator, I find that School A spends about 76.80% on salaries (key sequence: 190 300, ÷, 247 780, %), whereas School B spends about 75.74% on salaries (key sequence: 341 340, ÷, 450 700, %). Now I can make a direct comparison: School A spends about £76.80 in every £100, School B spends about £75.74 in every £100.

There are other occasions, however, when the tendency always to put proportions into percentage terms seems a bit daft. For example, I come from a family of 3 boys and 1 girl. I could say that 75% of the children in my family are boys. I suppose there's no harm in this, but remember that what this is saying is effectively: '75 out of each 100 children in my family are boys!'

How do percentages relate to decimals?

In the previous chapter we saw how a decimal such as 0.37 means 37 hundredths. Since 37 hundredths also means 37 per cent, we can see a direct relationship between decimals with two digits after the point and percentages. So, 0.37 and 37% are two ways of expressing the same thing. Here are some other examples: 0.50 is equivalent to 50%, 0.05 is equivalent to 5%, 0.42 is equivalent to 42%. It really is as easy as that: you just move the digits two places to the left, because effectively what we are doing is multiplying the decimal number by 100. This works even if there are more than two digits, for example, 0.125 = 12.5% and 1.01 = 101%.

This means that we have effectively three ways of expressing proportions of a quantity or of a set: using a fraction, using a decimal or using a percentage. It is useful to learn by heart some of the most common equivalences, such as the following:

Fraction	Decimal	Percentage
½	0.5 (0.50)	50%
¼	0.25	25%
¾	0.75	75%
⅕	0.2 (0.20)	20%
⅖	0.4 (0.40)	40%
⅗	0.6 (0.60)	60%
⅘	0.8 (0.80)	80%
1/10	0.1 (0.10)	10%
3/10	0.3 (0.30)	30%
7/10	0.7 (0.70)	70%
9/10	0.9 (0.90)	90%
1/20	0.05	5%
⅓	0.33 (approx.)	33% (approx.)

Knowledge of these equivalences is useful for estimating percentages. For instance, in example (2) above, 130 out of 250 pupils were girls. This is just over half the population, so I would expect the percentage to be just a bit more than 50% (it is 52%). A proportion of 145 girls out of 450 pupils is a bit less than a third, so I would expect a percentage of around 33% (it is about 32.22%).

Also, because it is so easy to change a decimal into a percentage, and since we can convert a fraction to a decimal (see Chapter 17) just by dividing the top number by the bottom number, using a calculator, this gives us another direct way of expressing a fraction or a proportion as a percentage. For example, 23 out of 37 corresponds to the fraction $^{23}/_{37}$. On a calculator enter: '23, ÷, 37, ='. This gives the decimal equivalent, 0.6216216. Since the first two decimal places correspond to the percentage, we can just read this straight off as 'about 62%'. If we wish to be more precise, we could include a couple more digits, such as 62.16%. (See Chapter 12 for a discussion of rounding.)

So, in summary, we now have these four ways of expressing a proportion of '*A* out of *B*' as a percentage: 1) use *ad hoc* multiplication and division to change the proportion to an equivalent number out of 100; 2) work out *A/B* × 100, using a calculator, if necessary; 3) just enter on to a calculator: *A*, ÷, *B*, % (but note that calculators may vary in the precise key sequence to be used); and 4) use a calculator to find '*A* ÷ *B*' and read off the decimal answer as a percentage, by shifting all the digits two places to the left.

How can you have a hundred and one per cent?

Since 100% represents the whole quantity being considered, or the whole population, it does seem a bit odd at first to talk about percentages greater than 100. Football managers are well known for abusing mathematics in this way, for example, by talking about their team having to give a hundred and one per cent – meaning, presumably, everything they have plus a little more.

However there are perfectly correct uses of percentages greater than 100, not for expressing a proportion of a whole unit but for comparing two quantities. Just as we use fractions to represent the ratio of two quantities, we can also use percentages in this way. So, for example, if in January a window-cleaner earns £500 and in February he earns only £400, one way of comparing the two month's earnings would be to say that February's were 80% of January's. The 80% here is simply an equivalent way of saying four-fifths (⅘). If then in March he was to earn £600 then we could quite appropriately record that March's earning were 120% of January's. This is equivalent to saying 'one and a fifth' of January's earnings.

How do you calculate a percentage of a quantity?

The most common calculation we have to do with percentages is to find a percentage of a given quantity, particularly in the context of money. In cases where the percentage can be converted to a simple equivalent fraction, there are often very obvious *ad hoc* methods of doing this. For example, to find 25% of £48, simply change this to ¼ of £48, which is £12. Then when the quantity in question is a nice multiple of 100, we can often find easy ways to work out percentages. First, let us note that, for example, 37% of 100 is 37. So, if I had to work out 37% of £600, we could reason that, since 37% of £100 is £37, we simply need to multiply £37 by 6 to get the answer required, namely, £222.

It is also possible to develop *ad hoc* methods for building up a percentage, using easy components. One of the easiest percentages to find is 10% and most people intuitively start with this. (Note, however, that the fact that 10% is the same as a tenth makes it a very special case: 5% is not a fifth, 7% is not a seventh, and so on. Because we often start with 10% and make so much use of it, pupils can often get confused about this and teachers should make a special point of explaining that this connection works *only* with 10%.) So to find, say, 35% of £80, I could build up the answer like this:

    10% of £80 is £8
 so 20% of £80 is £16 (doubling the 10%)
and 5% of £80 is £4 (halving the 10%)
Adding the 10%, 20% and 5% gives me the 35% required: £29

It is often the case that 'intuitive' approaches to finding percentages, such as this one, are neglected in schools, in favour of more formal procedures. This is a pity, since success with this kind of manipulation all contributes to greater confidence with numbers generally.

When such methods as these fail, then we should turn to a calculator. For example, to find 37% of £946, we need to find $^{37}/_{100}$ of 946. This can be evaluated on a calculator. An appropriate key sequence is: 37, ÷, 100, ×, 946, =. This gives the result, 350.02, so we conclude that 37% of £946 is £350.02. Personally, I use a more direct method on the calculator. Since 37% is equivalent to 0.37, I just enter the key sequence: 0.37, ×, 946, =. There is another way, of course, using the percentage key. On my calculator the appropriate key sequence is: 946, ×, 37, %.

What about percentage increases and decreases?

One of the most common uses of percentages is to describe the size of a change in a given quantity, by expressing it as a proportion of the starting value. We are all familiar with percentage increases in salaries, for example. So if your monthly salary of £1500 is increased by 5%, to find your new salary you would have to find 5% of £1500 (£75) and add this to the existing salary. There is a more direct way of doing this: since your new salary is the existing salary (100%) plus 5%, it must be 105% of the existing salary. So you could get your new salary by finding 105% of the existing salary, i.e. by multiplying by 1.05 (remember that 105% = 1.05 as a decimal).

Similarly, if an article costing £200 is reduced by 15%, then to find the new price we have to find 15% of £200 (£30) and deduct this from the existing price, giving the new price as £170. More directly, we could reason that the new price is the existing price (100%) subtract 15%, so it must be 85% of the existing salary. Hence we could just find 85% of £200, for example, by multiplying 200 by 0.85.

There is an interesting phenomenon related to percentage increases and decreases which often puzzles people. If you apply a given percentage increase and then apply the same percentage decrease, you do not get back to where you started! For example, the price of an article is £200. The price is increased one month by 10%. The next month the price is decreased by 10% What is the final price? Well, after the 10% increase the price has gone up to £220. Now we apply the 10% decrease to this. This is a decrease of £22, not £20, because the percentage change always applies to the existing value. So the article finishes up costing £198.

Self-assessment questions

18.1: A department store is advertising '25% off' for some items and 'one-third off' for others. Which is the greater reduction?

18.2: Use *ad hoc* methods to find what percentage of pupils in a year group achieve level 5 in a mathematics test, if there are: a) 50 pupils in the year group and 13 achieve level 5; b) 300 in the year group and 57 achieve level 5; c) 80 in the year group and 24 achieve level 5; and d) 130 in the year group and 26 achieve level 5. In each case, state what percentage do not achieve level 5.

18.3: On a page of an English textbook there are 1249 letters, of which 527 are vowels. In an Italian text it is found that there are 277 vowels in a page of 565 letters. Use a calculator to determine approximately what percentage of letters are vowels in each case.

18.4: Change: a) ³⁄₂₀ into a percentage; and b) 65% into a fraction.

18.5: Use informal, intuitive methods to find: a) 30% of £120; and b) 17% of £450.

18.6: The price of a television costing £275 is increased by 12% one month and decreased by 12% the next. What is the final price? Use a calculator, if necessary.

18.7: A shop is advertising a stereo system for £600. But the manager tells you that there must be 20% tax added to this price. However, he is also offering 10% discount. Which would you prefer the manager to apply first? The tax or the discount?

Summary of teaching points

1. Explain the meaning of *per cent* as 'for each hundred' and show how percentages are used to describe a fraction of a quantity or of a set.
2. Encourage pupils to find examples of percentages used in newspapers and advertising and discuss with them what is being claimed.
3. Encourage the use of *ad hoc* methods of expressing a proportion as a percentage, using numbers that relate easily to 100.
4. Allow pupils to use calculators to express more difficult proportions as percentages, showing them the various different ways of doing this.
5. Emphasise the equivalence between fractions and percentages.
6. Show pupils how simple it is to change a percentage into an equivalent decimal and vice versa, by moving the digits two places.
7. Encourage pupils to memorise common equivalences between fractions, decimals and percentages.
8. Encourage pupils to use informal, intuitive methods for finding a percentage of a quantity, particularly building up a percentage using easy proportions such as 10% and 5%.
9. Let pupils use calculators for the more difficult examples of finding a percentage of a quantity, and explain to them some of the different ways of doing this.
10. Emphasise that 10% being equivalent to one-tenth is a special case.
11. Be aware that not all calculators follow the same key sequence for expressing a proportion as a percentage or for calculating percentages of a quantity.

19

Handling Data

Pupils should be taught to: interpret and create frequency tables, including those for grouped discrete data; collect and represent data appropriately using graphs and diagrams, including block graphs, pictograms and line graphs; interpret a wider range of graphs and diagrams that represent data, including pie charts.

In this chapter there are explanations of

- the four stages of handling data: collecting, organising, representing, interpreting;
- the use of tallying and frequency tables for collecting and organising data;
- the differences between discrete data, grouped discrete data and continuous data;
- the representation of discrete and grouped discrete data in block graphs;
- the misleading effect of suppressing zero in a frequency graph; and
- other ways of representing data: set diagrams, pictograms, pie charts and line graphs.

What do pupils have to learn about handling statistical data?

Essentially there are four stages involved in handling data: collecting it, organising it, representing it and interpreting it. (NB: I adopt the current usage of *data* as a singular noun, meaning 'a collection of information'.) Pupils should therefore have experience of all four of these stages.

They should learn how to collect data as part of a purposeful enquiry, setting out to answer specific questions which they might raise. This might involve the skills associated with designing simple questionnaires. For example, as part of a geography-focused project on transport, they might decide to collect data about how pupils travel to school and seek to make comparisons between, say, pupils in a rural school and those in a city school. A useful technique here is that of *tallying*, based on counting in fives. Data should then be organised in a *frequency table*. Figure 19.1 shows both these processes for the information collected from a year-5 class in a rural school.

Various kinds of graphs and diagrams can then be used to represent the data, before the final step of interpreting it. To involve pupils in this important

	tallying		How we travel	Number of pupils
Bus	卌 |		Bus	7
Bike	||		Bike	2
Car	卌 卌		Car	10
Walk	卌 |		Walk	6
			Total	25

tallying — *frequency table*

Figure 19.1   Using tallying and a frequency table

step of interpretation, I have found three approaches useful in the classroom:
1) pupils just write about what the graph tells them, particularly in relation to
the questions and issues which prompted the collection of the data; 2) pupils
write sentences about what the graph tells us, incorporating key words, such as
'most', 'least', 'more than', 'less than'; and 3) pupils make up a number of
questions which can be answered from the graph, to pose to each other.

What is discrete data?

The word *discrete* means 'separate'. Discrete data is information about a particular population (such as the children in a class), which automatically sorts
the members of the population into quite distinct, separate subsets. The information about travelling to school, shown in Figure 19.1, is a good example of
discrete data, since it sorts the pupils automatically into four separate, distinct
subsets: those who come by bus, by car, by bicycle or on foot. Other examples
of this kind of discrete data which pupils might collect, organise, display and
interpret would include: favourite TV programme, chosen from a list of six
possible programmes; daily newspaper taken at home, including 'none'; and
month in which they were born. In each case the question asked (e.g. how did
you travel to school today?) identifies a 'variable' (e.g. means of transport) and
the answer determines a 'value' for the variable (e.g. bus, car, bike, on foot).
Separate subsets are formed for each individual 'value' taken by the variable.
The number in each subset is called the *frequency*. Sometimes the variable is
numerical, rather than just descriptive; for example, pupils might be asked
how many children are there in their family (the possible values of this variable
are 1, 2, 3, 4, . . .), or what size shoes they wear, or how many pets they have.
Initially, we should use variables which have no more than a dozen values,
otherwise we finish up with too many subsets to allow any meaningful interpretation. We can then display the data in a conventional *block graph*. There
are two important stages in the development of this type of graph. In Figure
19.2a each square is shaded individually, as though each square represents one
child. In interpreting the graph the pupil can count the number of squares, as
though counting the number of children in each subset, so there is no need for
a vertical axis. (In an earlier stage still, children would write their names on
squares of gummed paper which would be arranged in columns, so that the

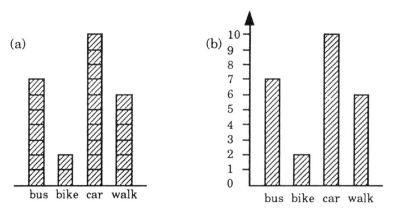

Figure 19.2   Two stages in the use of block graphs

individual contribution of each child can be identified.) Figure 19.2b is based on a more sophisticated idea. Now, the individual contributions are lost and it is the height of the column which indicates the frequency, rather than the number of squares in the column. We read off this frequency by relating the tops of the columns to the scale on the vertical axis, where, it should be noted, the numbers label the points on the axis, not the spaces between them. We have progressed from counting to measurement. This is an important step because, even though we may still use squared paper to draw these graphs, we now have the option of using different scales on the vertical axis, appropriate to the data: for example, with larger populations we might take one unit on the vertical scale to represent 10 people. Notice that, in Figure 19.2, I have used the convention, sometimes used for discrete data, of leaving gaps between the columns; this is an appropriate procedure because it conveys pictorially the way in which the variable sorts the population into discrete subsets.

In order to present an appropriate picture of the distribution of the data, it is essential that the columns in a block graph be drawn with equal widths. There

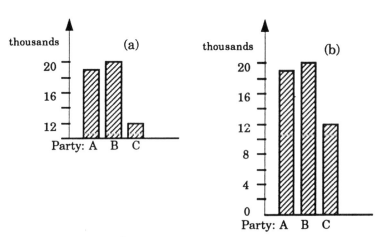

Figure 19.3   Suppression of zero

is a further important point to make about using block graphs to represent frequencies, illustrated by the graphs shown in Figure 19.3. This was produced prior to a general election to show the numbers of votes gained by three political parties (which I have called A, B and C) in the previous general election. The graph in Figure 19.3a was the version put out by our local Party A candidate to persuade us that we would be wasting our vote by voting for Party C. By not starting the frequency axis at zero a totally false picture is presented of the relative standing of Party C compared to A and B. Because the purpose of drawing a graph is to give us an instant overview of the relationships within the data, this procedure (called *suppression of zero*) is nearly always inappropriate or misleading and should be avoided. The graph in Figure 19.3b, properly starting the vertical axis at zero, presents a much more honest picture of the relative share of the vote.

So what is meant by 'grouped discrete data?'

Discrete data like that in the examples above is the simplest kind of data to handle. Sometimes, however, there are just too many values of the variable concerned for us to sort the population into an appropriate number of subsets. So the data must first be organised into groups. For example, a group of year-5 pupils were asked how many writing implements (pencils, pens, felt-tips, etc.) they had with them one day at school. The responses were as follows: 1, 2, 2, 3, 4, 4, 5, 5, 5, 6, 6, 8, 8, 8, 9, 9, 10, 10, 11, 13, 14, 14, 14, 15, 15, 18, 19, 25, 26, 32. Clearly, there are just too many possibilities here to represent this data in a block graph as it stands. The best procedure, therefore, is to group the data, for example, as shown in Figure 19.4. Notice that the range of values in the subsets (0–4, 5–9, 10–14, 15–19, etc.) should be the same in each case; that the groups should not overlap; that they must between them cover all the values of the variable; and that groups with zero frequency (like 20–24 in Figure 19.4) should not be omitted from the table or from the graph. Of course, the data could have been grouped in other ways, producing either more subsets (e.g. 0–1, 2–3, 4–5, and so on: 17 groups), or fewer (e.g. 0–9, 10–19,

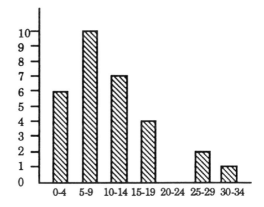

Figure 19.4   Handling grouped discrete data

20–29, 30–39). When working with *grouped discrete data* like this we should aim for between five and a dozen groups: more than a dozen, we have too much information to take in; less than five, we have lost too much information.

What other kind of data is there apart from discrete?

Discrete data contrasts with what is called *continuous data*. This is the kind of data produced by a variable which can theoretically take any value on a continuum. For example, if we were collecting data about the waist sizes of a group of adults, the measurements could come anywhere on a tape measure from, say, 50 cm to 120 cm. They are not just restricted to particular, distinct points on the scale. For example, the waist measurement for one individual might be about 62.5 cm. If he or she put on some weight and the measurement increases to about 64.5 cm, then we know that the waist size would increase continuously from one measurement to the next, on the way taking every possible value in between; it would not suddenly jump from one value to the other! This is a characteristic of a continuous variable. The contrast with a discrete variable like, for example, the number of pets you own, is clear. If you have three pets and then get a fourth, you suddenly jump from three to four, without having to pass through 3.1 pets, 3.2 pets, and so on. Measurements of length, mass, volume and time intervals are all examples of continuous data.

Having said that, we always have to record measurements 'to the nearest something' (see the discussion on rounding in Chapter 12). The effect of this is immediately to change the values of the continuous variable into a set of discrete data! For example, we might measure waist size to the nearest centimetre. This now means that our data is restricted to the following, separate, distinct values: 50 cm, 51 cm, 52 cm, and so on. This means that, in practice, the procedure for handling this kind of data, produced by recording a series of measurements to the nearest something, is no different from that for handling discrete data with a large number of potential values, by grouping it as explained above, thus making it an appropriate activity for primary-school

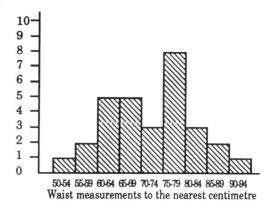

waist measurements to nearest centimetre	frequency
50 - 54	1
55 - 59	2
60 - 64	5
65 - 69	5
70 - 74	3
75 - 79	8
80 - 84	3
85 - 89	2
90 - 94	1

Figure 19.5   A graph derived from a continuous variable

children. Pupils can collect data about, for example, their heights (to the nearest centimetre), their masses (to the nearest tenth of a kilogram), the circumferences of their heads (to the nearest millimetre), the volume of water they can drink in one go (to the nearest tenth of a litre), the time taken to run 100 metres (to the nearest second), and so on. Each of these is technically a continuous variable, but by being measured to the nearest something generates a set of discrete data, which can then be grouped appropriately and represented in a graph. The only difference I would suggest is that we should reflect the fact that the data originated from a continuous variable by drawing the columns in the graph with no gaps between them, as shown in Figure 19.5. Any further development of handling of continuous data than this would be beyond the scope of primary-school mathematics.

What other ways are there of representing data?

Figure 19.6 shows two further ways of representing the data used in Figure 19.1. The most elementary method, picture (a), is a *set diagram*, with the actual names of the pupils written in the various subsets. Then in picture (b), a *pictogram*, the names have been replaced by pictures, organised in neat rows and columns. The pictogram is clearly only a small step from a block graph, with the pictures replaced by individual shaded squares. It is also possible with larger populations to use pictograms where each icon (picture) represents a number of individuals rather than just one.

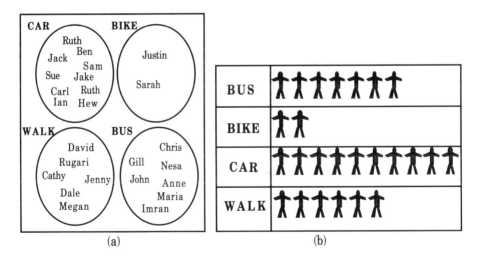

(a)   (b)

Figure 19.6   A set diagram and a pictogram

Much more sophisticated is the *pie chart*, shown in Figure 19.7. Here it is the angle of each slice of pie which represents the proportion of the population in each subset. It is usual practice to write these proportions as percentages (see Chapter 18) within the slice itself, if possible. Pie charts are really only appropriate for discrete data with a small number of subsets, say, six or less. They are often used to show what proportions of a budget are spent in various

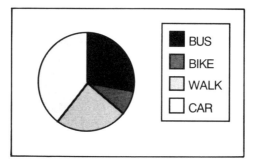

Figure 19.7   A pie chart

categories. The mathematics for producing a pie chart can be quite complicated for primary-school children, unless the data is chosen very carefully. For
example, to determine the angle for the slice representing travel by bus, in
Figure 19.7, we would have to divide 360 degrees by 25, to determine how
many degrees per person in the population, then multiply by 7. Using a calculator, the key sequence is: $360 \div 25 \times 7 =$ (answer 100.8, i.e. about 101 degrees).
This angle then has to be drawn using a protractor. Fortunately, this can all be
done nowadays by a computer. If the data in question is entered on a database
or on a spreadsheet – many simple examples of these kinds of programs are
available for use in primary schools – then usually there is available a choice of
a block graph, a pie chart or a line graph (see below) at the press of a button.
This certainly means that primary-school children should learn how to interpret pie charts – but it also means that they do not need really to learn how to
draw them for themselves.

The other type of graph used sometimes for representing statistical data is
the *line graph*. An example of a line graph is shown in Figure 19.8. This shows

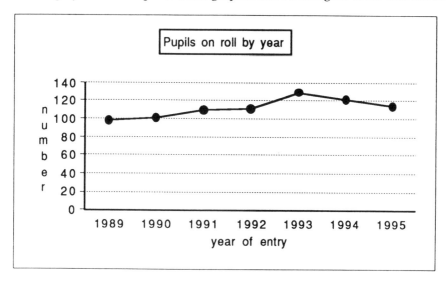

Figure 19.8   A line graph

the number of pupils on a primary-school roll at the beginning of each school year for a number of years. A line graph is really only appropriate for statistical data where the variable along the horizontal axis is 'time', since the movement of the line, up and down, gives a picture of how the number on roll is changing with time. It would be useful for showing, for example, the average mid-day temperature over a series of months, the number of pupils absent each day one week, the number of pupils who have completed their mathematics work by various numbers of minutes past ten o'clock, and so on. A line graph would therefore be totally inappropriate as a means of presenting discrete data such as that relating to travelling to school in Figure 19.1, and fairly inappropriate for all the other examples of statistical data used in this chapter.

Self-assessment questions

19.1: Make up two questions which can be answered from the graphs shown in each of: a) Figure 19.2; b) Figure 19.4; and c) Figure 19.5.

19.2: Which of these variables are discrete? Which would generate discrete data which should be grouped? Which are continuous? a) The time it takes a person to count to a thousand; b) your height; c) the number of living grandparents; d) the amount of money in coins in a person's possession; e) a person's favourite kind of music chosen from a list of ten possibilities; f) the number of A-levels a person has passed; and g) the mass of the classroom guinea-pig recorded each Monday morning for a term.

19.3: Which of the examples in Question 19.2 would be best represented in a pie chart? Which would be best represented in a line graph?

19.4: For example (d) in Question 19.2, the data collected from a group of students ranged from zero to £4.59. How would you choose to group this data in order to represent it in a bar chart?

19.5: (a) In a class of 36 pupils, 14 come to school by car. What angle would be needed in the slice of a pie chart to represent this information? (b) What would it be for 14 pupils out of a class of 33?

Summary of teaching points

1. Pupils should have experience of all four stages of handling data: collecting, organising, representing, interpreting.
2. Motivation is higher when the data is collected by the pupils themselves, higher still when it is collected to answer some questions they have posed themselves and even higher when it is about themselves!
3. The skills of handling data and pictorial representation are best taught through purposeful enquiries related to topics focusing on other areas of the curriculum, such as geography, history or science.
4. Teach the technique of tallying and encourage pupils to use it when collating data.
5. Pupils should first handle discrete data with non-numerical variables (e.g. means of travel to school), then discrete data using numerical

variables (e.g. number of pets owned). Use examples with no more than a dozen subsets.

6. Introduce pupils to set diagrams and pictograms as ways of representing discrete data.

7. Block graphs are introduced first by sticking on or shading individual squares, the number of which represents the frequency, and then by columns, the heights of which represent the frequency.

8. Later pupils can learn to interpret pie charts: these are best used when there is only a small number of subsets.

9. Pupils should progress to handling discrete data with so many subsets that the data has to be organised into groups covering a range of values.

10. Finally they can deal with continuous variables, such as measurements of length, mass, time and volume, by recording measurements to the nearest something and thus converting the values of the variable to discrete data, which can then be grouped appropriately.

11. Pupils should use database and spreadsheet programs to organise data and to generate graphs (particularly block graphs and pie charts) for them to interpret.

12. Encourage pupils to collect examples of graphs and tables of data from the press and advertising – and discuss whether they are helpful or misleading.

13. Introduce line graphs for data related to the passing of time.

20

Averages

Pupils should be taught to: understand and use measures of average, leading towards the mode, the median and the mean in relevant contexts, and the range as a measure of spread.

In this chapter there are explanations of

- the idea of an average as a representative figure for a set of data;
- three measures of average: the mean, the median and the mode;
- the need for a measure of spread and the idea of range; and
- the concept of average speed.

I thought an average was what you get by adding up some numbers and dividing by how many there are in the set: is there more to it than that?

The process outlined in the question posed here produces one kind of average figure, called the *mean* (or, to use its full title, the *arithmetic mean*). The purpose of finding an average is to produce a *representative figure* for a set of numerical data. The mean is just one way of doing this which is appropriate in many circumstances. But it is not the only way. Sometimes it makes more sense to use other kinds of average, in particular, the *median* and the *mode*. The important purpose shared by all three of these measures of average is to find a suitable way of obtaining one number which can represent the whole set of numbers. This 'average' figure will then enable us to: 1) to make comparisons between different sets of data, by comparing their means, medians or modes; and 2) to make sense of individual numbers in a set by relating them to these averages.

In the discussion below we will use these different kinds of average to consider the marks out of 100 gained by two groups of pupils (Group A, 14 pupils; Group B, 11 pupils) in the same mathematics and English tests, as follows:

Group A: Mathematics	23, 25, 46, 48, 48, 49, 53, 60, 61, 61, 61, 62, 69, 85
Group B: Mathematics	36, 38, 43, 43, 45, 47, 60, 63, 69, 86, 95
Group A: English	45, 48, 49, 52, 53, 53, 53, 53, 54, 56, 57, 58, 59, 62
Group B: English	45, 52, 56, 57, 64, 71, 72, 76, 79, 81, 90

What is the logic behind the process of finding the mean?

To find the mean value of a set of numbers three steps are involved: 1) find the sum of all the numbers in the set; 2) divide by the number of numbers in the set; and 3) round the answer appropriately, if necessary (see Chapter 12).

For example, to find the mean score of Group A above in mathematics: 1) the sum of the scores is 751; 2) divide 751 by 14, using a calculator to get 53.642857; and 3) round this to, say, one decimal place, to determine the mean score to be about 53.6. The logic behind using this as a representative figure is that the total marks obtained by the group would have been the same if all the pupils had scored the mean score (allowing for the possibility of a small error introduced by rounding: for example, if the 14 pupils had all scored 53.6, the total of their marks would have been 750.4). I imagine the process to be one of pooling. All the pupils put all their marks into a pool, which is then shared out equally between all 14 of them. This is an application of the concept involved in division structures associated with the word 'per' (see Chapter 10): we are finding the 'marks per student', assuming an equal sharing of all the marks awarded between them. An example which illustrates this well would be to find the mean amount of money which a group of people have in their possession. This could be done by putting all their money on the table and then sharing it out again equally between the members of the group. This is precisely the process which is modelled by the mathematical process of finding the mean.

We can now use this process to make comparisons. For example, to compare Group A with Group B in mathematics, we could compare their mean scores. Group B's mean score is about 56.8 (625 ÷ 11). This would lend some support to an assertion that, on the whole, Group B (mean score 56.8) has done better in the test than Group A (mean score 53.6).

We can also use average scores to help make sense of individual scores. For example, Cathy in Group B scored 60 in mathematics and 64 in English. Reacting naively to the raw scores, we might conclude that she did better in English than in mathematics. But by comparing the marks with the mean scores for her group leads to a different interpretation: Cathy's mark for mathematics (60) is above the mean (56.8), whilst the higher mark she obtained for English (64) is actually below the mean for her group (which works out to be 67.5). This would lend some support to the view that Cathy has done better in mathematics than in English.

What is the median?

The *median* is simply the number which comes in the middle of the set when the numbers are arranged in numerical order. Finding this average figure is much easier therefore than calculating the mean. The only complication arises when there is an even number of elements in the set, because then there is not a middle one. So the process of finding the median is as follows: 1) arrange all the numbers in the set in order from smallest to largest; 2) if the number of numbers in the set is odd, the median is the number in the middle; and 3) if the number of numbers in the set is even, the median is the mean of the two numbers in the middle, i.e. halfway between them.

For example, for Group B mathematics, with a set of 11 pupils, the median is the 6th mark when the marks are arranged in order; hence the median is 47. For Group A mathematics, with a set of 14, the median comes halfway between the 7th and 8th marks, i.e. halfway between 53 and 60; hence the median is 56.5. Interestingly, if we use the median rather than the mean as our measure of average we would draw a different conclusion altogether when comparing the two groups: that on the whole Group A (median mark of 56.5) has done rather better than Group B (median mark of 47)! The median is often a more appropriate representative figure than the mean when working with a small set of numbers, as in these examples. The reason for this is that the median is not affected by one or two extreme values, such as the 86 and 95 in Group B; a couple of scores much larger than the rest, like these two, can increase the value of the mean quite significantly and produce an average figure which does not represent the group in the most appropriate way. To take an extreme case, imagine that in a test nine pupils in a group score 1 and the other one pupil scores 100: this data produces a mean score of 10.9 and a median of 1! There is surely no argument here that the median 'represents' the performance of the group as a whole most appropriately. All this simply serves to illustrate the fact that most sets of statistics are open to different interpretations – which is why I have used the phrase 'lend some support to . . .' when drawing conclusions from the data in these examples.

Returning to our pupil Cathy, who scored 60 for mathematics and 64 for English, we can compare her performance with the median scores for her group, of 47 and 71 respectively. These statistics again lend support to the assertion that she has done better in mathematics than in English.

What is the mode and when would you use it?

The mode is simply the number in the set which occurs most frequently. For example, for Group A mathematics, the mode (or the modal mark) is 61, because this occurs three times, which is more than any other number in the set. For Group B mathematics, the mode is 43. This is actually a pretty daft way of determining representative marks for these sets of data. The mode is really only any use as a measure of average when you are dealing with a large set of data and when the range of values covered by the data is quite small. A good example of the use of a mode would be when discussing an 'average' family. In the UK, the modal number of children in a family is two, because more families have two children than any other. So if I were to write a play featuring an 'average' family, there would be two children in it. Clearly the mode is more use here than the mean, since '2.4 children' would be difficult to cast. Like the mean and the median, the mode enables us to make useful comparisons between different sets, when it is an appropriate and meaningful measure of average; for example, when comparing social factors in, say, parts of China, some countries in Africa and European states, the modal number of children per family would be very significant statistics to consider.

What is meant by 'the range as a measure of spread'?

If we compare Group A's marks for mathematics (mean score 53.6) with their marks for English (mean score 53.7), looking just at the means we might conclude that the sets of marks for the two subjects were very similar. Looking at the actual data it is clear that they are not. The most striking feature is that the mathematics marks are widely spread and the English marks are relatively closely clustered together. Statisticians have various ways of measuring the degree of 'spread' (sometimes called 'dispersion') in a set of data: the reader may have heard, for example, of the 'standard deviation'. These measures of spread have a similar purpose to the measures of average: they enable us to compare sets of data and to make sense of individual items of data. For primary-school work we would only introduce the simplest measure of spread, the *range*. This is as simple as it sounds: the range is just the difference between the largest and the smallest values in the set.

So, when comparing Group A's mathematics and English we would say that although they have about the same mean scores the range for mathematics is 62 marks (85 – 23), whereas the range for English is only 17 marks (62 – 45).

How does the idea of 'average speed' fit in with the concept of an average?

Pupils' first experience of speed is usually the speed of a vehicle, measured in 'miles per hour'. It is therefore a bit perverse for us to use 'kilometres per hour' when discussing speed in primary schools, as occurs in many primary mathematics schemes, since this is mostly unrelated to the children's experience. Note that average speed gives us another example of that important little word, 'per'. The idea of average speed derives from the concept of a mean. Over the course of a journey in my car, my speed will be constantly changing; sometimes it will even be zero. When we talk about the average speed for a journey, then it is as though we add up all the miles covered during various stages of the journey and then share them out equally 'per hour', using the same idea of 'pooling' which was the basis for calculating the mean of a set of numbers. So if my journey covers 400 miles in total and takes 8 hours, the average speed is 50 miles per hour (400 ÷ 8). The logic here is that if I had been able to travel at a constant speed of 50 miles in each hour, then the journey would have taken the same time (8 hours). So the average speed (in miles per hour) is the total distance travelled (in miles) divided by the total time taken (in hours). We can then extend this definition of average speed to apply to journeys where the time is not a whole number of hours; for example, for a journey of 22 miles in 24 minutes (0.4 hours) the average speed is '22 ÷ 0.4', which is 55 miles per hour. And, of course, the same principle applies whatever units are used for distance and time; for example, if the toy car takes 5 seconds to run down a ramp of 150 centimetres, the average speed is 30 centimetres per second (150 ÷ 5).

Self-assessment questions

20.1: Compare the mean and median scores for English for Groups A and B, using the data given above. Which group did better for English on the whole?

20.2: Find the mean score for English for the two groups combined. Is the mean score of the two groups combined equal to the mean of the two separate mean scores?

20.3: Find the median scores and the ranges for English and Mathematics for the two groups combined.

20.4: John, in Group A, scored 49 for mathematics. How does this score compare to the performance of Group A as a whole?

20.5: Compile a frequency table for the numbers of letters in the last one hundred words in this chapter (ignoring numbers). What is the modal number of letters per word?

20.6: Toy car P travels 410 centimetres in 6 seconds; toy car Q travels 325 centimetres in 5 seconds. Which had the greater average speed?

20.7: On a car journey of 400 miles I average a speed of 40 miles per hour: how long does the journey take? On the way back I average a speed of 50 miles per hour: how long does the return journey take? Now (be careful!), what is the average speed for the whole journey, there and back?

Summary of teaching points

1. The idea of an average is appropriately introduced to pupils towards the upper end of the primary range. Explain to pupils the idea of an average being a representative figure for a set of numbers, enabling us to make comparisons between different sets.

2. Explain the idea of the mean, first using the example of pooling money and sharing it out equally, then extending it to other examples.

3. Emphasise that the median is just the one in the middle when the numbers are arranged in order, but point out how to deal with a set with an even number of numbers.

4. Introduce pupils to the idea of using the mode as a measure of average when appropriate, for example, when dealing with a large set of numbers with a limited range of possible values.

5. Show pupils, using examples of sets with approximately the same mean but very different spreads, the importance of looking at the range of values when comparing sets of numbers.

6. Pupils should use and apply these concepts to make comparisons between sets of data and to make sense of individual items of data, using information they have collected themselves in the course of purposeful enquiries.

7. Useful sources of data for applying these concepts are: the pupils themselves (their ages, their heights, distance of home from school, children in their family, and so on), the weather, sport, science experiments (repeating a measurement several times and recording a mean value) and most geography-focused topics (particularly for making comparisons between different areas).

8. Pupils must learn that conclusions drawn from statistics, such as averages, can be uncertain or even misleading.

21

Probability

Pupils should be taught to: develop understanding of probability, through experience, as well as experiment and theory; understand that the probability of an event lies between impossibility and certainty, leading to the use of the scale from 0 to 1; recognise situations where probabilities can be based on equally likely outcomes, and others where estimates must be based on experimental evidence.

In this chapter there are explanations of

- the meaning of probability as a measurement applied to events;
- some of the language we use to indicate probability subjectively;
- the use of a numerical scale from 0 to 100%, or from 0 to 1, for measuring probability;
- estimating probability from statistical data;
- estimating probability from data obtained by repeating an experiment a large number of times;
- estimating probability by using theoretical arguments based on symmetry and equally likely outcomes; and
- the use of two-way tables for identifying all the possible equally likely outcomes from an experiment involving two independent events.

What is probability?

First of all we should recognise that in mathematics probability is a measurement, just like any other measurement such as length or mass. Secondly, it is a measurement which is applied to *events*. But what it is about an event which is being measured is surprisingly elusive. My view is that what we are measuring is how strongly we believe that the event will happen. We describe this level of belief with words ranging from 'impossible' to 'certain' and compare our assessment of different events by talking about one being 'more likely' or 'less likely' than another. This strength of belief is determined by different kinds of *evidence* which we may assemble.

Sometimes this evidence is simply the accumulation of our experience, in which case our judgement about how likely one event may be compared to others is fairly *subjective*. For example, one group of students wrote down some events which might occur during the following twelve months and ranked them in order from the least likely to the most likely as follows: a) it will snow in Norwich during July; b) Norwich City will win the FA Cup; c) Steve will get a teaching post; d) there will be a general election in the UK; and e) someone will reach the summit of Mount Everest. When they were then told that Steve had an interview at a school the following week for a post for which he was ideally suited, this extra piece of evidence had an immediate effect on their strength of belief in event (c) and they changed its position in the ranking.

By using 'more likely than' and 'less likely than', this activity is based on the ideas of comparison and ordering, always the first stages of the development of any aspect of measurement. Then we would need to introduce some kind of measuring scale. For measuring probability, this can be done at first using everyday language. For example, we might judge that event (a) is 'almost impossible', event (b) is 'fairly unlikely' and event (e) is 'almost certain'. When we feel that an event is as likely to happen as not to happen, we say that 'the chances are evens'. To introduce a numerical scale, we can think of awarding marks out of 100 for each event, with 0 marks for an event we believe to be impossible, 100 marks for an event we judge to be certain, and 50 marks for 'evens'. For example, purely subjectively, the students in the group awarded 1 mark for event (a), 5 marks for event (b), 50 marks for event (d) and 99 marks for event (e). Event (c) started out at 40, but moved to 75 when the new evidence was obtained.

If these marks out of 100 are now thought of as percentages and converted to decimals (see Chapter 18 for how to do this), we have the standard scale used for measuring probability, ranging from 0 (impossible), through 0.5 (evens), to 1 (certain). For example, our subjective assessment of the probabilities of events (b) and (e) are 0.05 and 0.99 respectively.

How can you measure probability more objectively?

There are three ways of collecting evidence which can be used for a more objective estimate of probability: 1) we can collect statistical data and use the idea of relative frequency; 2) we can perform an experiment a large number of times and use the relative frequency of different outcomes; and 3) we can use theoretical arguments based on symmetry and equally likely outcomes.

The first of these is used extensively in the world of businesses, such as insurance and marketing, where probabilities are often assessed by gathering statistical data. For example, to determine an appropriate premium for a life insurance policy for a person such as myself, an insurance company would use the probabilities that I might live to 60, to 70, to 80, and so on. To determine these probabilities they could collect statistical data about university lecturers living in East Anglia and find what proportion of these survive to various ages. If it is found that out of 250 cases, 216 live to 70, then this evidence would suggest that a reasonable estimate for the probability of my living to this age is 86.4% (216 ÷ 250) or, as a decimal, 0.864. Since it is normally impractical to obtain data from the entire population, this application of probability is usually based on evidence collected from a *sample*. For example, what is the probability that a word chosen at random from a page of text in this book will have four letters in it? To answer this we could use the last hundred words of the previous chapter as a sample. Since 18 of these words have four letters, the *relative frequency* of four-letter words in the sample is 18%. So an estimate for the probability, based on this evidence, would be 0.18. In general, the larger the sample, the more reliable is the relative frequency as an estimate of the probability.

The second procedure for obtaining objective estimates for probabilities applies the same idea, but to an *experiment*, often the kind of thing that can be experienced in the classroom. Now the 'event' in question is an *outcome* of the experiment. For example, the experiment might be to throw three identical dice simultaneously. The outcome we are interested in is that the score on one of them should be greater than the sum of the scores on the other two. What is the probability of this outcome? A useful experience for pupils is to make a subjective estimate of the probability, based purely on intuition, and then to perform the experiment a large number of times, recording the numbers of successes and failures. For example, they might make a subjective estimate that the chances of this happening would be a bit less than evens, so the probability is, say, about 0.40. Then the dice are thrown, say, 200 times and it is found that the number of successes is 58. Hence the relative frequency of successes is 29% (58 ÷ 200) and so the best estimate for the probability, based on this evidence, would be 0.29.

For some experiments, however, we can consider all the possible outcomes theoretically and make estimates for probability using an argument based on symmetry. Experiments with coins and dice lend themselves to this kind of argument. The simplest argument would be about tossing one coin. There are only two possible outcomes, heads and tails. Given the symmetry of the coin, there is no reason to assume that any one outcome is more or less likely than the other. So we would conclude that the probability of a head is 0.5 and the probability of a tail is 0.5. Notice that the sum of the probabilities of all the possible outcomes must be 1. This represents 'certainty': we are certain that the coin will come down either heads or tails. Similarly, if we throw a conventional, six-faced die, there are six possible outcomes, all of which, on the basis of symmetry, are equally likely. We therefore determine the probability of each number turning up to be one-sixth, or about 0.17 (1 ÷ 6 = 0.1666666 on a calculator). We can also determine the probability of events which are made up of various outcomes. For example, there are two scores on the die which are multiples of three, so the probability of throwing a multiple of three would be two sixths, or about 0.33 (²⁄₆ = ⅓ = 0.3333333 on a calculator). So the general procedure for determining the probability of a particular event by this theoretical approach is: 1) list all the possible equally likely outcomes from the experiment, being guided by symmetry, but thinking carefully to ensure that the outcomes listed really are equally likely; 2) count up in how many of these outcomes the event in question occurs; and 3) divide the second number by the first. For example, to find the probability that a card drawn from a conventional pack of playing cards will be less than 7: 1) there are 52 equally likely outcomes from the experiment, i.e. 52 possible cards which can be drawn; 2) the event in question (the card is less than 7) occurs in 24 of these; and 3) so the probability is 24 ÷ 52, or about 0.46.

It is important to remember at this stage what I said at the beginning of this chapter about the meaning of probability. It is a measure of how strongly you believe an event will happen. So when I say the probability of a coin turning up heads is 0.5, I am making a statement about how strongly I believe that it will come up heads. This kind of theoretical probability, provided the argument based on symmetry was valid, does not change from one outcome to the next. So the statement that the probability of getting a head is 0.5 does not tell me anything about what will happen next. If I have just thrown a head, the probability of the next toss being a head is still 0.5. If I have just thrown 20 tails in succession, the probability of the next one being a head is still 0.5. (Of course, there might be something peculiar about the coin, but I am assuming that it is not bent or weighted in any way which might distort the results.) What the probability does tell me, however, is that *in the long run*, if you go on tossing the coin long enough, you will see the relative frequency of heads (and tails) gradually getting closer and closer to 50%. This does not mean that with a thousand tosses I would *expect* 500 of each; in fact, that would be very surprising! But I would expect the proportion of heads to be about 50% and getting closer to 50% the more experiments I perform. It is therefore important for pupils actually to do such experiments a large number of times, obtain the relative frequencies of various outcomes for which they have determined the theoretical probability and observe and discuss the fact that the two are not usually exactly the same. There is a wonderfully mystical idea here: that in an experiment with a number of equally likely possible outcomes we have no way of predicting what will be the outcome of any given experiment, but we can predict with confidence what will happen in the long run! (This for me seems to provide a mathematical model for resolving the theological paradox of free will and predestination.)

How do you deal theoretically with tossing two coins or throwing two dice?

We do have to be careful when arguing theoretically about possible outcomes to ensure that they are really all equally likely. For example, one class of pupils decided there were three possible outcomes when you toss two coins – two heads, two tails, one of each – and determined the probabilities to be one-third for each. Then performing the experiment 1000 times between them (40 times each for 25 pupils) they found that two heads turned up 256 times, two tails turned up 234 times and one of each turned up 510 times. So the relative frequencies were 25.6%, 23.4% and 51%, obviously not getting close to the 'theoretical' 33.3% . The problem is that these three outcomes are *not equally likely*. Calling the two coins A and B, we can identify *four* possible outcomes: A and B both heads, A head and B tail, A tail and B head, A and B both tails. So the theoretical probabilities of two heads, two tails and one of each are 0.25, 0.25 and 0.50 respectively.

Second coin

		Head(H)	Tail(T)
First	**Head(H)**	H+H	H+T
coin	**Tail(T)**	T+H	T+T

(a) outcomes from tossing two coins

Second die

+	1	2	3	4	5	6
1	2	3	4	5	6	7
2	3	4	5	6	7	8
3	4	5	6	7	8	9
4	5	6	7	8	9	10
5	6	7	8	9	10	11
6	7	8	9	10	11	12

First die

(b) outcomes from throwing two dice

Figure 21.1 Two-way tables for an experiment with two independent events

With experiments involving two independent events, such as two coins being tossed or two dice being thrown, a useful device for listing all the possible outcomes is a two-way table. Figure 21.1a is such a table, showing the four possible outcomes from tossing two coins. Figure 21.1b similarly gives all 36 possible outcomes, shown as total scores in the table, when two dice are thrown: from this table we can discover, for example, that the probability of scoring seven (7 occurs 6 times out of 36: $6/36 = 0.17$ approximately) is much higher than, say, scoring eleven (11 occurs 2 times out of 36: $2/36 = 0.06$ approximately).

Self-assessment questions

21.1: What would be the most appropriate way to determine the probability that: a) a drawing-pin will land point up when tossed in the air; b) a person aged 50–59 years in England will have two living parents; and c) the total score when two dice are thrown is an even number?

21.2: What is the probability that a word chosen at random in this book will have less than than six letters in it? Use the sample of data collected in Question 20.5 in the previous chapter to make an estimate for this.

21.3: If I throw a dodecahedron die (with twelve faces, numbered one to twelve): a) what is the probability that I will score a number with two digits? b) what is the probability that I will score a number with one digit?

21.4: See Figure 21.1b. When two conventional dice (with six faces, numbered one to six) are thrown, what is the probability of: a) Scoring a multiple of 3? b) Scoring a multiple of 4? c) Scoring a number which is a multiple of 3 or 4 (or both)?

21.5: I throw two conventional dice. Write down an outcome which has a probability of 0 and another outcome which has a probability of 1.

Summary of teaching points

1. Introduce probability by getting pupils to write down events which may occur in the next 12 months and then to rank them in order from least

likely to most likely. Use this to introduce some of the language of probability, particularly 'more likely than' and 'less likely than'.

2. Pupils should describe events which might occur with such labels as 'impossible', 'nearly impossible', 'not very likely', 'evens', 'fairly likely', 'almost certain', 'certain'.

3. Introduce the idea of measuring probability on a numerical scale, by subjectively assigning points out of 100 (i.e. percentage scores) to various events which might occur; then use these to introduce the probability scale from 0 to 1, by changing the percentages to decimals.

4. Pupils can be introduced to the idea of relative frequency, expressed as a percentage and as a decimal, using statistical data they have gathered themselves, as part of a purposeful enquiry.

5. Then explain to them how to apply the idea of relative frequency to the outcomes of experiments, interpreting these as estimates of probability.

6. Give pupils opportunities to compare their intuitive estimates of probabilities of various outcomes from an experiment with the estimates of probabilities obtained by repeating the experiment a large number of times.

7. In using theoretical arguments based on symmetry, emphasise the importance of identifying equally likely outcomes.

8. Let pupils compare probabilities determined theoretically with the results of performing experiments a large number of times.

9. Emphasise the idea that probability does not tell you anything about what will happen next, but predicts what will happen in the long run.

10. One obvious application of probability is to betting and lotteries. Be aware that some parents will hold strong views about gambling, so handle this subject in a way which is sensitive to different perspectives on the morality and acceptability of gambling as a pastime.

22

Algebra

Pupils should be taught to: explore number sequences, explaining patterns and using simple relationships; interpret, generalise and use simple mappings, relating to numerical, spatial or practical situations, expressed initially in words and then using letters as symbols.

In this chapter there are explanations of

- the difference in the meaning of letters used as abbreviations in arithmetic and as used in algebra;
- the idea of a letter representing a variable;
- some other differences between arithmetic thinking and algebraic thinking;
- precedence of operators;
- ways of introducing pupils to the idea of a letter as a variable;
- the important role played by tabulation;
- the ideas of sequential and global generalisation;
- independent and dependent variables;
- the meaning of the word 'mapping' in an algebraic context; and
- the usefulness of the trial-and-improvement method for solving equations arising from problems.

What do the letters used in algebra, like '*x*' and '*y*', actually mean?

To answer this important question I will start by posing two problems, using letters as symbols. The reader is invited to write down his or her answers to these two problems before reading on:

- Problem 1: You can get 10 francs to the pound. You have *P* pounds. You exchange this money for *F* francs. What is the relationship between *P* and *F*?
- Problem 2: *S* is the number of students in a school. *T* is the number of teachers. There are 20 times as many students as teachers. Write down an equation using *S* and *T*.

Most people write down '$10F = P$' for Problem 1 (or '$10F = 1P$' or '$P = 10F$' or '$1P = 10F$', which are all different ways of saying the same thing). The correct answer is actually '$F = 10P$'. The table in Figure 22.1a shows various values for P and F. For example, if I have 1 pound ($P = 1$) I can exchange this for 10 francs ($F = 10$); if I have 2 pounds ($P = 2$) I can exchange this for 20 francs ($F = 20$); similarly, when $P = 3$, $F = 30$, and so on. The table makes it clear that whatever number is chosen for P (1, 2, 3, . . .) the value of F is ten times this number (10, 20, 30, . . .). This is precisely what is meant by the algebraic statement, '$F = 10P$'. Even people who are apparently quite well qualified in mathematics get this the wrong way round when this problem is given to them, so it is instructive to analyse the thinking which leads to this misunderstanding. What those who write down '$10F = P$' are thinking, of course, is that they are writing a statement which is saying '10 francs makes a pound'. The F and P are being used as abbreviations for 'franc' and 'pound'. This is, of course, how we use letters in *arithmetic*, when they are actually abbreviations for fixed quantities or measurements. When we write '10p' or '5 m' the 'p' stands for 'a penny' and the 'm' stands for 'a metre'. But this is precisely what the letters do *not* mean in *algebra*. They are not abbreviations for measurements. They do not represent 'a thing' or an object. They are *variables*. The letter 'P' in Problem 1 stands for 'whatever number of pounds you choose'. It does not stand for a pound, but for the *number* of pounds.

No. of pounds	No. of francs		No. of teachers	No. of students
P	**F**		**T**	**S**
1	10		1	20
2	20		2	40
3	30		3	60
4	40		4	80
5	50		5	100
(a)			(b)	

Figure 22.1   Tabulating values for Problems 1 and 2

So, in Problem 2, the relationship between S and T is *not* '$20S = T$'. Those who write this down think that what they are saying is, '20 students for 1 teacher'. Here they are using the S to stand for 'a student' and T to stand for 'a teacher'. Again, we see the same misunderstanding. S and T are not abbreviations for a student and a teacher. They stand for 'the number of students' and 'the number of teachers'. They are variables. T can be any number and whatever number is chosen, S is 20 times this. So the relationship is '$S = 20T$'. This means 'the number of students is 20 times the number of teachers' or, referring to the tabulation of values in Figure 22.1, 'the number in column S is 20 times whatever number is in column T'.

It is understandable that so many people get the algebraic statements in these problems the wrong way round. First of all, the choice of P, F, S, T as letters to represent the variables in the problems is actually unhelpful (deliberately, I have to admit). Using the first letters of the words 'pound', 'franc', 'student' and 'teacher' does rather suggest that they are abbreviations for these things.

(Fewer people get these relationships the wrong way round if other letters are used for the variables, such as N and M.) Then, so many of us have been subjected to explanations in 'algebra lessons' which reinforce this misconception that the letters stand for things. For example, it does not help to explain '$2a + 3a = 5a$' by saying '2 apples plus 3 apples makes 5 apples'. This again makes us think of a as an abbreviation for apples. What this statement means is: whatever number you choose for a, then 'a multiplied by 2' plus 'a multiplied by 3' is the same as 'a multiplied by 5'.

Are there other differences between arithmetic and algebra in the way symbols are used that I should be aware of?

The distinction between the meaning of letters used in algebra (as variables) and in arithmetic (as abbreviations) is undoubtedly one of the most crucial differences between these two branches of mathematics. But there are a number of other significant differences of which teachers should be aware:

- The use of the equals sign.
- The need to recognise the mathematical structure of a problem.
- The distinction between solving a problem and representing it.
- The need to recognise 'precedence of operators'.

Surely the equals sign always means the same thing, doesn't it?

What the equals sign means strictly in mathematical terms is not the same thing necessarily as the way it is interpreted in practice. When doing arithmetic, that is manipulating numbers, pupils mostly think of the equals sign as an instruction to do something with some numbers, to perform an operation. They see '$3 + 5 =$' and respond by doing something, i.e. adding the 3 and the 5 to get 8. So, given the question, '$3 + \square = 5$', many younger pupils put 8 in the box; they see the equals sign as an instruction to perform an operation on the numbers in the question, and naturally respond to the '+' sign by adding them up. Pupils also use the equals sign simply as a device for connecting the calculation they have performed with the result of the calculation. It means simply, 'This is what I did and this is what I got . . .' Given the problem, 'You have £28, earn £5 and spend £8, how much do you have now?' pupils will quite happily write something like: '$28 + 5 = 33 - 8 = 25$'. Purists may object to this way of recording the calculations, arguing that '$28 + 5$' does not equal '$33 - 8$'. But this is not what the pupil means, of course. What is written down accurately represents the pupil's thinking about the problem, or the buttons he or she has pressed on a calculator to solve it. It simply means something like, 'I added 28 and 5, and got the answer 33, and then I subtracted 8 and this came to 25'. In algebra, however, the equals sign usually represents *equivalence*. It means that what is written on one side 'is the same as' what is written on the other side. Of course, it has this meaning in arithmetic as well: '$3 + 5 = 8$' does mean that '$3 + 5$' is the same as 8. But pupils rarely use it to mean this; their experience reinforces the perception of the equals sign as an instruction to perform an operation with some numbers. In algebraic statements it is the idea of equivalence which is strongest in the way the equals sign is used. For example, when we write '$p + q = r$', this is not actually an instruction to add p and q. In fact, we may not have to do anything at all with the statement. It is simply a statement of equivalence between one variable and a combination of two others.

What is different about arithmetic and algebra in relation to recognising the mathematical structure of a problem?

In arithmetic, pupils often succeed through adopting informal, intuitive, context-bound approaches to solving problems. Often they do this without having to be aware explicitly of the underlying mathematical structure. For example, many pupils will be able to solve, 'How much for 10 grams of chocolate if you can get 2 grams per penny?' without recognising the formal structure of the problem as that of division. But even with a calculator, they may then be unable to solve the same problem with more difficult numbers: "How much for 75 grams of chocolate if you can get 1.35 grams per penny?' The corresponding algebraic problem is a generalisation of all problems with this same structure: 'How much for A grams of chocolate if you can get B grams per penny?' It is often no use in trying to explain this just putting in some simple numbers for A and B and asking what you do to these numbers to answer the question, because the pupils do not recognise the existence of a division structure here at all. The primitive, intuitive thinking about the arithmetic problem with simple numbers does not make the mathematical structure explicit in a way which supports the algebraic generalisation, '$A \div B$'. It is partly because of this that I have put so much stress on the *structures* of addition, subtraction, multiplication and division in Chapters 4, 6, 8 and 10, and encouraged the frequent use of the question, 'what is the calculation you enter on a calculator to answer this?', as a device for making the mathematical structure explicit.

Can you explain the distinction between solving a problem and representing it?

The discussion above leads to a further significant difference between arithmetic and algebra. Given a problem to solve in arithmetic involving more than one operation, the question we ask ourselves is, 'What sequence of operations is needed to *solve* this problem?' In algebra, the question is, 'What sequence of operations are needed to *represent* this problem?' For example, consider this problem:

- Problem 3: A plumber's call-out charge is £15, then you pay £12 an hour. How many hours work would cost £75?

The arithmetic thinking might be: $75 - 15 = 60$, then $60 \div 12 = 5$. This is the sequence of operations required to *solve* the problem. But the algebraic approach would be to let N stand for the number of hours (which is therefore a variable and can take any value) and then to write down: $12N + 15 = 75$. This is the sequence of operations which *represents* the problem. (Then to solve the problem we have to find the value of N which makes this algebraic equation true.) It is quite possible, therefore, that the two approaches, as illustrated here, result in the use of inverse operations. To solve the problem we think: subtraction, then division; but to represent the problem algebraically we think: multiplication, then addition. It is this kind of difference in the thinking involved which makes it so difficult for many pupils to make generalised statements using words or algebraic symbols, even of the simplest kind.

What is meant by 'precedence of operators'?

A statement like '3 + 5 × 2' is potentially ambiguous. If you do the addition first the answer is 16. But if you do the multiplication first the answer is 13! Which is correct? Well, if you enter this calculation as it stands on to the kind of basic calculator used in primary schools (using the key sequence: 3, +, 5, ×, 2, =) , you get 16. The calculator does the operations in the order they are entered. However, if you use a more advanced, scientific calculator, with the same key sequence, you will probably get the answer 13. These calculators use what is called an *algebraic operating system.* (As do many computer applications, such as spreadsheet programs.) This means that they adopt the convention of giving precedence to the operations of multiplication and division. So, when you enter '3 + 5', the calculator waits to determine whether there is a multiplication or a division following the 5; if there is, this is done first. If you actually mean to do the addition first you would have to use brackets to indicate this: for example, (3 + 5) × 2. (This can also be written as 2(3 + 5), with the multiplication sign omitted but understood.)

Now this convention of precedence of operators is always applied strictly in algebra and is essential for avoiding ambiguity, particularly because of the way symbols are used in algebra to represent problems not just to solve them. So, for example, $A + B \times C$ (which is usually written $A + BC$, with the understanding that BC means $B \times C$) stands for 'B multiplied by C, add A'; whereas to represent 'A added to B, then multiply by C' we would write $(A + B) \times C$. [This is usually written $C(A + B)$.] But in arithmetic – and therefore in number work in primary schools – we do not actually need this convention. The calculations we have to do should always arise from a practical context which will naturally determine the order in which the various operations have to be performed, so there is not usually any ambiguity. Since the basic calculators we use in primary schools deal with operations in the order they arrive, there is little point in giving pupils calculations like '3 + 5 × 2' and insisting that this means you do the multiplication first. But as soon as we get into using algebra to express generalisations, we need this convention for precedence of operators, so pupils have to learn to recognise it and to use brackets as necessary to over-ride it.

How can the idea of a letter being a variable be introduced to pupils?

The central principle in algebra is the use of letters to represent *variables* which enable us to express *generalisations*. Pupils should therefore first encounter the use of letters as algebraic symbols for this purpose. The most effective way of doing this is through the tabulation of number patterns in columns, with the problem being to express the pattern in the numbers, first in words and later in symbols. A useful game in this context is *What's My Rule?* Figure 22.2 shows some examples of this game. In each case the pupils are challenged to say what is the rule which is being used to find the numbers in Column B and then to use this rule to find the number in Column B when the number in Column A is 100. In example (a), pupils usually observe first that the rule is 'adding 2'. Here they have spotted what I refer to when talking to children as the 'up-and-down rule'. When talking to teachers I call it the *sequential generalisation*. This is the pattern which determines how to continue the sequence. Asking what answer do you get when the number in A is 100, or some other large number, makes us realise the inadequacy of the sequential generalisation. We need a 'left-to-right rule': a rule which tells us what to do to the numbers in A to get the numbers in B. This is the *global generalisation*. Pupils towards the top end of the primary range can usually determine that when the number in A is 100, the number in B is 201, and this helps them to recognise that the rule is 'double and add 1'. Later this can be expressed algebraically as '$B = A \times 2 + 1$', or '$B = 2A + 1$'. This clearly uses the idea of letters as variables, expressing generalisations. The statement means essentially, 'The number in Column B is whatever number is in Column A multiplied by 2, add one'. Similarly, in Figure 22.2b, the sequential generalisation, 'add 4', is easily spotted; more difficult is the global generalisation, 'multiply by 4 and subtract 1', although again working out what is in B when 100 is in A helps to make this rule explicit. This leads to the algebraic statement, '$B = A \times 4 - 1$', or '$B = 4A - 1$'. In these kinds of examples, where A is chosen and a rule is used to determine B, A is called an *independent variable* and B a *dependent variable*.

A	B		A	B		A	B		A	B
1	3		1	3		1	3		1	99
2	5		2	7		2	8		2	98
3	7		3	11		3	13		3	97
4	9		4	15		4	18		4	96
5	11		5	19		5	23		5	95
6	13		6	23		6	28		6	94
7	15		7	27		7	33		7	93
8	17		8	31		8	38		8	92
9	19		9	35		9	43		9	91
10	21		10	39		10	48		10	90
100	?		100	?		100	?		100	?
(a)			(b)			(c)			(d)	

Figure 22.2   What's My Rule?

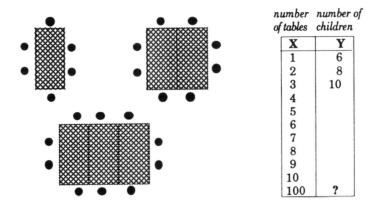

number of tables	number of children
X	**Y**
1	6
2	8
3	10
4	
5	
6	
7	
8	
9	
10	
100	?

Figure 22.3   An investigation leading to a generalisation

This experience of tabulation and finding generalisations to describe the patterns occurs very often in *mathematical investigations*, particularly those involving a sequence of geometric shapes, such as those discussed in Chapter 14 (see, for example, Figures 14.3 and 14.4). Figure 22.3 provides another example: the problem is how many children can sit around various numbers of tables, arranged side by side, if six children can sit around one table. The number of tables here is the independent variable and the number of children the dependent variable. With 2 tables we can seat 8 children; with 3 tables we can seat 10. These results are already tabulated. The tabulation can then be completed for other numbers of tables, the sequential generalisation can be articulated, the answer for 100 tables can be predicted and finally the global generalisation can be formulated, first in words and then in symbols, with X, representing the independent variable, i.e. the number of tables, and Y the dependent variable, i.e. the number of children. This is left as an exercise for the reader, in Question 22.6 below.

So what is a mapping?

In the examples of tabulation used above there have always been three components: a set of input numbers (the values of the independent variable), a rule for doing something to these numbers and a set of output numbers (the values of the dependent variable). These three components put together – input set, rule, output set – constitute what is sometimes called a *mapping*.

This is an all-pervading idea in algebra. In fact, most of what we have to learn to do in algebra fits into this simple structure. Sometimes we are given the input and the rule and we have to find the output: this is substituting into a formula. Then sometimes we are given the input and the output and our task is to find the rule: this is the process of generalising (as in the examples of tabulation above). Then finally, we can be given the output and the rule and be required to find the input: this is the process of solving an equation. That just about summarises the whole of algebra!

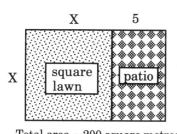

side of lawn	area of garden
X	**Y**
20	500
10	150
13	234
11	176
12	204
11.9	201.111
11.8	198.24
11.85	199.6725
etc....	

Figure 22.4   A problem solved by trial and improvement

Is solving equations something to introduce in primary schools?

As a formal algebraic process, I would definitely not introduce solving equations in primary schools, especially since the techniques involved can so easily reinforce the idea that the letters stand for 'things', or even specific numbers, rather than variables. What is appropriate, however, is to introduce pupils to the algebraic thinking involved in solving problems through the *trial-and-improvement* approach (see Chapter 14). These can be purely numerical problems, which cannot be solved by a simple arithmetic procedure, such as finding square roots and cube roots, as explained in Chapter 14. Or they can be practical problems; problems about area and perimeter are particularly useful here. In Figure 22.4, the problem posed is: 'What should be the length of the side of a square lawn if the area of the whole garden is to be 200 square metres? (The width of the patio is fixed as 5 metres.)' This is approached by trying various inputs (for the side of the square) and using an appropriate rule to determine the outputs (the corresponding area of the garden). One possible rule is 'add 5 to the side of the square and multiply by the side of the square'. Expressed in symbols this is '$X(X + 5)$'. (So we are actually solving the equation, $X(X + 5) = 200$.) The first trial is $X = 20$. This gives an area of 500, which is too large. Next we try 10, which gives an area of 150, which is too small. So we try something in between, say, $X = 13$. This gives an area of 234, too large . . . and so on, until we get an answer to whatever level of accuracy we require. The point about solving equations this way is that the letter involved (X standing for the side of the square) is genuinely perceived as a variable – and our task is to find the value of this independent variable which generates the required value for the dependent variable. This is much more sophisticated and powerful than the idea that 'X stands for an unknown number'. I remember being told this at school and spending a whole year doing things like $2X + 3X = 5X$, all the time believing that the teacher actually knew what this unknown number was and that one day he would tell us.

Self-assessment questions

22.1: The length of a garden is F feet. Measured in yards, it is Y yards long. What is the relationship between F and Y? (There are three feet in one yard.) What criticism could you make of this question?

22.2: If I buy A apples at 10p each and B bananas at 12p each, what is the meaning of: a) $A + B$; b) $10A$; c) $12B$; and d) $10A + 12B$? What criticism could you make of this question?

22.3: The first 5 rides in a fair are free. The charge for all the other rides is £2 each. If Jenny has £12 to spend, how many rides can she have? What are the arithmetic steps you used in answering this question? How would you *represent* the problem algebraically, using N to stand for the number of rides?

22.4: What answer would you get if you entered '25 − 5 × 3' onto: a) a basic calculator; and b) a scientific calculator using an algebraic operating system?

22.5: For each of Figure 22.2c and 22.2d, write down: a) the sequential generalisation; b) the value of B when A is 100; c) the global generalisation in words; and d) the global generalisation in symbols ($B = . . .$).

22.6: Complete the tabulation of results in Figure 22.3; write down: a) the sequential generalisation; b) the number of children if there are 100 tables; c) the global generalisation in words; and d) the global generalisation in symbols ($Y = . . .$). Now repeat this investigation with the tables arranged end to end, rather than side by side.

22.7: I choose a number, double it, add 3 and multiply the answer by my number. The result is 3654. What is my number? Use a calculator and the trial-and-improvement method to answer this. What equation have you solved?

Summary of teaching points

1. Use the *What's My Rule?* game to introduce pupils to algebraic thinking through making generalisations, first in words, then in symbols.

2. Reinforce this with tabulated results from investigations, where pupils can find patterns in the sequence of numbers obtained.

3. Use this procedure: tabulate results in an orderly fashion; articulate the sequential generalisation (the up-and-down rule); predict the result for a big number, such as 100; articulate the global generalisation (the left-to-right rule) in words; check this on some results you know; and express the global rule in symbols.

4. Avoid the fruit-salad approach to explaining algebraic statements, e.g. referring to '$3a + 5b$' as '3 apples and 5 bananas', or anything which reinforces the ideas that the letters stand for objects or specific numbers.

5. Emphasise the idea that a letter in algebra stands for 'whatever number is chosen', i.e. a variable.

6. Reinforce through your own language the idea that the equals sign means 'is the same as', even in the early stages of recording the results of calculations.

7. Use the question, 'What is the calculation you would enter on a calculator to solve this problem?', to help make the underlying structures of problems explicit (see summaries in Chapters 4, 6, 8 and 10).

8. Do not worry about precedence of operators when doing number work: the context giving rise to the calculation will determine the appropriate sequence of operations.

9. But make this principle explicit when algebraic notation is introduced, explaining the different systems used by various calculators, and showing the need for brackets when some rules are written algebraically.

10. Use trial-and-improvement methods, with a calculator, to solve equations arising from practical or numerical problems, to reinforce the idea of a variable.

23

Coordinates

Pupils should be taught to: use coordinates to specify location; recognise the number relationships between coordinates in the first quadrant of related points on a line or in a shape.

In this chapter there are explanations of

- how the coordinate system enables us to specify location in a plane;
- axis, *x*-coordinate and *y*-coordinate, origin;
- the meaning of 'quadrant' in the context of coordinates;
- the difference between the coordinate system for labelling points in a plane and other systems which label spaces;
- some of the ways in which the coordinate system enables us to connect algebraic and geometric relationships;
- how to plot an algebraic relationship as a graph; and
- linear relationships, including those where one variable is directly proportional to another.

What is meant by 'coordinates in the first quadrant'?

The coordinate system is a wonderfully simple but elegant device for specifying location in two dimensions. Two number lines are drawn at right angles to each other, as shown in Figure 23.1. These are called *axes* (plural of *axis*). Of course, the lines can continue as far as we wish at either end. The point where the two lines meet (called the *origin*) is taken as the zero for both number lines. The vertical line is called the *y*-axis, and the horizontal line the *x*-axis. Then any point in the plane can be specified by two numbers, called its *coordinates*. The *x*-coordinate of a point is the distance moved along the *x*-axis and the *y*-coordinate is the distance moved vertically, in order to get from the origin to the point in question. For example, to reach the point P shown in Figure 23.1 we would move 3 units along the *x*-axis and then 4 units vertically, so the *x*-coordinate of P is 3 and the *y*-coordinate is 4. We then state that the coordinates of P are (3,4). The convention is always to give the *x*-coordinate first and the *y*-coordinate second.

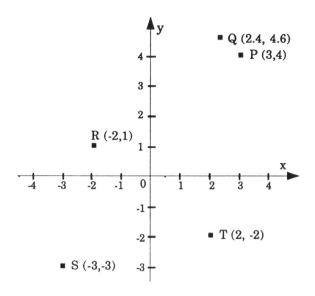

Figure 23.1   The coordinate system

The axes divide the plane into four sections, called *quadrants*. The first quadrant consists of all the points which have a positive number for each of their two coordinates. The points P and Q in Figure 23.1 are in the first quadrant. The point R (–2,1) is then in the second quadrant, S (–3, –3) in the third quadrant and T (2, –2) in the fourth quadrant.

The beauty of this system is that we can now refer specifically to any point in the plane. And, of course, we are not limited to integers, as is shown by the point Q, with coordinates (2.4, 4.6). We can also use the coordinate system to describe the movement from one point to another. For example, from R to P is a movement of 5 units in the *x*-direction and 3 units in the *y*-direction; from T to S is a movement of –5 in the *x*-direction and –1 in the *y*-direction.

An important feature of this system is that it is the *points* in the plane which are labelled by the coordinates, not the *spaces*. This is a similar point to that made in Chapter 19, with reference to Figure 19.2b, where the numbers on the vertical axis labelled the points on the scale, not the spaces between them. This is an important teaching point, because there are a number of situations pupils will encounter which use coordinate systems based on the idea of labelling the spaces – for example, a number of board games and computer games, city street-maps, and computer spreadsheets. A common system employed in these and other similar examples is to use the labels for the columns (A, B, C . . .) and the labels for the rows (1, 2, 3 . . .) to specify individual cells or squares (e.g. B3). So, moving from this kind of labelling of spaces to the labelling of points is an important and significant step in the development of the idea of a coordinate system.

How do coordinates help to understand number relationships and geometry?

The system described above is sometimes called the *Cartesian coordinate system*. It takes its name from René Descartes (1596–1650), a prodigious French mathematician, who first made use of the system to connect geometry and algebra. He discovered that by interpreting the inputs and outputs from an algebraic mapping (see Chapter 22) as coordinates, and then plotting these as points, you could generate a geometric picture of the relationship. Then by the reverse process, starting with a geometric picture drawn on a coordinate system you can generate an algebraic representation of geometric properties. At primary-school level, we can only just touch on these massive mathematical ideas, so a couple of simple examples will suffice here.

First, we can take any simple algebraic relationship of the kind considered in Chapter 22 and explore the corresponding geometric picture. The convention is to use the x-axis for the independent variable. For example, the table shown in Figure 22.2a is generated by the algebraic rule, $B = 2A + 1$. In this case, A is the appropriate variable to be represented by the x-axis. The pairs of values in the table can be written as coordinates, as follows: (1, 3), (2, 5), (3, 7), and so on. When these are plotted, as shown in Figure 23.2a, it is clear that they lie on a straight line. These points can then be joined up and the line continued indefinitely, as shown in Figure 23.2b. This straight line is a powerful geometric image of the way in which the two variables, A and B, are related. An algebraic rule like this which produces a straight-line graph is sometimes called a *linear relationship*. We can use the straight-line graph to read off values of B for values of A other than those plotted; for example, the arrow in Figure 23.2b shows that when $A = 3.5$, $B = 8$.

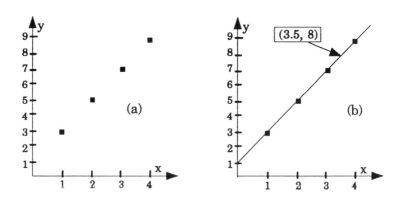

Figure 23.2   The rule B = 2A + 1 *represented by coordinates*

Using this process to explore different algebraic rules leads us to recognise a linear relationship as one in which the rule is simply a combination of multiplying or dividing by a fixed number and addition or subtraction. For example, all these rules are linear relationships:

multiply by 7 and subtract 5   [y = 7x – 5]
divide by 6 and add 4   [y = x/6 + 4]
multiply by 3 and subtract from 100 [y = 100 – 3x]
add 1 and multiply by 2   [y = 2(x + 1)]

There are, of course, non-linear relationships. These are other kinds of rules, for example, those involving squaring (e.g. multiply the input by itself) and other powers (cubes, and so on) which produce sets of coordinates that do not lie on straight lines. These are beyond the scope of this book.

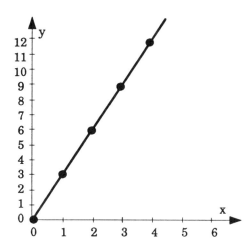

Figure 23.3   The variable y *is directly proportional to* x

The simplest kind of linear relationship is where *y* is *directly proportional* to *x*. This means that *y* is obtained by multiplying *x* by a constant factor. Examples of this kind of relationship abound in everyday life. If a bottle of wine costs £3, *x* is the number of bottles I buy and *y* is the total cost in pounds, then the rule for finding *y* is 'multiply *x* by 3' or '*y* = 3*x*'. This rule generates the coordinates, (1, 3), (2, 6), (3, 9), and so on, and, including the possibility that I do not buy any bottles, (0, 0). As shown in Figure 23.3, this rule produces a straight-line graph which, noting again the significance of the (0, 0) possibility, passes through the origin. Any rule of this kind, in which *y* is directly proportional to *x*, such as *y* = 7*x*, *y* = 0.5*x*, *y* = 2.75*x*, will produce a straight-line graph passing through the origin. An interesting point for discussion in the example above relates to the fact that the number of bottles bought is a 'discrete' variable (see Chapter 19): you cannot buy 3.6 bottles, for example. This means that the points on the line between the whole number values do not actually have any meaning. By contrast, if *x* had been the number of litres of petrol being bought at £3 per litre (price used for demonstration purposes only), then the rule would have been the same, *y* = 3*x*, but this time *x* would be a continuous variable and all the points on the straight-line graph in the first quadrant would have meaning. For example, when *x* is 3.6, *y* is 10.8, corresponding to a charge of £10.80 for 3.6 litres of petrol.

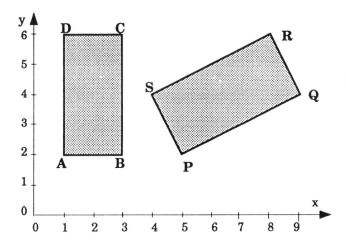

Figure 23.4   Using coordinates to draw rectangles

Can you give an example of how coordinates might be used to investigate a geometric property?

Using coordinates we can easily communicate a geometric shape, made up of straight lines, to someone else. For example, I could ask a class of pupils to plot the points (1, 2), (3, 2), (3, 6) and (1, 6) and to join these points up, in order to produce the rectangle ABCD in Figure 23.4. The corners A, B, C and D are sometimes called the *vertices* of the rectangle (each one is a *vertex*). Similarly, rectangle PQRS is produced by plotting (5, 2), (9, 4), (8, 6) and (4, 4). An interesting question is now raised: what rules or numerical patterns determine the coordinates of the four vertices of a rectangle? For example, we might notice that the movement from P to S (–1 in the *x*-direction, 2 in the *y*-direction) is the same as that from Q to R; and similarly for S to R and P to Q. A particularly interesting rule relates the coordinates of opposite vertices. I will leave the reader to discover this for him or herself (see Question 23.4 below). In this way we can analyse geometric properties, such as the characteristics of a rectangle, by means of algebraic relationships. It is the potential for exploring the connection between algebraic and geometric relationships which makes the coordinate system such a fundamental part of mathematics at every level.

Self-assessment questions

23.1: A knight's move in chess is two steps horizontally (left or right) and one step vertically (up or down), or two steps vertically and one step horizontally. Starting at (3,3), which points can be reached by a knight's move? Plot them and join them up.

23.2: On squared paper, plot some of the points corresponding to each of the tables (b), (c) and (d) in Figure 22.2. Are the algebraic rules here linear relationships?

23.3: Give an example of a variable which is directly proportional to each of the following independent variables: a) the number of boxes of eggs bought, with six eggs in each; b) the number of pounds exchanged at a bank for some foreign currency; and c) the bottom number in a set of equivalent fractions.

23.4: Plot the three points, (1, 2), (0, 3) and (3, 6), on squared paper. Join them up and find the fourth point needed to complete a rectangle. Looking at this example and the two rectangles in Figure 23.4, what is the rule connecting the coordinates of opposite vertices of a rectangle? Use this rule to determine the fourth vertex of a rectangle, if the first three vertices are (4, 4), (5, 8), (13, 6). Check your answer by plotting the points and joining them up.

23.5: Plot these points and join them up in order to form a rectangle: A (0, 0), B (4, 0), C (4, 3) and D (0, 3). Now keep A and B fixed, but change C and D by adding 1 to each of their x-coordinates. What happens to the shape? Repeat this procedure and produce another shape. And again. The shapes you are making are all examples of parallelograms. What rules can you find for connecting the coordinates of the four vertices of a parallelogram? Use these rules to find the fourth vertex if the first three are (1, 1), (4, 2) and (4,4).

Summary of teaching points

1. The use of coordinates to specify the location of points in a plane, rather than spaces, as in street-maps, is a significant point to be explained to pupils carefully.

2. Give pupils experience of activities where they use the coordinate system to describe movements from one point to another.

3. There is actually no need to limit primary-school pupils' experience of coordinates to the first quadrant, since the principles are the same in the other quadrants and these provide some useful experience of interpreting and applying negative numbers.

4. Pupils should interpret tables of values obtained by exploring algebraic relationships (as in Chapter 22) as sets of coordinates, plot these and discuss the results.

5. Pupils should investigate whether or not a particular relationship produces a straight-line graph when plotted as coordinates.

6. When a real-life relationship produces a straight-line graph, pupils should discuss whether or not the points between those plotted have meaning.

7. Show pupils how relationships where one variable is directly proportional to another can be shown as a straight-line graph passing through the origin.

8. Give pupils the opportunity to analyse simple properties of geometric shapes such as rectangles and parallelograms, by looking for patterns and rules in the coordinates of their vertices.

24

Measurement

Pupils should be taught to: choose appropriate standard units of length, mass, capacity and time; make sensible estimates with them in everyday situations; convert one metric unit to another; know the rough metric equivalents of imperial units still in daily use.

In this chapter there are explanations of

- the distinction between mass and weight;
- the distinction between volume and capacity;
- two aspects of the concept of time: time interval and recorded time;
- the role of comparison and ordering as a foundation for measurement;
- the principle of transitivity in the context of measurement;
- conservation of length, mass and liquid volume;
- non-standard and standard units;
- the idea that all measurement is approximate;
- the difference between a ratio scale and and interval scale;
- SI and other metric units of length, mass and time, including the use of prefixes;
- the importance of estimation and the use of reference items; and
- imperial units still in use and their relationship to metric units.

What is the difference between mass and weight?

There is a real problem here about the language we use to describe what we are measuring when, for example, we put a book in one pan of a balance and equalise it with, say, two hundred grams in the other. Colloquially, most people say that what we have found out is that the book *weighs* two hundred grams, or that its *weight* is two hundred grams. This is technically incorrect. What we have discovered is that the book *weighs the same as* a mass of two hundred grams, or that the *mass* of the book is two hundred grams. This conflict between everyday language usage and the scientifically correct usage is not resolved simply by using the two words, mass and weight, interchangeably.

The units we use for weighing, such as grams and kilograms, or pounds and ounces, are actually units for measuring the mass of an object, not its weight. The mass is a measurement of the quantity of matter there is in the object. This is not the same thing as the amount of space it takes up – that is the *volume* of the object. A small lump of lead might have the same mass as our book, but take up much less space, because the molecules making up the piece of lead are much more tightly packed together than those in the book. The problem with this concept of mass is that we cannot actually experience it directly. I cannot see the mass of the book, feel it or perceive it in any way. When I hold the book in my hand what I experience is the weight of the book. The weight is the force exerted on the book by the pull of gravity. I can feel this, because I have to exert a force myself to hold the book up. Of course, the weight and the mass are directly related: the greater the mass, the greater the weight, and therefore the heavier the object feels when I hold it in my hand. However, the big difference between the two is that, whereas the mass of an object is invariant, the weight changes depending on how far you are from the centre of the earth (or whatever it is that is exerting the gravitational pull on the object). We are all familiar with the idea that an astronaut's weight changes in space, or on the Moon, because the gravitational pull being exerted on the astronaut is less than it is on the earth's surface. In some circumstances, for example when in orbit, this gravitational pull can effectively be cancelled out and the astronaut experiences 'weightlessness'. The astronaut can then place a book on the palm of his or her hand and it weighs nothing. On the Moon's surface the force exerted on the book by gravity, that is the weight of the book, is about one-sixth of what it was back on the earth's surface. But throughout all this the mass of the astronaut and the mass of the book remain unchanged. The book is still two hundred grams, as it was on earth, even though its weight has been changing constantly. (So a good way of losing weight is to go to the Moon, but this does not affect your waist size because what you really want to do is to lose mass!)

An important point to note is that the balance-type weighing devices do actually measure mass. We put the book in one pan, balance it with a mass of 200 g in the other pan, and because the book 'weighs the same as' a mass of 200 g we conclude that it also has a mass of 200 g. Note that we would get the same result using the balance on the Moon. However, the pointers on spring-type weighing devices, such as many kitchen scales and bathroom scales, actually respond directly to weight. This means that they would give a different reading if we took them to the Moon, for example. But, of course, they are calibrated for use on the earth's surface, so when I stand on the bathroom scales and the pointer indicates 72 kg I can rely on that as a measurement of my mass. On the Moon it would point to 12 kg; this would just be totally wrong.

Because weight is a force, it should be measured in the units of force. The standard unit of force in the metric system is the *newton*, appropriately named after Sir Isaac Newton (1642–1727), the mathematical and scientific genius who first articulated this distinction between mass and weight. A newton is defined as the force required to increase the speed of a mass of one kilogram by one metre per second every second. A newton is actually about the weight of a small apple and a mass of a kilogram has a weight of nearly 10 newtons. But you don't have to know any of this. You may come across spring-type weighing devices with a scale graduated in newtons, but these would not be appropriate for use in primary schools.

One way to introduce the word 'mass' to primary-school pupils is to refer to those plastic or metal things we use for weighing objects in a balance as 'masses' (rather than 'weights'). So we would have a box of ten-gram masses and a box of hundred-gram masses, and so on. Then when we have balanced an object against some masses, we can say that the object weighs the same as a mass of so many grams, as a step towards using the correct language, that the mass of the object is so many grams.

Can you explain the distinction between volume and capacity?

The volume of an object is the amount of three-dimensional space that it occupies. By historical accident, liquid volume and solid volume are conventionally measured in different units, although the concepts are exactly the same. Liquid volume is measured in litres and millilitres, and so on, whereas solid volume would have to be measured in units such as cubic metres and cubic centimetres. In the metric system the units for liquid and solid volume are related in a very simple way: one millilitre is the same volume as one cubic centimetre; or one litre is the same volume as one thousand cubic centimetres (see Figure 24.1).

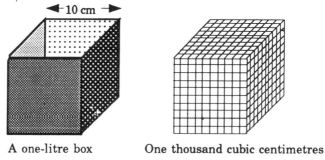

Figure 24.1   A litre is the same volume as a thousand cubic centimetres

Only containers have *capacity*. The capacity of a container is the maximum volume of liquid which it can hold. Hence capacity is measured in the same units as liquid volume. For example, if a wine glass holds 180 millilitres of wine when filled to the brim then its capacity is 180 millilitres.

What about measuring time?

There are two quite different aspects of time which pupils have to learn to handle. First of all there is the idea of a *time interval*. This refers to the length of time occupied by an activity, or the time that passes from one instant to another. Time intervals are measured in units such as seconds, minutes, hours, days, weeks, years, decades, centuries, millennia. Then there is the idea of *recorded time*, the time at which an event occurs. To handle recorded time, we use the various conventions for reading the time of day, such as o'clocks, a.m. and p.m., the 24-hour system, together with the different ways of recording the date, including reference to the day of the week, the day in the month and the year. So, for example, we might say that the meeting starts at 1530 on Monday 7 October 1996, using the concept of 'recorded time', and that it is expected to last for 90 minutes, using the concept of 'time interval'.

Time is one aspect of measurement which has not gone metric, so the relationships between the units (60 seconds in a minute, 60 minutes in an hour, 24 hours in a day, and so on) are particularly challenging. This makes it difficult, for example, to use a subtraction algorithm for finding the time intervals from one time to another. I strongly recommend that problems of this kind are done by an *ad hoc* process of adding-on. For example, to find the length of time of a journey starting at 10.45 a.m. and finishing at 1.30 p.m., reason like this: 15 minutes to 11 o'clock, then 2 hours to 1 o'clock, then a further 30 minutes, making a total of 2 hours and 45 minutes. Setting this out as a formal subtraction would be highly inadvisable.

Learning about time is also complicated by the fact that the hands on a conventional dial-clock go round twice in a day; it would have been so much more sensible to go round once a day! Because of the association of a circle with 12 hours on a clock face, I always avoid using a circle to represent a day: for example, a pie chart for 'how I spend a day', or a circular diagram showing the events of a day. For this last illustration I would recommend a diagram like the one shown in Figure 24.2. Pupils can add to this pictures or verbal descriptions of what they are doing at various times of day.

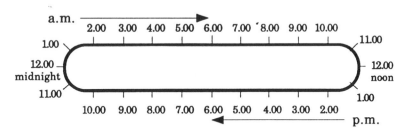

Figure 24.2   A picture of a day

Then there are the added complications related to the variety of watches and clocks which pupils may use, as well as the range of ways of saying the same time. For example, as well as being able to read a conventional dial-clock and a digital display in both 12-hour and 24-hour versions, pupils have to learn that these represent the same time of day: twenty to four in the afternoon, 3.40 p.m., 1540 (also written sometimes as 15:40 or 15.40). Incidentally, the colloquial use of, for example, 'fifteen hundred' to refer to the time 1500 in the 24-hour system is an unhelpful abuse of mathematical language. It reinforces the misunderstanding, mentioned in Chapter 2, of thinking that '00' is an abbreviation for 'hundred'. I prefer the BBC World Service convention: 'The time is fifteen hours.' A couple of further small points relate to noon and midnight. First, note that 'a.m.' and 'p.m.' are abbreviations for *ante-meridian* and *post-meridian*, meaning 'before noon' and 'after noon', respectively. This means that 12 noon is neither a.m. nor p.m. It is just 12 noon. Similarly, 12 o'clock midnight is neither a.m. nor p.m. Then, in the 24-hour system, midnight is the moment when the recorded time of day starts again, so it is not 2400, but 0000, i.e. 'zero hours'.

What principles are central to teaching measurement in the primary age range?

Some of the central principles in learning about measurement relate to the following headings: 1) comparison and ordering; 2) transitivity; 3) conservation; 4) non-standard and standard units; 5) approximation; 6) a context for developing number concepts; and 7) the meaning of zero.

First, the foundation of all aspects of measurement is direct comparison, putting two and then more than two objects (or events) in order according to the attribute in question. The language of comparison, discussed in relation to subtraction in Chapter 6, is of central importance here. Two objects are placed side by side and pupils determine which is the longer, which is the shorter. Two items are placed in the pans of a balance and pupils determine which is the heavier, which is the lighter. Water is poured from one container to another to determine which holds more, which holds less. Two pupils perform specified tasks, starting simultaneously, and observe which takes a longer time, which takes a shorter time. No units are involved at this stage, simply direct comparison leading to putting two or more objects or events in order. The reader may note here that the first stage of learning about probability (Chapter 21) employed this same procedure: simply to compare two or more events and decide which was more likely or less likely than which.

An important mathematical principle here is that of *transitivity*. In Chapter 13 we saw that this mathematical property applied to the relationships 'is a multiple of' (illustrated in Figure 13.1) and 'is a factor of' (illustrated in Figure 13.3). The principle of transitivity is shown in Figure 24.3. If we know that A is related to B (indicated by an arrow) and B is related to C, the question is whether A is related to C as a logical consequence. With some relations (such as 'is a factor of') it does follow logically and we can draw in the arrow connecting A to C. In other cases it does not. For example, the relationship 'is a mirror image of' can be applied to a set of shapes: if shape A is a mirror image of shape B, and B is a mirror image of shape C, then it is *not* true that A must automatically be a mirror image of C, so this is not a transitive relationship. We can now see that whenever we compare two objects (or events) using a measuring attribute such as their lengths, their masses, their capacities or the length of time (for events), then we are again making use of a transitive relationship. The arrow used in Figure 24.3 could represent any one of the measuring relationships used to compare two objects or events, such as: 'is longer than', 'is lighter than', 'holds more than' or 'takes less time than'. In each case, because A is related to B and B is related to C, then it follows

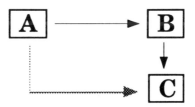

Figure 24.3   The transitive property

logically that A is related to C. This principle is fundamental to ordering a set of more than two objects or events: once we know A is greater than B and B is greater than C, for example, it is this principle which allows us not to have to check A against C. Grasping this is a significant step in the development of a pupil's understanding of measuring.

Next we should note the principle of *conservation*, another fundamental idea in learning about measurement of length, mass and liquid volume. Pupils meet this principle first of all in the context of conservation of number: they have to learn, for example, that if you rearrange a set of counters in different ways you do not alter the number of counters. Similarly, if two objects are the same length, they remain the same length when one is moved to a new position: this is the principle of conservation of length. Conservation of mass is experienced when pupils balance two lumps of Plasticine, then rearrange each lump in some way, such as breaking one up into small pieces and moulding the other into some shape or other, and then check that they still balance. Conservation of liquid volume is the one that catches many pupils out. When they empty the water from one container into another, differently shaped container, as shown in Figure 24.4, by focusing their attention on the heights of the water in the containers, pupils often lose their grip on the principle that the volume of water has actually been unchanged by the transformation.

Fundamental to the idea of measuring is the use of a 'unit'. The use of non-standard units to introduce the idea of measuring in units is a well established tradition in primary-school mathematics teaching. For example, they might measure the length of items of furniture in spans, the length of a wall in cubits (a cubit is the length of your forearm), the mass of a book in conkers, the capacity of a container in egg-cups. Many adults make use of non-standard units of length in everyday life, especially, for example, when making rough-and-ready measurements for practical jobs around the house and garden. The

Figure 24.4   Conservation of liquid volume

value of this approach is that children get experience of the idea of measuring in units, but using familiar, unthreatening objects first, rather than going straight into the use of mysterious things called millilitres and grams, and so on. Also, it is often the case that the non-standard unit is a more appropriate size of unit for early measuring experiences. For example, most of the things around the classroom the pupils might want to weigh will have a mass of several hundred grams. The gram is a very small mass for practical purposes to begin with, and the kilogram is far too large; conkers and glue-sticks are much more appropriate sizes of units for measuring mass in the early stages. Eventually, of course, we must learn that there is a need for a standard unit. The experience of working with non-standard units often makes this need explicit, as, for example, when two pupils measure the length of the hall in paces and get different answers.

The next major principle of measurement is that nearly all measurements are *approximate*. If you are measuring length, mass, time or capacity, all you can ever achieve is to make the measurement to the nearest something, depending on the level of accuracy of your measuring device. The principle of measuring to the nearest something and the associated language (see Chapter 12 for a discussion on rounding) should be introduced to primary-school pupils from the earliest stages. Even when measuring in non-standard units they will encounter this idea, as, for example, when determining that the length of the table is 'nearly 9 spans' or 'about 9 spans' or 'between 8 and 9 spans'.

Then we should stress the central importance of measurement experiences as a context for developing number concepts. Throughout this book I have used measurement problems and situations to reinforce ideas such as place value (Chapter 2), the various structures for the four operations (Chapters 4, 6 , 8 and 10) and calculations with decimals (Chapter 17).

Finally in this section, a comment on the meaning of zero. Measurements such as length, mass, liquid volume and capacity, and time intervals, are examples of what are called *ratio scales*. These are scales where the ratio of two quantities has a real meaning. For example, if a child is 90 cm tall and an adult is 180 cm tall, we can legitimately compare the two heights by means of ratio, stating that the adult is twice as tall as the child. Similarly, we can compare masses, capacities and time intervals by ratio. However, recorded time is not like this: it would make no sense to compare, say, 6 o'clock with 2 o'clock by saying that one is three times the other. This is an example of what is called an *interval scale*. Comparisons can only be made by reference to the difference (i.e. the interval) between two measurements, for example, saying that 6 o'clock is 4 hours later than 2 o'clock. Of course, you can compare the measurements in a ratio scale by reference to difference (e.g. the adult is 90 cm taller than the child), but the point about an interval scale is that you cannot do it by ratio, you can only use difference. Temperature measured in degrees centigrade (or Fahrenheit) is another example of an interval scale. It would be meaningless to assert that 15°C is three times as hot as 5°C; the two temperatures should be compared by their difference. The interesting mathematical point here is that the thing which really distinguishes a ratio scale from an interval scale is that in a ratio scale the zero means *nothing*, but in an interval scale it does not. When the recorded time is 'zero hours', time has not disappeared. When the temperature is 'zero degrees', there is still a temperature out there and we can feel it! But a length of 'zero metres' is no length; a mass of 'zero grams' is nothing; a bottle holding 'zero millilitres' of wine is empty; a time of 'zero seconds' is no time at all.

What metric units and prefixes do I need to know about?

There is an internationally accepted system of metric units called *SI units* (Système International). This system specifies one base unit for each aspect of measurement. For length the SI unit is the *metre*, for mass it is the *kilogram* (not the gram), for time it is the *second*. There is not a specific SI unit for liquid volume, since this would be measured in the same units as solid volume, i.e. cubic metres. However, the *litre* is a standard unit for liquid volume and capacity which is used internationally. Other units can be obtained by various prefixes being attached to these base units. There is a preference for those related to a thousand: for primary-school use this would be just *kilo* (*k*), meaning 'a thousand', and *milli* (*m*), meaning 'a thousandth'. So, for example, throughout this book we have used kilograms (kg) and grams (g), where 1 kg = 1000 g, and litres (l) and millilitres (ml), where 1 litre = 1000 ml. (NB the symbol l used for litre can be confused in print with the numeral 1.) Similarly we can have kilometres (km) and metres (m), with 1 km = 1000 m, and metres and millimetres (mm), with 1 m = 1000 mm. These are the only uses of the prefixes kilo and milli likely to be needed in the primary school. For practical purposes we will need other prefixes, especially *centi* (*c*), meaning 'a hundredth'. This gives us the really useful unit of length, the centimetre (cm), where 1 m = 100 cm. We might also find it helpful, for example when explaining place value and decimals with length (see Chapter 2), to use the prefix *deci* (*d*), meaning 'a tenth', as in decimetre (dm), where 1 m = 10 dm. We might also note that some wine bottles are labelled 0.75 litres, others are labelled 7.5 dl (decilitres), others 75 cl (centilitres) and others 750 ml (millilitres).

I grew up using mainly imperial units: how can I get better at thinking metric?

Take every opportunity to practise *estimation* of lengths, heights, widths and distances, liquid volume and capacity, and mass. In the supermarket, take note of which items are sold by mass (although they will call it weight) and which by volume; estimate the mass or volume of items you are purchasing and check your estimate against what it says on the packet. This all helps significantly to build up confidence in handling less familiar units.

One way of becoming a better estimator is to learn by heart the sizes of some specific *reference items*. Pupils should be encouraged to do this for length, mass and capacity, and then to relate other estimates to these. Here are some that I use personally:

- A child's finger is about 1 cm wide.
- The pupils' rulers are 30 cm long.

- A sheet of A4 paper is about 21 cm by 30 cm.
- The distance from my nose to my outstretched finger-tip is about one metre (100 cm).
- The classroom door is about 200 cm or 2 m high.
- The mass of an individual packet of crisps is 30 g.
- The mass of a standard packet of tea is 125 g.
- The mass of a standard-size tin of baked beans is about 500 g (including the tin).
- A standard can of drink has a capacity of 330 ml.
- A wine bottle holds 750 ml of wine.
- Standard cartons of milk or fruit juice are 1 litre (1000 ml).
- A litre of water has a mass of a kilogram (1000 g).

What imperial units are still important?

The attempt to turn the UK into a fully metricated country has not been entirely successful. A number of popular units of measurement stubbornly refuse to go away. For example, many people still find temperatures given in degrees Fahrenheit to be more meaningful than those in centigrade. The prime candidate for survival would seem to be the *mile*: somehow I cannot imagine in the foreseeable future all the road signs and speed limits in the UK being converted to kilometres. Because pupils cannot possibly have practical experience of measuring distances in kilometres to compensate for the lack of experience of this metric unit in everyday life, it makes sense for any work we do in primary schools related to journeys and average speeds (see Chapter 20) to be done in miles and miles per hour.

For those who wish to relate miles to kilometres the most common equivalence used is that 5 miles is about 8 kilometres. A simple method for doing conversions is to read off the corresponding speeds on the speedometer in a car, most of which are given in both miles per hour and kilometres per hour. For example, you can read off that 30 miles is about 50 km, 50 miles is about 80 km, 70 miles is about 110 km. There is also an intriguing connection between this conversion and a sequence of numbers called the *Fibonacci sequence*, named after Leonardo Fibonacci, a twelfth/thirteenth-century Italian mathematician: 1, 2, 3, 5, 8, 13, 21, 34, 55, 89, etc. The sequential generalisation here is to add the two previous numbers to get the next one. So, for example, the next number after 89 is 144 (55 + 89). Now, purely coincidentally, it happens that one of these numbers in miles is approximately the same as the next one in kilometres. For example, 2 miles is about 3 km, 3 miles is about 5 km, 5 miles is about 8 km, 8 miles is about 13 km, and so on. This works remarkably well to the nearest whole number for quite some way! (See Question 24.1 below.)

Other common measurements of length likely to survive through everyday usage, together with an indication of the kinds of equivalences which might be useful to learn, are: the inch (about the width of an adult thumb, around two and a half centimetres), the foot (about the length of a standard class ruler or a sheet of A4 paper, i.e. about 30 cm) and the yard (a bit less than a metre, about 91 cm).

Units of mass still met in the delicatessen are: the ounce (about the same as a small packet of crisps, i.e. about 30 g), the pound (getting on for half a kilogram, about 450 g). Many people still like to weigh themselves in stones: a stone is a bit more than 6 kg. And, for those who enjoy this kind of thing, a hundredweight is just over 50 kg, and a metric tonne (1000 kg) is therefore just a little more than an imperial ton (20 hundredweight).

Gallons have just about disappeared from the petrol station, but still manage to survive in common usage; for example, people still tell me how many miles per gallon their car does, even though petrol is almost universally sold in litres. My car, incidentally, does 9 miles to the litre. A gallon is about four and a half litres. Given the drinking habits of the British public, another contender for long-term survival must be the pint. I have noticed that many primary-school pupils refer to any carton of milk as 'a pint of milk', regardless of the actual volume involved. A pint is just over half a litre. Milk is sold in both half-litre and pint containers, depending on your supplier.

Self-assessment questions

24.1: Given that 1 mile is 1.6093 km, use a calculator to find how far the rule for changing miles to kilometres based on the Fibonacci sequence is correct to the nearest whole number.

24.2: The mass of a litre of water is 1 kg (1000 g). What will it be on the Moon?

24.3: Are these relationships transitive? a) 'Is earlier than' applied to times of the day; and b) 'is half of' applied to lengths.

24.4: Measure the length of a sheet of A4 paper to the nearest millimetre. Give the answer: a) in millimetres; b) in centimetres; c) in decimetres; and d) in metres.

24.5: Which is the greater: a) half a pound or 250 grams; b) 2 pints or a litre; c) 6 feet or 2 metres; d) 50 miles or 100 kilometres; e) 4 ounces or 100 grams; f) 10 stone or 50 kilograms; and g) 9 miles to the litre or 35 miles to the gallon?

Summary of teaching points

1. Pupils should develop their skills and understanding of measurement through practical, purposeful activities.

2. Introduce new aspects of measurement through direct comparison and ordering.

3. Introduce the idea of measuring in units via non-standard units which are familiar and appropriately sized, and use these experiences to establish the need for a standard unit.

4. Refer to the things we use for weighing objects on a balance as 'masses' and use the language 'weighs the same as a mass of so many grams'. Then encourage pupils to say 'the mass is so many grams', whilst acknowledging that most people incorrectly say 'the weight is so many grams'.

5. With older pupils in the primary range you can discuss the effect of gravity and space travel on weight and the idea that mass does not change.

6. It is not necessary to do much work on solid volume, measured in cubic centimetres, in the primary age-range.

7. But the measurement of liquid volume and capacity, in litres and millilitres, because of the scope for practical experience with water and various containers, is an important component of primary-school mathematics.

8. Restrict the range of metric units used for practical work in the primary school to metre, centimetre, millimetre, litre, millilitre, kilogram, gram. Reference may also be made to kilometre and decimetre.

9. Work on journeys and average speeds is most appropriately done in miles and miles per hour.

10. Make considerable use of estimation as a class activity, encouraging pupils to learn by heart the measurements of specific reference items.

11. Make collections and displays of packages, discussing which items are sold by mass or by volume, the units used, which are metric and which imperial.

12. Do not use formal subtraction algorithms for finding the length of time from one recorded time to the next; teach an *ad hoc* adding-on approach.

13. Do not use a circle to represent a day, because of the association with a 12-hour clock-face.

14. Pupils should learn to choose and use appropriate measuring devices, discussing the idea of accuracy. Make explicit the notion that measurement is always to the nearest something.

15. Discuss imperial units still in everyday use. Give pupils practical experience which will enable them to become familiar with some useful equivalences between metric and imperial units.

25

Angle

Pupils should be taught to: use right angles, fractions of a turn and, later, degrees, to measure rotation, and use the associated language.

In this chapter there are explanations of

- the dynamic and static views of angle;
- comparison and ordering of angles;
- the use of turns and fractions of a turn for measuring angle;
- degrees;
- acute, right, obtuse, straight, reflex angles; and
- the sum of the angles in a triangle, a quadrilateral, and so on.

What is an angle?

An angle is a measurement. When we talk about the angle between two lines we are not referring to the shape formed by the two lines, nor to the point where they meet, nor to the space between the lines, but to a particular kind of measurement. There are two ways in which we can think of what it is that is being measured. First there is the *dynamic* view of angle: the angle between the lines is a measurement of the size of the *rotation* involved when you point along one line and then turn to point along the other. This is the most useful way of introducing the concept of angle to children, because it lends itself to practical experience, with the children themselves pointing in one direction and then turning themselves through various angles to point in other directions. Also, when it comes to measuring angles between lines drawn on paper, pupils can physically point something, such as a pencil or a finger, along one line and rotate about the intersection of the lines to point along the other line. We should note that there are always two angles involved when turning from one direction to another, depending on whether you choose to rotate clockwise or anticlockwise, as shown in Figure 25.1.

Secondly, there is the *static* view of angle. This is where we focus our attention on how pointed is the shape formed by the two lines. But the angle is still a measurement: we can think of it as a measurement of the difference in

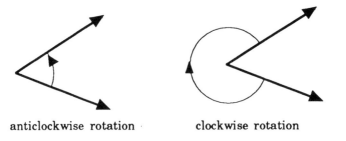

anticlockwise rotation   clockwise rotation

Figure 25.1   Angle as a measure of rotation

direction between the two lines. So, for example, in Figure 25.2, the angle marked in (a) is greater than that marked in (b), because the two lines in (b) are pointing in nearly the same direction, whereas the difference in the direction of the two lines in (a) is much greater. Thinking of angle as the difference in direction between two lines helps to link the static view of angle with the dynamic one of rotation, because the obvious way to measure the difference in two directions is to turn from one to the other and measure the amount of turn.

Figure 25.2   Angle as a measure of the difference in direction

Figure 25.2 illustrates that, like any aspect of measurement, the concept of angle enables us to make comparisons and to order (see Chapter 24). This can be dynamically, by physically doing the rotations involved (for example, with a pencil) and judging which is the greater rotation, which the smaller. It can also be experienced more statically, by cutting out one angle and placing it over another to determine which is the more pointed (the smaller angle). Figure 25.3 shows a set of angles, (a)–(f), ordered from smallest to largest.

The equivalent to making measurements of length, mass and capacity in non-standard units is to measure angle in turns and fractions of a turn, using the dynamic view. Figure 25.3f shows a whole turn, pointing in one direction and rotating until you point again in the same direction. Then, for example, if a pupil points North and then turns to point South they have moved through an angle which can be called a half-turn. Similarly, rotating from North, clockwise, to East is a quarter-turn. Figure 25.3b shows a quarter-turn from a horizontal position to a vertical position. This explains why a quarter-turn is also called a *right angle*: it is an *upright* angle. Figure 25.3d illustrates why a half-turn, formed by two lines pointing in opposite directions, is also called a *straight angle*.

The next stage of development is to introduce a standard unit for measuring angles. For primary-school use this unit is the degree, where 360 degrees (360°)

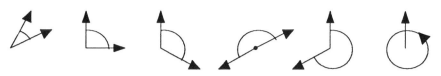

(a) acute angle (b) right angle (c) obtuse angle (d) straight angle (e) reflex angle (f) whole turn

Figure 25.3   A set of angles in order from smallest (a) to largest (f)

is equal to a complete turn. Hence a right angle (quarter-turn) is 90° and a straight angle (half-turn) is 180°. There is evidence that this system of measuring angles in degrees based on 360 was used as far back as 2000 BC by the Babylonians, and it is thought that it may be related to the Babylonian year being 360 days. So we have here another example of a non-metric measurement in common use. There is actually a metric system for measuring angle, used in some European countries, in which '100 grades' is equal to a right angle, but this has never caught on in the UK. Interestingly, it is because 'centigrade' would then be one hundredth of a grade, and therefore a measure of angle, that the 'degree centigrade' as a measure of temperature is now officially called the 'degree Celsius', to avoid confusion.

The device used to measure angles in degrees is, of course, the *protractor*. I personally recommend the use of a 360° protractor, preferably marked with only one scale and with a pointer which can be rotated from one line of the angle being measured to the other, thus emphasising the dynamic view of angle. Even if there is not an actual pointer, pupils can still be encouraged to imagine the rotation always starting at zero on one line and rotating through 10°, 20°, 30° . . . to reach the other.

Can you remind me about acute, obtuse and reflex angles?

Mathematicians can never resist the temptation to put things into categories, thus giving them opportunity to invent a new collection of terms. Angles are classified, in order of size, as: acute, right, obtuse, straight, reflex, as illustrated in Figure 25.3. An *acute* angle (a) is an angle less than a right angle. An *obtuse* angle (c) is an angle between a right angle and a straight angle. A *reflex* angle (e) is an angle greater than a straight angle, but less than a whole turn.

I remember that the three angles in a triangle add up to 180 degrees, but what about shapes with more than three sides?

A popular way of seeing this property of the angles of a triangle is to draw a triangle on paper, mark the angles, tear off the three corners and fit them together, as shown in Figure 25.4, to discover that together they form a straight angle, or two right angles (180°). The same thing can be done with the four angles of a quadrilateral (a shape with four straight sides), to discover that they fit together to make a whole turn, or four right angles (360°).

This illuminative experience uses the static view of angle. It is also possible to illustrate the same principle using the dynamic view, as shown in Figure

Figure 25.4   The three angles of a triangle fitted together to make a straight angle

25.5, by taking an arrow (or, say, a pencil) for a walk round a triangle. Step 1 is to place an arrow (or the pencil) along one side of the triangle, for example on AC. Step 2 is to slide the arrow along until it reaches A, then rotate it through the angle at A. Now, for Step 3, slide it up to B and rotate through that angle. Finally, Step 4, slide it down to C and rotate through that angle. The arrow has now rotated through the sum of the three angles and is facing in the opposite direction to which it started! Hence the three angles together make a half-turn, or two right angles. Clearly this will work for any triangle, not just the one shown here.

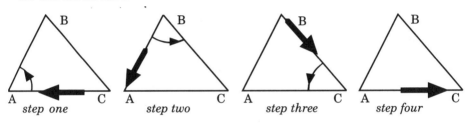

Figure 25.5   The three angles of a triangles together make a half-turn

The same procedure can then be applied to a four-sided figure, such as the quadrilateral shown in Figure 25.6. Now we find that the arrow does a complete rotation, finishing up pointing in the same direction as it started, so we conclude that the sum of the four angles in a four-sided figure is four right angles.

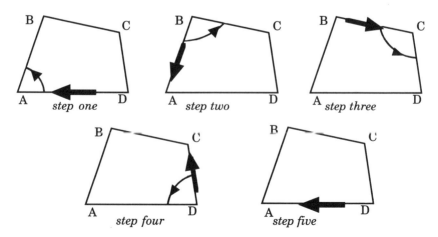

Figure 25.6   The four angles of a quadrilateral together make a whole turn

The delight of this activity is that it can easily be extended to five-sided figures, six sided, seven sided, and so on. The results can then be tabulated, using the approach given in Chapter 21, in order to formulate a sequential generalisation and a global generalisation. This is left as an exercise for the reader in Question 25.2 below.

Self-assessment questions

25.1: Put these angles in order and classify them as acute, right, obtuse, straight or reflex: 89°, ⅛ of a turn, 150°, 90°, ¾ of a turn, 200°, 2 right angles, 95°.

25.2: Use the idea of taking an arrow round a shape, rotating through each of the angles in turn, to find the sum of the angles in: a) a five-sided figure; b) a six-sided figure; and c) a seven-sided figure. Give the answers in right angles, tabulate them and formulate both the sequential and the global generalisations. What would be the sum of the angles in a figure with 100 sides?

Summary of teaching points

1. Emphasise especially the dynamic view of angle, giving plenty of practical experience of rotating objects, themselves and pointers (such as fingers and pencils).

2. Include the important stages of developing a measurement concept when teaching angle: comparison, ordering and the use of non-standard units (turns and fractions of turns).

3. Get pupils to compare and order angles by cutting them out and placing them on top of each other.

4. I recommend the use of a 360° protractor for measuring angles in degrees. Emphasise the idea of rotation from zero when explaining to pupils how to use a protractor.

5. Use a transparent protractor on an overhead projector to demonstrate to pupils how to use this device for measuring angles.

6. When explaining about angles, do not always draw diagrams in which one of the lines is horizontal (see my example in the figures in this chapter!)

7. Pupils can cut out pictures from magazines, mark angles on them and display them in sets as acute, right, obtuse, straight and reflex.

8. Use both the static and the dynamic methods for discovering the sum of the angles in a triangle, a quadrilateral, and so on.

26

Transformations and Symmetry

Pupils should be taught to: understand the congruence of simple shapes; recognise reflective . . . and rotational symmetries; transform 2-D shapes by translation, reflection and rotation.

In this chapter there are explanations of

- the fundamental ideas of transformation and equivalence;
- translation, reflection and rotation as types of congruence; and
- reflective and rotational symmetry for two-dimensional shapes.

What is a congruence?

To answer this question I will discuss the general ideas of *transformation* and *equivalence*, apply these to shapes and identify three types of transformation, *translations*, *rotations* and *reflections,* which, whilst changing shapes in some way or other, all produce *congruent* shapes. In general we call these transformations *congruences*.

Two fundamental questions in mathematics are: 1) How are they the same? 2) How are they different? The first question directs our attention to what is called an *equivalence*, the second to a *transformation*. For example, in Chapter 16 we saw that we could *transform* a fraction such as ⅔ into an *equivalent* fraction such as ⁴⁄₆, by multiplying top and bottom numbers by 2. The two fractions are, in a sense, different. For a start they use different top and bottom numbers; and two pieces of a pizza cut into three is not exactly the same situation in every respect as four pieces of a pizza cut into six. But you do get the same amount of pizza. So there is an important sense in which they *are* the same. A similar line of reasoning applied in Chapter 24, when discussing conservation of liquid volume. In the example shown in Figure 24.4, the water in the container is transformed in some way when it is poured into another container. It is a different 'shape', it has a different height, and so on. But something very important stays the same, namely, the volume of the water. Then if I draw a large diagram on the board and ask the class to copy it on to their paper, they all dutifully do this, even though none of them has a piece of paper anything like large enough to produce a diagram as big as mine. Their diagrams are different from mine, that is different in size, whilst in many respects they might be the same as mine. Much of what we have to understand in mathematics comes down to recognising the equivalences which exist within various transformations, which transformations preserve which equivalences, how things can be different yet be the same. This way of thinking is central to developing an understanding of shape and space.

In a mathematics lesson Cathy was asked to draw on squared paper as many different shapes as possible which are made up of five square units. Figure 26.1 shows four of the shapes which she drew. Her teacher told her that they were all the same shape. Cathy insisted they were all different. Who was right? The answer is, of course, that they are both right. The shapes are all the same in some senses and all different in others.

First, consider how they are the same. All four shapes are made up of five square units; they have the same number of sides (six); each shape has one side of length four units, one side of length three units, one side of length two units and three sides of length one unit; each shape has five 90° angles and one 270° angle; and the sides and the angles are arranged in the same way in each of the shapes to make what we might recognise as a letter 'L'. Surely they are identical, the same in every respect? Well, they certainly are *congruent*. This word describes the relationship between two shapes which have sides of exactly the same length, angles of exactly the same size, all arranged in exactly the same way, as in the four shapes shown in Figure 26.1. A practical definition would be that you could cut out one shape and fit it exactly over the other one. The pages in this book are congruent: as you can see, one page fits exactly over the next. The computer discs I am using whilst writing the book are all congruent: I can see them sitting on the desk at this moment in a neat pile, one placed exactly over the other, the bevelled corners and indentations along the edges matching perfectly.

So, how are the shapes in Figure 26.1 different? For example, how is Shape 2 different from Shape 1? Cathy's argument is that they are in different positions on the paper: Shape 1 is here and Shape 2 is over there, so they are not the same shape. Surely every time I draw the shape in a different position I have drawn a different shape, in a sense. So the shapes are different if you decide to take

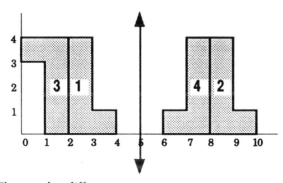

Figure 26.1   The same but different

position into account. In order to do this we need a system of coordinates, as outlined in Chapter 23. The transformation which has been applied to Shape 1 to produce Shape 2 is called a *translation*. We saw in Chapter 23 that we can use the coordinate system to describe movements. So this translation can be specified by saying, for example, that to get from Shape 1 to Shape 2 you have to move 6 units in the *x*-direction and 0 units in the *y*-direction. Any movement of our shape like this, so many units in the *x*-direction and so many in the *y*-direction, is a translation.

If we now decide that, for the time being, we will not count translations as producing shapes which are 'different', what about Shape 3? Is that different from Shape 1? Cathy's idea is that Shape 1 is an L-shape the right way up, but Shape 3 is upside down, so they are different. So the shapes are different if you decide to take their orientation on the page into account. In order to take this into account we need the concept of direction, and, as we saw in Chapter 25, to describe a difference in direction we need the concept of angle. To transform Shape 1 into Shape 3 we can apply a *rotation*. To specify a rotation we have to indicate the point about which the rotation occurs and the angle through which the shape is rotated. If Shape 1 is rotated through an angle of 180° (either clockwise or anticlockwise), about the middle of its left-hand side – the point with coordinates (2,2) – then it is transformed into Shape 3. Imagine copying Shape 1 on to tracing paper, placing a pin in the point (2,2) and rotating the tracing paper through 180°. The shape would land directly on top of Shape 3. Any movement of our shape like this, turning through some angle about a given centre, is a rotation.

Now if we decide that, for the time being, we will not count rotations or translations as producing shapes which are 'different', what about Shape 4? Is that different from Shape 1? Cathy's idea is that they are actually mirror images of each other. This difference can be made explicit by colouring the shapes, say, red, before cutting them out. Shapes 1, 2 and 3 can all be placed on top of each other and match exactly, with the red faces uppermost. But Shape 4 only matches if we turn it over so that it is red face down. This surely makes it different from all the others! The transformation which has been applied now to Shape 1 to produce Shape 4 is a *reflection*. To specify a reflection all you have to do is to identify the mirror line. In the case of Shapes 1 and 4 the mirror line is the vertical line passing through 5 on the *x*-axis, shown as a double-headed arrow in Figure 26.1. Each point in Shape 1 is matched by a corresponding point in Shape 4, the other side of the mirror line and the same distance from it. For example, the corner of the letter L with the reflex angle in Shape 1 is 2 units to the left of the mirror line, but the corresponding point in Shape 4 is 2 units to the right of the mirror line. Any movement of our shape like this, obtained by producing a mirror image in any given mirror line, is a reflection.

What is reflective symmetry?

Sometimes when we reflect a shape in a particular mirror line it matches *itself* exactly, in the sense that the mirror image coincides precisely with the original

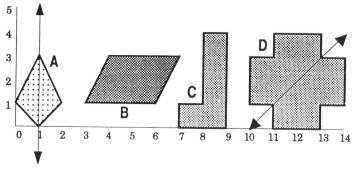

Figure 26.2   Are these shapes symmetrical?

shape. Shape A in Figure 26.2 is an example of this phenomenon. The mirror line is shown as a double-headed arrow. This divides the shape into two identical halves which are mirror images of each other. If we cut the shape out we could fold it along the mirror line and the two halves would match exactly. Another approach is to use the idea employed above of colouring the shape, cutting it out and turning it face down: we find that the shape turned face down could still fit exactly into the hole left in the paper. The shape is said to have *reflective symmetry* (sometimes called line symmetry) and the mirror line is called a *line of symmetry*. Shape D in Figure 26.2 also has reflective symmetry. There are actually four possible lines which divide this shape into two matching halves with one half the mirror image of the other, although only one of these is shown in the diagram. Finding the other three lines of symmetry is an exercise for the reader (Question 26.2). Again, notice that if you coloured the shape, cut it out and turned it face down, it could fit exactly into the hole left in the paper. Shape C does not have reflective symmetry. The colouring, cutting out and turning face down routine demonstrates this nicely, since it is clear that we would not then be able to fit the shape into the hole left in the paper.

Shape B is perhaps a surprise, because this too does *not* have reflective symmetry. (If you think, for example, that one of the diagonals is a line of symmetry, copy the shape on to paper and use the colouring, cutting out and turning face-down procedure; or try folding it in half along the diagonal.) But it does have a kind of symmetry. To see this we can use the tracing-paper idea employed above. Trace the shape on to tracing paper and then rotate it around the centre point through a half-turn. The shape matches the original shape exactly. A shape which can be rotated on to itself like this is said to have *rotational symmetry*. The point about which we rotate it is called the *centre of rotational symmetry*. If we coloured Shape B and cut it out, there would be two ways in which we could fit it into the hole left in the paper, by rotating it, without turning the shape face down. We therefore say that the shape has rotational symmetry of *order two*. Shape D also has rotational symmetry (see Question 26.2 below). Shapes A and C do not have rotational symmetry. Well, not really. I suppose you could say that they have rotational symmetry of order one, since there is *one* way in which their cut-outs could fit into the hole left in the paper, without turning them face down. In this sense all two-dimensional shapes would have rotational symmetry of at least order one. Personally, whilst recognising this, I would usually say that shapes like A and C do not have rotational symmetry.

These ideas of reflective and rotational symmetry are fundamental to the creation of attractive designs and patterns, and are employed effectively in a number of cultural traditions, particularly the Islamic. Pupils can learn first of all to recognise these kinds of symmetry in the world around them, and gradually to learn to analyse them and to employ them in creating designs of their own.

Self-assessment questions

26.1: Describe the congruences which transform Shape 2 in Figure 26.1 into: a) Shape 1; b) Shape 4; and c) Shape 3.

26.2: In Shape D in Figure 26.2, where are the other three lines of symmetry? What is the order of rotational symmetry of this shape?

26.3: Is it possible to draw a two-dimensional shape with exactly two lines of symmetry, where the lines of symmetry are not at right angles to each other?

26.4: Is it possible to draw a shape with exactly two lines of symmetry which does not have rotational symmetry?

Summary of teaching points

1. Use geometrical designs from different cultural traditions, such as Islamic patterns, to provide a rich experience of transformations and symmetry.

2. Use some of the numerous computer programs which are available to provide primary pupils with some fascinating opportunities to explore transformations and symmetry.

3. The most important emphasis for pupils' learning about shape and space in the primary school is the opportunity for masses of practical experience of colouring in shapes, cutting them out, folding them, turning them over, rotating them, looking at them in mirrors, fitting them together, making patterns, matching them, sorting them, classifying them, and so on. Our approach here can be much less structured than in other aspects of the mathematics curriculum.

4. Frequently use the two questions about transformation and equivalence to promote useful discussion in work with shapes: a) How are they the same? b) How are they different?

5. Use the tracing paper approach to explore the ideas of rotation and rotational symmetry.

6. Use the colouring, cutting-out, turning face-down approach to explore the ideas of reflection and reflective symmetry.

7. An interesting project is to make a display of pictures cut from magazines which illustrate different aspects of symmetry.

27

Classifying Shapes

Pupils should be taught to: recognise . . . geometrical features and properties and use these to classify shapes.

In this chapter there are explanations of

- the importance of classification as a process for making sense of the shapes in the world around us;
- polygons, including the meaning of 'regular polygon';
- acute-angled, right-angled and obtuse-angled triangles;
- equilateral, isosceles and scalene triangles;
- parallelograms, rectangles, squares, rhombuses, and the relationships between them;
- tessellations;
- polyhedra, including the meaning of 'regular polyhedron';
- prisms and pyramids; and
- reflective symmetry applied to three-dimensional shapes.

Why are there so many technical terms to learn in geometry?

We need the special language of geometry in order to classify shapes into categories. Classification is an important intellectual process which helps us to make sense of our experiences. By coding information into categories we condense it and gain some control over it. Classification is at the heart of mathematics. The intellectual process involved is another example of the 'same but different' principle discussed in Chapter 26. We form categories in mathematics by recognising attributes shared by various elements (such as numbers or shapes). These elements are then formed into a set. Although the elements in the set are different they have something the same about them. When it is a particularly interesting or significant set we give it a name. Because it is important that we should be able to determine definitely whether or not a particular element is in the set, the next stage of the process is often to formulate a precise definition.

For example, in Chapter 13 we recognised the attribute shared by these numbers, (2, 3, 5, 7, 11, 13, 17 . . .), that they had no factors apart from 1 and themselves. This led to putting them into a set and giving them a name, 'prime numbers'. Because of some uncertainty about whether or not the number 1 was prime, a definition was then produced, namely, that a prime number is one which has precisely two factors. I suggested in Chapter 13 that awareness of various ways of classifying numbers contributes to a greater confidence with number. The same is true of shapes. Just as with numbers, we might recognise an attribute common to certain shapes (such as having three sides), form them into a category, give the set a name (e.g. the set of triangles) and then, if necessary, make the classification more explicit with a precise definition. This process of classifying and naming leads to a greater confidence in handling shapes and a better awareness of the shapes which make up the world around us.

So, to participate in this important process of classification of shapes, we need, first of all, a whole batch of mathematical ideas related to the significant properties of shapes which are used to put them into various categories. This will include, for example, reference to whether the edges of the shape are straight, the number of sides and angles, whether various angles are equal or right angled, and whether sides are equal in length or parallel. Then, secondly, we need to know the various terms used to name the sets, supported where necessary by a definition. My experience is that many primary teachers and student-teachers have a degree of uncertainty about some of these terms which undermines their confidence in teaching mathematics. For their sake the following material is provided for reference purposes.

What are the main classes of two-dimensional shapes?

The first classification of two-dimensional shapes we should note separates out those with only straight edges from those, such as circles, semi-circles and ellipses, which have curved edges. A two-dimensional closed shaped made up entirely of straight edges is called a *polygon*.

Polygons can then be further classified depending on the number of sides: *triangles* with three sides, *quadrilaterals* with four, *pentagons* with five, *hexagons* with six, *heptagons* with seven, *octagons* with eight, and so on.

Then we can also categorise polygons into those which are *regular* and those which are not. A *regular polygon* is one in which all the sides are the same length and all the angles are the same size. For example, a regular octagon has eight equal sides and eight angles, each of which is equal to 135°. To work out the angles in a regular polygon, use the rule $(2n - 4$ right angles) deduced in Question 25.2 (Chapter 25) to determine the total of the angles in the polygon (e.g. for an octagon the sum is $2 \times 8 - 4 = 12$ right angles, i.e. 1080°), then divide this by the number of angles (e.g. for the octagon, 1080° ÷ 8 = 135°) The word 'regular' is often misused when people talk about shapes, as though it were synonymous with 'symmetric' or even 'geometric'. For example, the rectangular shape of the cover of this book is *not* a regular shape, because two of the sides are longer than the other two.

There is a fascinating way of forming the regular polygons, using the fact that the number of lines of symmetry increases as the number of sides increases. (For example, a regular triangle has three lines of symmetry, a regular quadrilateral has four, and so on.) You need two mirrors taped together, so that they can open out like the covers of a book. Draw a straight line on a sheet of paper and place the two mirrors, opened at 120° across the line, so that you can see the reflections in the mirrors. With care, you should be able to arrange the mirrors so that you can see a regular triangle in them. Then slowly close the two mirrors. As you do this the image will successively form each of the regular polygons. This is a delightful experience, not to be missed!

What are the different categories of triangles that I should know about?

There are basically two ways of categorising triangles. The first is based on their angles, the second on their sides. Figure 27.1 shows examples of triangles categorised in these ways.

First we can categorise a triangle as being *acute angled, right angled* or *obtuse angled.* (See Chapter 25 for the classification of angles.) An *acute-angled triangle* is one in which all three angles are acute, i.e. less than 90°. A *right-angled triangle* is one in which one of the angles is a right angle; it is not possible, of course, to have two right angles since the sum of the three angles has to be 180°, and this would make the third angle zero! The right angles are indicated in Figure 27.1 in the conventional fashion. An *obtuse-angled triangle* is one with an obtuse angle, i.e. one angle greater than 90° and less than 180°; again it is only possible to have one such angle because of the sum of the three angles having to equal 180°. This condition also makes it impossible to have a triangle containing a reflex angle.

Then, secondly, we can categorise triangles as being *equilateral, isosceles* or *scalene.* An *equilateral* (i.e. equal-sided) triangle is one in which all three sides are equal. Because of the rigid nature of triangles, the only possibility for an equilateral triangle is one in which the three angles are also equal (to 60°). So an equilateral triangle must be a regular triangle. This is only true of triangles. For example, you can have an equilateral octagon (with eight equal sides) in which the angles are not equal: just imagine joining eight equal strips of card with paper-fasteners and manipulating the structure into many different shapes, all of which are equilateral octagons but only one of which is a regular octagon.

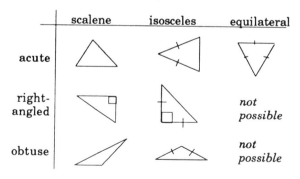

Figure 27.1   Categories of triangles

An *isosceles* triangle is one with two sides equal. In Figure 27.1 the equal sides are those marked with a small dash. An isosceles triangle has a line of symmetry passing through the middle of the angle formed by the two equal sides. If the triangle is cut out and folded in half along this line of symmetry the two angles opposite the equal sides match each other. So we can discover practically that a triangle with two equal sides always has two equal angles.

Finally, a *scalene* triangle is one with no sides equal. Using these different categorisations it is then possible to determine seven different kinds of triangle, as shown in Figure 27.1.

What are the different categories of quadrilaterals that I should know about?

The most important set of quadrilaterals is the set of *parallelograms*, i.e. those with two pairs of opposite sides parallel. Figure 27.2 shows some examples of parallelograms. Two lines drawn in a two-dimensional plane are said to be *parallel* if theoretically they would never meet if continued indefinitely. This describes the relationship between the opposite sides in each of the shapes drawn in Figure 27.2. In Chapter 26 we saw that not all parallelograms have reflective symmetry: in Figure 27.2, only the special parallelograms A, B and C, have reflective symmetry. But they do all have rotational symmetry of at least order two. This means that the opposite angles match on to each other, and the opposite sides match on to each other, when the shape is rotated through a half-turn. In other words, the opposite angles in a parallelogram are always equal and the opposite sides are always equal. There are then two main ways of classifying parallelograms. One of these is based on the angles, the other on the sides.

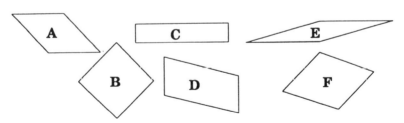

Figure 27.2   Examples of parallelograms

The most significant aspect of the angles of a parallelogram concerns whether or not they are right angled. If they are, as, for example, in shapes B and C in Figure 27.2, the shape is called a *rectangle*. Note that if one angle in a parallelogram is a right angle, because opposite angles are equal and the four angles add up to four right angles, all the angles must be right angles. The rectangle is probably the most important four-sided shape from a practical perspective, simply because our artifical world is so much based on the rectangle. It is almost impossible to look anywhere and not see rectangles. (Interestingly, however, there are children who grow up in rural areas of some African countries where their environment is based on the circle – they sit on circular stools in circular houses in circular villages – and this is often reflected in their relative confidence in handling the mathematics of circles and rectangles, compared to, say, British children.)

Then a *rhombus* is a parallelogram in which all four sides are equal, as, for example, in shapes A and B in Figure 27.2. A *square* (shape B) is therefore a rhombus which is also a rectangle, or a rectangle which is also a rhombus. It is, of course, a quadrilateral with all four sides equal and all four angles equal (to 90°), so 'square' is another name for a regular quadrilateral.

There is an important point about language to make here. A square is a rectangle (a special kind of rectangle) and a rectangle is a parallelogram (a special kind of parallelogram). Likewise, a square is a rhombus (a special kind of rhombus) and a rhombus is a parallelogram (a special kind of parallelogram). Sometimes one hears teachers talking about 'squares or rectangles', for example, as though they were different things, neglecting the fact that squares are a subset of rectangles. If you need to distinguish between rectangles which are squares and those which are not, then you can refer to *square rectangles* (such as B in Figure 27.2) and *oblong rectangles* (such as C).

What is a tessellation?

One further way of classifying two-dimensional shapes is to distinguish between those which *tessellate* and those which do not. A shape is said to tessellate if it can be used to make a tiling pattern, or a *tessellation*. This means that the shape can be used over and over again to cover a flat surface, the shapes fitting together without any gaps. In practical terms we are asking whether the shape can be used as a tile to cover the kitchen floor (without worrying about what happens when we reach the edges). The commonest shapes used for tiling are, of course, squares and other rectangles, which fit together so neatly without any gaps, as shown in Figure 27.3a. This is no doubt part of the reason why the rectangle is such a popular shape in a technological world. Figure 27.3b demonstrates a remarkable fact, that *any* triangle tessellates. If the three angles of the triangle are called A, B and C, then it is instructive to identify the six angles which come together at a point where six triangles meet in the tessellation, as shown. Because A, B and C add up to 180°, a straight angle, we find that they fit together at this point, neatly lying along straight lines. By repeating this arrangement in all directions the triangle can clearly be used to form a tessellation.

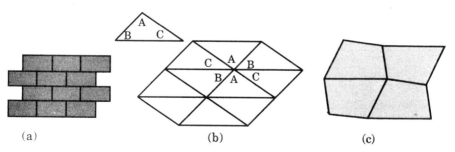

Figure 27.3   Tessellations

It is also true that *any* quadrilateral tessellates, as illustrated in Figure 27.3c. Because the four angles add up to 360°, we can arrange for four quadrilaterals to meet at a point with the four different angles fitting together without any gaps. This pattern can then be continued indefinitely in all directions. Interestingly, apart from the equilateral triangle and the square, the only other regular polygon which tessellates is the regular hexagon, as seen in the familiar honeycomb pattern.

What are the main classes of three-dimensional shapes?

The first classification of three-dimensional shapes is to separate out those that have curved surfaces, such as a sphere (a perfectly round ball), a hemisphere (a sphere cut in half), a cylinder (like a baked-bean tin) and a cone (see the nearest motorway). A shape which is made up entirely of flat surfaces (also called *plane* surfaces) is called a *polyhedron* (plural: *polyhedra*). To describe a polyhedron we need to refer to the flat surfaces, which are called *faces* (not sides, incidentally), the lines where two faces meet, called *edges*, and the points where edges meet, called *vertices* (plural of *vertex*).

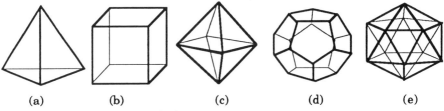

(a)   (b)   (c)   (d)   (e)

Figure 27.4   The regular polyhedra

As with polygons, the word *regular* is used to identify those polyhedra in which all the faces are the same shape, all the edges are the same length and all the angles between edges are equal. Whereas there was an infinite number of different kinds of regular polygons, there are, in fact, only five kinds of regular polyhedra. These are shown in Figure 27.4: a) the regular *tetrahedron* (four faces, each of which is an equilateral triangle); b) the regular *hexahedron* (usually called a *cube*; six faces, each of which is a square); c) the regular *octahedron* (eight faces, each of which is an equilateral triangle); d) the regular *dodecahedron* (twelve faces, each of which is a regular pentagon); and e) the regular *icosahedron* (twenty faces, each of which is an equilateral triangle).

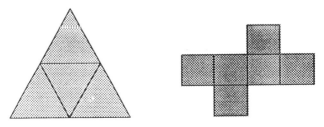

Figure 27.5   Nets for a regular tetrahedron and a cube

These and other solid shapes can be constructed by drawing a two-dimensional *net*, such as those shown for the regular tetrahedron and cube in Figure 27.5, cutting these out, folding and sticking. (It is advisable to incorporate some flaps for gluing in appropriate positions before cutting out.) This is an excellent mathematical activity for primary-school pupils, in which a whole range of spatial concepts and practical skills come together.

A *prism* is a shape made up of two identical polygons at opposite ends, joined up by parallel lines. Figure 27.6 illustrates a) a triangular prism, b) a rectangular prism and c) a hexagonal prism. I like to think of prisms as being made from cheese: a shape is a prism if you can slice the cheese along its length in a way in which each slice is identical. Note that they are all called prisms, although colloquially the word is often used to refer just to the triangular prism. Note also that another name for a rectangular prism is a *cuboid*: this is a three-dimensional shape in which all the faces are rectangles.

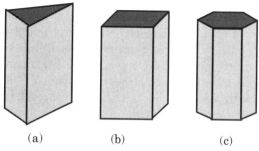

(a)   (b)   (c)

Figure 27.6   Some prisms

Another category of three-dimensional shapes to be mentioned here is the set called pyramids, illustrated in Figure 27.7. A *pyramid* is made up of a polygon forming the *base*, and then lines drawn from each of the vertices of this polygon to some point above, called the *apex*. The result of this is to form a series of triangular faces rising up from the edges of the base, meeting at the apex. Note that a triangular-based pyramid – (a) – is actually a tetrahedron by another name, and that a square-based pyramid – (b) – is the kind we associate with ancient Egypt.

To conclude this chapter I will make a brief mention of *reflective symmetry* as it is applied to three-dimensional shapes. In Chapter 26 we saw how some two-

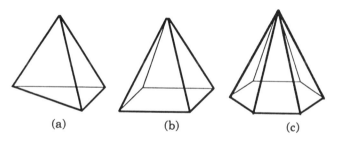

(a)   (b)   (c)

Figure 27.7   Pyramids

Figure 27.8   A plane of symmetry

dimensional shapes have reflective symmetry, with a line of symmetry dividing the shape into two matching halves, one a mirror image of the other. The same applies to three-dimensional shapes, except that it is now a *plane of symmetry* which divides the shape into the two halves. This is like taking a broad, flat knife and slicing right through the shape, producing two bits which are mirror images of each other, as illustrated with a cone in Figure 27.8. The cone, of course, has an infinite number of planes of symmetry, since any vertical slice through the apex of the cone can be used. All the three-dimensional shapes illustrated in the figures in this chapter have reflective symmetry. For example, the regular tetrahedron in Figure 27.4 has three planes of symmetry. Children can experience this idea by slicing various fruits in half, or by using solid shapes made out of Plasticene or similar moulding material.

Self-assessment questions

27.1: Why is it not possible to have an equilateral, right-angled triangle or an equilateral, obtuse-angled triangle? (See Figure 27.1.)

27.2: What are the sizes of the three angles in a right-angled, isosceles triangle?

27.3: What is another name for: a) a rectangular rhombus; b) a regular quadrilateral; c) a triangle with rotational symmetry; d) a rectangular prism; and e) a triangular-based pyramid?

27.4: Which of the following shapes tesselate? (a) A parallelogram; b) a regular pentagon; and c) a regular octagon.

27.5: How many planes of symmetry can you identify for a cube?

Summary of teaching points

1. Pupils will develop geometric concepts, such as those discussed in this chapter, by experiences of classifying, using various attributes of shapes, informally in the first instance, looking for exemplars and non-exemplars, and discussing the relationships between shapes in terms of samenesses and differences.

2. The role of the definition is not to enable pupils initially to formulate a concept, but to sharpen it up once the concept has been formed informally, and to deal with doubtful cases.

3. Give pupils opportunity to explore the properties of various shapes, including the different kinds of triangles and quadrilaterals, and regular and

irregular shapes, by folding, tracing, matching, looking for reflective and rotational symmetries, and drawing out the implications of these.

4. Remember when talking about various special quadrilaterals that a square is a rectangle, and that a rectangle is a parallelogram.

5. Pupils can investigate which shapes tessellate and which do not, discovering, for example, that all triangles and all quadrilaterals do. They should use a plastic or card shape as a template, drawing round it in successive positions.

6. Construction of three-dimensional shapes from nets is an excellent practical activity drawing on a wide range of geometric concepts and practical skills.

28

Perimeter and Area

Pupils should be taught to: find perimeters of simple shapes; find practically the circumferences of circles, being introduced to the ratio π; find areas and volumes.

In this chapter there are explanations of

- the concepts of area and perimeter;
- the ideas of varying the area for a fixed perimeter, and varying the perimeter for a fixed area;
- a similar idea with volume and surface area; and
- the ratio π and its relationship to the circumference and diameter of a circle.

How do you explain the ideas of perimeter and area so that pupils don't get them confused?

Area is a measure of the amount of two-dimensional space inside a boundary. The *perimeter* is the length of the boundary. I always use *fields* and *fences* to explain these ideas. The area is the size of the field and the perimeter is the amount of fencing around the edge. Pupils can draw pictures of various fields on squared paper, such as that shown in Figure 28.1. They can then count up the number of units of fencing around the edge, to determine the perimeter, which in this case is 18 units. Make sure that they count the units of fencing and not the squares around the edge, being especially careful going round corners not to miss out any units of fencing. To determine the area they can fill the field with 'sheep', using small cubes to represent sheep; the number of sheep they can

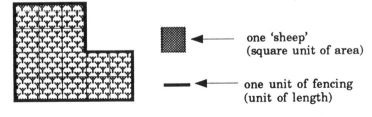

Figure 28.1   Fields and fences

188

get into the field is a measure of the area. This is, of course, the same as the number of square units inside the boundary, in this case 16 square units.

What is the relationship between perimeter and area?

In general, there is no relationship. This is something of a surprise for many people. It provides us with an interesting counter-example of the principle of conservation (see Chapter 24). When, for example, you rearrange the fencing around a field into a different shape, without changing the overall perimeter, the area is *not* conserved. For any given perimeter there is a range of possible areas. This makes an interesting investigation for pupils. Again it is best couched in terms of fields and fences. The first challenge is to find as many different fields as possible which can be enclosed within a given amount of fencing. Figure 28.2 shows a collection of shapes, drawn on squared paper, all of which represent fields made up from rearranging 12 units of fencing. They all have different areas! An important discovery is that the largest area is obtained with a square field. This is the best use of the farmer's fencing material. (If we were not restricted to the grid lines on squared paper the largest area would actually be provided by a circle: imagine the fencing to be totally flexible and push it out as far as you can in all directions in order to enclose the maximum area.)

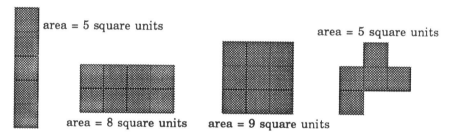

Figure 28.2   All these shapes have a perimeter of 12 units

The second challenge is the reverse problem: keep the area fixed and find the different perimeters. In other words, what amounts of fencing would be required to enclose differently shaped fields all with same area? Figure 28.3

Figure 28.3   All these shapes have an area of 16 square units

shows a collection of fields all with same area, 16 square units. Once again, we find the square to be the superior solution, requiring the minimum amount of fencing for the given area.

If it is not possible actually to make a square, using only the grid lines drawn on the squared paper (for example, with a fixed perimeter of 14 units, or a fixed area of 48 square units), we still find that the shape which is 'nearest' to a square gives the best solution. (The more general result, getting away from squared paper, is that the minimum perimeter for a given area is provided by a circle.) It is interesting to note that in some ancient civilisations land was priced by counting the number of paces around the boundary, i.e. by the perimeter. A shrewd operator in such an arrangement could buy square pieces of land and sell them off in long thin strips!

There is an interesting parallel here with volume and surface area in solid shapes. Figure 28.4 illustrates two cuboids (see Chapter 27) with the same volume, 12 cubic units. They have been made by arranging 12 unit cubes in different ways. In cuboid (a) the total surface area (that is the total number of square units on the six faces of the cuboid) is 32 square units, and in cuboid (b) it is 40 square units. This means that to cover (b) with paper you would need 40 square units of paper, but to cover (b) you would need only 32 square units. The fact that rearranging the volume changes the surface area actually explains why you sometimes need less wrapping paper if you arrange the contents of your parcel in a different way. The closer you get to a cube (or more generally to a sphere) the smaller the surface area.

Figure 28.4   Two cuboids with the same volume, 12 cubic units

What is π?

A circle is the shape consisting of all the points at a fixed distance from a given point. The given point is called the *centre*. The distance from the centre to any point on the circle is called the *radius*. The distance from one point through the centre to the opposite point on the circle is called the *diameter*. Clearly the length of the diameter is twice the length of the radius. The perimeter of a circle is also called the *circumference* (see Figure 28.5).

One of the most amazing facts in all mathematics relates to circles. If you measure the circumference of a circle and divide it by the length of the diameter you always get the same answer! This can be done in the classroom practically, using lots of differently sized circular objects, such as tin lids and crockery. To measure the diameter, place the circular object on a piece of paper between two blocks of wood, remove the object, mark the edges of the blocks on the paper and measure the distance between the marks. To measure the circumference,

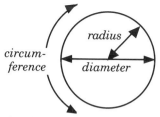

Figure 28.5   Terms used with circles

wrap some tape carefully around the object, mark where a complete circuit begins and ends, unwind the tape and measure the distance between the marks. Allowing for experimental error, which can be considerable with such crude approaches to measuring the diameter and the circumference, you should still find that in most cases the circumference divided by the diameter gives an answer of between about 3 and 3.3. Any results which are way out should be checked and measured again, if necessary. This result, that the circumference is always about three times the diameter, was clearly known in ancient civilisations and used in construction. It occurs in a number of places in the Bible; for example, in I Kings 7.23, we read of a construction, 'circular in shape, measuring ten cubits from rim to rim . . . taking a line of thirty cubits to measure around it.'

If we were able to measure more accurately, we might be able to determine that the ratio of the circumference to the diameter of a circle is about 3.14. This ratio is so important it is given a special symbol, the Greek letter π (pi). The value of π can be found theoretically to any number of decimal places. It begins like this: 3.14159265358979323384626433 . . . and actually goes on for ever, without ever recurring (see Chapter 3). For practical purposes, rounding this to two decimal places, as 3.14, is sufficient!

Once we have this value we can find the circumference of a circle, given the diameter, by multiplying the diameter by π, using a calculator if necessary. And we can find the diameter of a circle, given the circumference, by dividing the circumference by π.

There is a common misunderstanding, perpetrated I fear by some mathematics teachers who should know better, that π is *equal* to $^{22}/_7$ or three-and-one-seventh. This is not true. Three-and-one-seventh is an *approximation* for the value of π in the form of a fraction. As a decimal, three-and-one-seventh is equal to 3.142857 . . . , with the 142857 recurring. Comparing it with the value of π given above, we can see that it is only correct to two decimal places anyway, and therefore no better an approximation than 3.14. In the days of calculators 3.14 is bound to be a more useful approximation for π than $^{22}/_7$, which, along with quite a few of the things our teachers tell us at school, is probably best forgotten.

Self-assessment questions

28.1: Using just rectangular fields drawn on the grid lines on squared paper, what are the dimensions of the field which gives the maximum area for 20 units of fencing?

28.2: Using just rectangular fields drawn on the grid lines on squared paper, what are the dimensions of the field which gives the minimum length of fencing for an area of 48 square units?

28.3: How can a) 27 and b) 48 unit cubes be arranged in the shape of a cuboid to produce the minimum surface area?

28.4: How much ribbon will I need to go once round a cake with diameter 25 cm?

28.5: Roughly what is the diameter of a circular running-track 400 metres in circumference?

Summary of teaching points

1. Use the illustration of fields and fences to explain area and perimeter and pose problems about area and perimeter in these terms.

2. Let pupils investigate the way in which a fixed perimeter can produce a range of different areas, and vice versa.

3. Pupils can be introduced to solid volume by rearranging various numbers of unit cubes in the shape of cuboids; use numbers with plenty of factors, such as 12 and 24. Older primary pupils could investigate the way the surface area changes.

4. Give pupils practical experience of measuring the diameters and circumferences of circular objects, leading to the discovery that the ratio is always about three, or three and a bit.

5. Introduce older pupils to π, using, for practical purposes, the value 3.14 as an approximation for this ratio.

Answers to Self-Assessment Questions

Particularly where the question asks for the invention of a sentence, a question or a problem, the answers provided below are, of course, only examples of possible valid responses.

Chapter 2: Place value

2.1: CLXXXVIII, CCLXVII, CCC, DCXIII, DCC (188, 267, 300, 613, 700).
2.2: Four thousand one hundred (4099 + 1 = 4100).
2.3: (a) $516 = (5 \times 10^2) + (1 \times 10^1) + 6$; b) $3060 = (3 \times 10^3) + (6 \times 10^1)$; c) $2305004 = (2 \times 10^6) + (3 \times 10^5) + (5 \times 10^3) + 4$.
2.4: 6 one-pound coins, 2 ten-penny coins, 4 one-penny coins.
2.5: 3.2 is 3 flats and 2 longs; 3.05 is 3 flats and 5 small cubes; 3.15 is 3 flats, one long and 5 small cubes; 3.10 is 3 flats and 1 long. In order, they are: 3.05, 3.10, 3.15, 3.2.
2.6: 3.405 m and 2.500 m (or 2.5 m or 2.50 m).
2.7: (a) £0.25; b) 0.25 m; c) £0.07; d) 0.045 kg; e) 0.050 litres; f) 0.005 m.

Chapter 3: Mathematical modelling

3.1: Mathematical model is '4.95 + 5.90 + 9.95'; mathematical solution, using a calculator, is 20.8; interpretation is that the total cost is £20.80.
3.2: Mathematical model is 27.90 ÷ 3; mathematical solution (calculator answer) is 9.3; this is an exact but slightly inappropriate answer, because of the convention of 2 figures after the point for money; interpretation is that each person pays £9.30.
3.3: Mathematical model is 39.70 ÷ 3; mathematical solution (calculator answer) is 13.233333; this is an answer which has been truncated; interpretation is that each person owes £13.23 and a little bit; two people pay £13.23, but one has to pay £13.24.
3.4: Mathematical model is 50 ÷ 0.32; mathematical solution (calculator answer) is 156.25; this is an exact but inappropriate answer; interpretation is that John can buy 156 bars of chocolate.

3.5: Mathematical model is 500 ÷ 35; mathematical solution (calculator answer) is 14.285714; this is an answer which has been truncated; interpretation is that it will take me 15 months to reach my target.

Chapter 4: Addition structures

4.1: 'I buy two articles costing £5.95 and £6.99. What is the total cost?'

4.2: 'My salary was £9750 and then I had a rise of £145. What was my new salary?'

4.3: 'If the recipe requires 250 ml of water and 125 ml of milk, what is the total volume of liquid?'

4.4: 'The class's morning consists of 15 minutes registration, 25 minutes assembly, 55 minutes mathematics, 20 minutes break, 65 minutes English. What is the total time?'

Chapter 5: Addition calculations

5.1: Put out 2 pound coins, 8 pennies; then 1 pound coin, 5 ten-pences and 6 pennies; then 9 ten-pences and 7 pennies; there are 21 pennies; exchange 20 of these for 2 tens, leaving 1 penny; there are now 16 tens; exchange 10 of these for 1 pound, leaving 6 tens; there are then 4 pounds; the total is 4 pounds, 6 tens and 1 penny, i.e. 461.

5.2: 500 + 200 makes 700; 30 + 90 makes 120, that's 820 in total so far; 8 + 4 makes 12, add this to the 820, to get 832.

5.3: (a) 98 is 2 less than 100; 423 + 100 is 523, take off 2, answer 521; b) take 3 off 314 and add it to 297, so the sum becomes 300 + 311; answer is 611; c) take 8 off the 309 and add it to the 492, making 301 + 500; answer is 801.

Chapter 6: Subtraction structures

6.1: 54 years; 2050 – 1996; this is an example of the inverse-of-addition structure.

6.2: 78 pages; 256 – 178; this is an example of the inverse-of-addition structure.

6.3: 27 years; 52 – 25; this is an example of the comparison structure.

6.4: 185 points; 750 – 565; this is an example of the inverse-of-addition structure.

6.5: 'The Australian Chardonnay is £3.95 and the Hungarian is £2.99. How much cheaper is the Hungarian?'

6.6: 'The temperature in London is 25°C, in Oslo it is –6°C. What is the temperature difference between the two cities?'

6.7: 'There are 250 pupils in a school. 159 have school lunches. How many do not?'

6.8: 'I want to buy a computer costing £489, but have only £350. How much more do I need?'

Chapter 7: Subtraction calculations

7.1: Put out 6 one-pound coins, 2 tens and 3 pence; take away 1 penny, leaving 2 pence; not enough ten-pences, so exchange 1 pound for 10 tens, giving 12 tens; take away 7 of these, leaving 5 tens; now take away 4 pounds; the result is 1 pound, 5 tens and 2 pence, i.e. 152.

7.2: Put out 2 thousands and 6 units; not enough units to take away 8, no tens to exchange and no hundreds, so exchange 1 thousand for 10 hundreds, leaving 1 thousand; now exchange 1 hundred for 10 tens, leaving 9 hundreds; then exchange 1 ten for 10 units, leaving 9 tens and giving 16 units; can now take away 8 units, 3 tens and 4 hundreds; the result is 1 thousand, 5 hundreds, 6 tens and 8 units, i.e. 1568.

7.3: Add 42 to both numbers, to give '763 − 500'; answer, 263.

7.4: (a) '999 − 458' is 541, so '1000 − 458' is 542; b) '819 − 519' is 300, so '819 − 523' is 4 less than this, i.e. 296; c) '606 − 206' is 400, so '605 − 206' is 399.

Chapter 8: Multiplication structures

8.1: 'I bought 29 boxes of eggs with 12 eggs in each box . . .' (29 lots of 12); 'There are 12 classes in the school with 29 children in each class . . .' (12 lots of 29).

8.2: 'I bought 12 kg of potatoes at 25p per kilogram. What was the total cost?'

8.3: The box can be seen as 4 rows of 6 yoghurts or 6 rows of 4 yoghurts.

8.4: 'If the length of the wing in the model is 16 cm, how long is the length of the wing on the actual aeroplane?' ($16 \times 25 = 400$ cm).

8.5: $1827 \times 1.12 = 2046.24$; new monthly salary is £2046.24.

Chapter 9: Multiplication calculations

9.1: The four areas are '40 × 30', '40 × 7', '2 × 30' and '2 × 7', giving a total of $1200 + 280 + 60 + 14 = 1554$.

9.2: $4 \times 90 = 360$, $40 \times 9 = 360$, $40 \times 90 = 3600$, $4 \times 900 = 3600$, $400 \times 9 = 3600$, $40 \times 900 = 36\,000$, $400 \times 90 = 36\,000$, $400 \times 900 = 360\,000$.

9.3: The six areas are '300 × 10', '300 × 7', '40 × 10', '40 × 7', '5 × 10' and '5 × 7', giving a total of $3000 + 2100 + 400 + 280 + 50 + 35 = 5865$.

9.4: (a) $248 \times 25 = 124 \times 50 = 62 \times 100 = 6200$; b) think of the 16 as $10 + 5 + 1$; now 72×10 is 720; so 72×5 is 360; and 72×1 is 72; so $72 \times 16 = 720 + 360 + 72$.

Chapter 10: Division structures

10.1: Scale factor is 20 ($300 \div 15$); an example of the ratio structure.

10.2: Price is £0.25 per pound-weight ($7 \div 28$); an example of the equal-sharing structure.

10.3: Can afford 8 CDs ($100 \div 12.50$); an example of the inverse-of-multiplication structure, using the idea of repeated subtraction.

10.4: I need 25 months ($300 \div 12$); this is an example of the inverse-of-multiplication structure, using the idea of repeated addition.

10.5: 'A packet of four chocolate bars costs 60p; how much per bar?'

10.6: 'How many tapes costing £4 each can I afford if I have £60 to spend?'

10.7: 'A teacher earns £1200 a month, a bank manager earns £3000. How many times greater is the bank manager's salary?' ($3000 \div 1200 = 2.5$); the bank manager's salary is 2.5 times that of the teacher.

Chapter 11: Division calculations

11.1: In '288 ÷ 6', 288 is the dividend, 6 is the divisor.

11.2: From 126 take away 10 sevens (70), leaving 56, then 5 sevens (35), leaving 21, which is 3 sevens; answer is therefore 10 + 5 + 3, i.e. 18.

11.3: From 851 take away 20 twenty-threes (460), leaving 391, then 10 more (230), leaving 161, then 5 more (115), leaving 46, which is 2 twenty-threes; answer is therefore 20 + 10 + 5 + 2, i.e. 37.

11.4: From 529 take away 50 eights (400), then 10 more (80), then 5 more (40), then 1 more (8), leaving a remainder of 1; answer is 66 remainder 1.

11.5: '154 ÷ 22' is the same as '(88 + 66) ÷ 22' which equals '(88 ÷ 22) + (66 ÷ 22)'; hence the answer is 4 + 3, i.e. 7.

11.6: (a) Multiply both numbers by 2 to give '770 ÷ 110'; divide both by 10 to give '77 ÷ 11'; answer is therefore 7; b) '420 ÷ 21' would be 20, so '419 ÷ 21' is 19 remainder 20.

Chapter 12: Remainders and rounding

12.1: The mathematical model is: 124×5.95 (or 5.95×124); the mathematical solution is 737.8; interpretation: the total cost of the order will be £737.80; to the nearest ten pounds, the total cost of the order will be about £740; to three significant figures, the total cost of the order will be about £738.

12.2: The mathematical model is: 365 ÷ 7; the solution is: 52 remainder 1; the answer to Jackie's problem is: there are 52 weeks in a year, plus one extra day; the remainder represent the one extra day; the calculator solution is 52.142857; this is an answer which has been truncated; the figures after the point represent a bit of a week.

12.3: (a) 327 ÷ 40 = 8.175 (calculator), or 8 remainder 7. So 9 coaches are needed. We round *up* (otherwise we would have to leave 7 children behind); b) 500 ÷ 65 = 7.6923076 (calculator), or 7 remainder 45. So we can buy 7 cakes. We round *down* (and have 45p change for something else).

12.4: Calculator result is 131.88888; the average height is 132 cm to the nearest cm.

12.5: (a) 3; b) 3.2; c) 3.16.

12.6: 205 books per shop; that's 3485 books altogether, so remainder is 15 books.

Chapter 13: Multiples, factors and primes

13.1: $3 \times 37 = 111$, $6 \times 37 = 222$, $9 \times 37 = 333$, $12 \times 37 = 444$, $15 \times 37 = 555$, $18 \times 37 = 666$, $21 \times 37 - 777$, $24 \times 37 = 888$, $27 \times 37 = 999$ (pattern breaks down when four-digit answer are achieved).

13.2: (a) $47 \times 9 = 423$; sum of digits = 9; b) $172 \times 9 = 1548$; sum of digits = 18; sum of these digits = 9; c) $9876543 \times 9 = 88888887$; sum of digits = 63; sum of these digits = 9.

13.3: (a) 2652 is a multiple of 2 (ends in even digit), 3 (sum of digits is multiple of 3), 4 (last two digits multiple of 4), 6 (multiple of 2 and 3); b) 6570 is a multiple of 2 (ends in even digit), 3 (sum of digits is multiple of 3), 5 (ends in

0), 6 (multiple of 2 and 3), 9 (digital root is 9); c) 2401 is a multiple of none of these (it is actually 7 × 7 × 7 × 7).

13.4: A three-digit number is a multiple of 11 if the sum of the two outside digits subtract the middle digit is either 0 (e.g. 561, 594, 330) or 11 (418, 979).

13.5: 24 (the lowest common multiple of 8 and 12).

13.6: (a) Factors of 95 are 1, 5, 19, 95; b) factors of 96 are 1, 2, 3, 4, 6, 8, 12, 16, 24, 32, 48 and 96; c) factors of 97 are 1 and 97 (it is prime); clearly 96 is the most flexible.

13.7: Factors of 48 are 1, 2, 3, 4, 6, 8, 12, 16, 24, 48; factors of 80 are 1, 2, 4, 5, 8, 10, 16, 20, 40, 80; common factors are 1, 2, 4, 8, 16; could have 16 rows of 3 blue and 5 red, or 8 rows of 6 blue and 10 red, or 4 rows of 12 blue and 20 red, or 2 rows of 24 blue and 40 red, or 1 row of 48 blue and 80 red!

13.8: 71, 73, 79, 83, 89, 97 (NB not 91, because this is 9 × 13).

13.9: 4403 = 7 × 17 × 37.

13.10: 5, 7, 11, 13, 17, 19, 23, 25, 29, 31, 35, 37, 41, 43, 47, 49, 53, 55, 59, 61; they are all prime except 25, 35, 49 and 55.

13.11: 4 = 2 + 2, 6 = 3 + 3, 8 = 3 + 5, 10 = 3 + 7, 12 = 5 + 7, 14 = 7 + 7, 16 = 3 + 13, 18 = 5 + 13, 20 = 7 + 13, 22 = 11 + 11, 24 = 7 + 17, 26 = 3 + 23, 28 = 5 + 23, 30 = 13 + 17.

13.12: The smallest answer is 2520.

Chapter 14: Squares, cubes and number shapes

14.1: Some possible answers: 20 is a factor of 100; 21 is a triangle number; 22 is a multiple of 2 and 11; 23 is a prime number; 24 has eight factors; 25 is a square number; 26 is a multiple of 2 and 13; 27 is a cube number; 28 is a triangle number; 29 is a prime number.

14.2: 36 is both a triangle number and a square number.

14.3: The differences between successive square numbers are 3, 5, 7, 9, 11 . . . , the odd numbers; these are the numbers of dots added to each square in Figure 14.1a in order to make the next one in the sequence.

14.4: The answers should be the same. Whole numbers less than 100 which are both cubes and squares are 1 and 64.

14.5: (a) 57; b) 17.

14.6: 14.14 m.

14.7: The cube root of 500 is between 7.93 and 7.94; so the length of the side of the cube should be about 7.9 cm (79 mm).

14.8: The answers are the square numbers: 4, 9, 16, 25, 36, and so on; two successive triangles of dots in Figure 14.4 can be fitted together to make a square number.

Chapter 15: Integers: positive and negative

15.1: 472, 0 and –10 are integers.

15.2: The order is B (+3), A (–4), C (–5).

15.3: (a) The temperature one winter's day is 4°C; that night it falls by 12 degrees; what is the night-time temperature? (answer: –8); b) the temperature one winter's night is −6°C; when it rises by 10 degrees what is the tempera-ture? (Answer: 4).

15.4: (a) If I am overdrawn by £5, how much must be paid into my account to make the balance £20? (Answer 25); b) if I am overdrawn by £15, how much must be paid into my account so that I am only overdrawn by £10? (Answer 5); c) if I have £20 in my bank balance, what debit would produce a balance of £10 overdrawn? (−30).

15.5: My basic calculator displays −42 with the negative sign at one end of the display and the 42 at the other; this is rather unsatisfactory.

15.6: The mathematical model is '458.64 − (−187.85)'; the cheque paid in was £646.49.

Chapter 16: Fractions

16.1: (a) A bar of chocolate is cut into 5 equal pieces and I have 4 of them; b) $\frac{4}{5}$ of a class of 30 children is 24 children; c) share 4 pizzas equally between 5 people; d) if I earn £400 a week and you earn £500 a week, my earnings are $\frac{4}{5}$ of yours.

16.2: (a) $\frac{1}{4} = \frac{2}{8} = \frac{3}{12}$; b) $\frac{1}{2} = \frac{2}{4} = \frac{3}{6} = \frac{4}{8} = \frac{6}{12}$; c) $\frac{3}{4} = \frac{6}{8} = \frac{9}{12}$; d) $\frac{4}{4} = \frac{8}{8} = \frac{12}{12} = \frac{6}{6} = \frac{3}{3} = \frac{2}{2} = 1$; e) $\frac{2}{12} = \frac{1}{6}$; f) $\frac{4}{12} = \frac{2}{6} = \frac{1}{3}$; g) $\frac{8}{12} = \frac{4}{6} = \frac{2}{3}$; h) $\frac{10}{12} = \frac{5}{6}$.

16.3: $\frac{3}{5}$ is $\frac{24}{40}$; $\frac{5}{8}$ is $\frac{25}{40}$; the latter is the larger.

16.4: $\frac{1}{6}$ ($\frac{2}{12}$) , $\frac{1}{3}$ ($\frac{4}{12}$) , $\frac{5}{12}$, $\frac{2}{3}$ ($\frac{8}{12}$), $\frac{3}{4}$ ($\frac{9}{12}$).

16.5: Compare by ratio the prices of two coffee pots, pot A costing £15, pot B costing £25.

16.6: $\frac{9}{24}$ or $\frac{3}{8}$ (three-eighths).

16.7: (a) $\frac{1}{5}$ of £100 is £20, so $\frac{3}{5}$ is £60; b) £1562.50 (2500 ÷ 8 × 5).

Chapter 17: Calculations with decimals

17.1: (a) Mathematical solution is 6.90, total cost is £6.90; b) mathematical solution is 3.25, total length is 3.25 m; c) mathematical solution is 0.22, difference in height is 0.22 m or 22 cm; d) mathematical solution is 5.75, change is £5.75.

17.2: (a) I have a 1.500-litre bottle of wine (one and a half litres) and pour out one glass of 0.125 litres (125 ml); how much is left? Answer: 1.375 litres; b) find the total mass (weight) of a bag of potatoes of 2.500 kg (two and a half kilograms) and a bag of onions of 1.120 kg. Answer: 3.620 kg.

17.3: How much for 4 paperbacks costing £3.99 each? Answer: £15.96 (399 × 4 = 1596, so 3.99 × 4 = 15.96).

17.4: Divide a 4.40-m length of wood into 8 equal parts; each part is 0.55 m (55 cm) long. (Change the calculation to 440 cm divided by 8.)

17.5: (a) 18.4; b) 18.4; c) 0.00184.

17.6: (a) 18 (or 18.0); b) 18 (or 18.0); c) 0.0018 (or 0.00180).

17.7: 0.0001; find the area in square metres of a square of side 0.01 m (1 cm).

17.8: (a) 2 ÷ 0.5 = 20 ÷ 5 = 4; b) 5.5 ÷ 0.11 = 550 ÷ 11 = 50.

17.9: (a) 0.17; b) 0.6; c) 0.35; d) 0.6666666 (approximately); e) 0.1428571 (approximately).

17.10: (a) $\frac{9}{100}$; b) $\frac{79}{100}$; c) $\frac{15}{100} = \frac{3}{20}$.

Chapter 18: Percentages

18.1: Since one-third is about 33%, this is the greater reduction.

18.2: (a) 13 out of 50 is the same proportion as 26 out of 100. So 26% achieve level 5 and 74% do not; b) 57 out of 300 is the same proportion as 19 out of 100. So 19% achieve level 5 and 81% do not; c) 24 out of 80 is the same proportion as 3 out of 10, or 30 out of 100. So 30% achieve level 5 and 70% do not; d) 26 out of 130 is the same proportion as 2 out of 10, or 20 out of 100. So 20% achieve level 5 and 80% do not.

18.3: English, about 42%; Italian, about 49%.

18.4: (a) $3/20 = 15/100 = 15\%$; b) $65\% = 65/100 = 13/20$.

18.5: (a) 10% of £120 is £12, so 30% is three times this, i.e. £36; b) 10% of £450 is £45; so 5% is £22.50; 1% is £4.50, so 2% is £9; so 17% is £45 + £22.50 + £9 = £76.50.

18.6: £271.04 (one way of doing this is: $275 \times 1.12 \times 0.88$).

18.7: It makes no difference! In one case the calculation could be: $600 \times 1.20 \times 0.90$; in the other it could be: $600 \times 0.90 \times 1.20$; the results are the same, £648.

Chapter 19: Handling data

19.1: (a) Which way of travelling to school is used by most children? How many fewer children walk than come by car? (b) How many children have fewer than five writing implements? Which group has no children in it? (c) How many have waist measurements in the range 60 to 64 cm, to the nearest centimetre? How many have waist measurements to the nearest centimetre which are greater than 89 cm?

19.2: (a) Continuous; b) continuous; c) discrete; d) discrete, but should be grouped; e) discrete; f) discrete; g) continuous.

19.3: Examples (c) and (f), having a small number of possibilities, are best displayed on a pie chart. Example (g) is best displayed on a line graph, with the horizontal axis representing time.

19.4: Fifty-pence intervals will produce 10 groups: £0.00–£0.49, £0.50–£0.99, £1.00–£1.49, and so on.

19.5: (a) 140 degrees; b) about 153 degrees (calculator answer: 152.72726).

Chapter 20: Averages

20.1: Group A English, mean = 53.7, median = 53; Group B English, mean = 67.5, median = 71. Both averages support the view that Group B did better.

20.2: The mean for English for the two groups combined is 59.8 (1494 ÷ 25). This is less than the mean of the two separate means (the mean of 53.7 and 67.5 is 60.6). Because there are more pupils in Group A their mean has a greater 'weighting' in the combined mean.

20.3: With 25 in the set the median is the 13th value when arranged in order; so for English, median = 56; for mathematics, median = 53. The range for English is 45 (90–45) and the range for mathematics is 72 (95–23).

20.4: For mathematics, John's mark (49) is less than the mean (53.6) and less than the median (56.5), but well above the bottom of the range.

20.5: The mode is 4, thus lending support to the assertion that there are more four-letter words used in English than anything else. (There are 18 four-letter words, followed by 15 two-lettered and 13 five-lettered.)

20.6: P (about 68 cm per sec) had a greater average speed than Q (65 cm per sec).

20.7: Journey there takes 10 hours, journey back takes 8 hours. Total journey is 800 miles in 18 hours, so overall average speed is about 44.4 mph (800 ÷ 18).

Chapter 21: Probability

21.1: (a) By experiment: finding the relative frequency of successful outcomes in a large number of trials; b) by collecting data from a large sample of people aged 50–59 years in England; c) using an argument based on symmetry, considering all the possible, equally likely outcomes.

21.2: 59% in the sample have less than 6 letters; estimate of probability is 0.59.

21.3: (a) $^3/_{12}$ = 0.25; b) $^9/_{12}$ = 0.75.

21.4: (a) $^{12}/_{36}$ = 0.33 approximately; b) $^9/_{36}$ = 0.25; c) $^{20}/_{36}$ = 0.56 approximately.

21.5: Examples: probability of scoring 1 is 0; probability of scoring less than 13 is 1.

Chapter 22: Algebra

22.1: $F = 3Y$. Using F and Y is misleading, since they look like abbreviations for 'a foot' and 'a yard', instead of variables (e.g. the number of feet).

22.2: (a) The total number of pieces of fruit bought; b) the cost of the apples in pence; c) the cost of the bananas; d) the total cost of the fruit. Using A and B is misleading, since they look like abbreviations for 'an apple' and 'a banana'; so $10A + 12B$ looks like '10 apples and 12 bananas'.

22.3: Jenny has 11 rides. Arithmetic steps: 12 divided by 2, add 5. Algebraic representation: $2(N − 5) = 12$.

22.4: (a) 60; b) 10.

22.5: For Figure 22.2c: a) add 5; b) 498; c) multiply by 5, subtract 2; d) $B = 5A − 2$. For Figure 22.2d: a) subtract 1; b) 0; c) subtract from 100; d) $B = 100 − A$.

22.6: Side by side: a) add 2; b) 204; c) multiply by 2, add 4; d) $Y = 2X + 4$. End to end: a) add 4; b) 402; c) multiply by 4, add 2; d) $Y = 4X + 2$.

22.7: My number is 42; the equation is $X(2X + 3) = 3654$.

Chapter 23: Coordinates

23.1: The points are (1, 2), (1, 4), (2, 5), (4, 5), (5, 4), (5, 2), (4, 1) and (2, 1). Joined up in this order they form an octagon.

23.2: They are all linear relationships, producing straight-line graphs.

23.3: (a) The total number of eggs; b) the equivalent number of francs; c) the top number in the fractions in the set.

23.4: The fourth vertex is (4, 5). The sum of the x-coordinates of two opposite vertices is the same as the sum of the x-coordinates for the other two opposite vertices. The same is true of the y-coordinates. The fourth vertex to go with (4, 4), (5, 8) and (13, 6) is therefore (12, 2), because $4 + 13 = 5 + 12$, and $4 + 6 = 8 + 2$.

23.5: A sequence of parallelograms is produced. The rules are exactly the same as those given for rectangles. The fourth vertex is (1, 3); if you join the points in a different order it could also be (1, −1) or (7, 5).

Chapter 24: Measurement

24.1: It works as far as 55 miles, which is 89 km to the nearest km (88.5115). The next value, 89 miles, is 143 km to the nearest km (143.2277), rather than the Fibonacci number, 144.

24.2: It will still be 1 kg. It will weigh less, but the mass does not change.

24.3: (a) Yes; if A is earlier than B and B is earlier than C, then A must be earlier than C; b) no; for example, 20 cm is half of 40 cm and 40 cm is half of 80 cm, but 20 cm is not half of 80 cm.

24.4: (a) 297 mm; b) 29.7 cm; c) 2.97 dm; d) 0.297 m.

24.5: (a) 250 g; b) 2 pints; c) 2 metres; d) 100 kilometres; e) 4 ounces; f) 10 stone; g) 9 miles to the litre.

Chapter 25: Angle

25.1: ⅛ of a turn (acute), 89° (acute), 90° (right), 95° (obtuse), 150° (obtuse), 2 right angles (straight), 200° (reflex), ¾ of a turn (reflex).

25.2: (a) 6 right angles; b) 8 right angles; c) 10 right angles. The sequential rule is 'add two right angles'. For a figure with N sides the global rule for the sum of the angles is $2N − 4$. When $N = 100$, the sum of the angles is 196 right angles.

Chapter 26: Transformations and symmetry

26.1: (a) Translation, −6 units in x-direction, 0 units in y-direction; b) reflection in vertical line passing through (8, 0); c) rotation through half-turn about (5, 2), clockwise or anticlockwise.

26.2: (a) A diagonal line passing through (11, 3) and (13, 1); b) a vertical line passing through (12, 2); c) a horizontal line passing through (12, 2). Order of rotational symmetry is four.

26.3: No.

26.4: No.

Chapter 27: Classifying shapes

27.1: Because all the angles in an equilateral triangle must be 60 degrees.

27.2: 90, 45 and 45 degrees.

27.3: (a) Square; b) square; c) equilateral triangle; d) cuboid; e) tetrahedron.

27.4: The parallelogram tessellates, as do all quadrilaterals.

27.5: Nine.

Chapter 28: Perimeter and area

28.1: The maximum area is given by the square field, 5 units by 5 units, i.e. 25 square units.

28.2: The minimum length of fencing is 28 units, for a field which is 6 units by 8 units.

28.3: (a) As a cube with side 3 units; total surface area = 54 square units; b) as a cuboid, 4 units by 4 units by 3 units; total surface area = 80 square units (16 + 16 + 12 + 12 + 12 + 12).

28.4: About 78.5 cm (25 × 3.14); 80 cm to be on the safe side.

28.5: About 127 m (400 ÷ 3.14).

Index

Index